# THE FOOD LOVER'S GUIDE TO FLORENCE

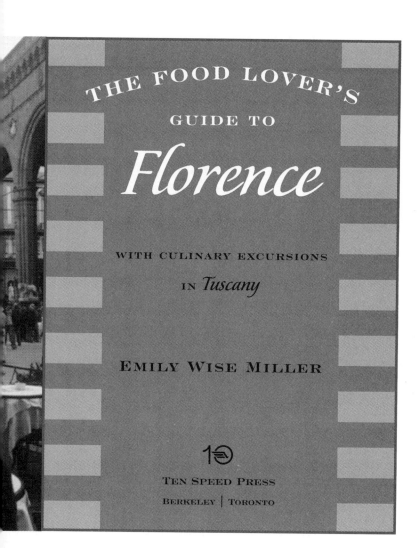

# THE FOOD LOVER'S
## GUIDE TO
# *Florence*

### WITH CULINARY EXCURSIONS
### IN *Tuscany*

## EMILY WISE MILLER

TEN SPEED PRESS
BERKELEY | TORONTO

Ten Speed Press
Box 7123, Berkeley, California 94707
www.tenspeed.com

Distributed in Australia by Simon & Schuster Australia, in Canada by Ten Speed Press Canada, in New Zealand by Southern Publishers Group, in South Africa by Real Books, and in the United Kingdom and Europe by Airlift Book Company.

Design by Nancy Austin
Map designs by Fineline Maps, Oakland, California

Library of Congress Cataloging-in-Publication Data

Miller, Emily Wise.
  The food lover's guide to Florence: with culinary excursions in Tuscany / Emily Wise Miller.
      p. cm.
Includes index.
  ISBN 1-58008-435-4
  1. Restaurants—Italy—Florence—Guidebooks. 2. Cookery, Italian.
3. Florence (Italy)—Guidebooks. I. Title.
  TX910.I8 M55 2003
  647.9545′51—dc21

                                    2003004344

Printed in Canada
First printing, 2003


1 2 3 4 5 6 7 8 9 10 - 07 06 05 04 03

# CONTENTS

Acknowledgments   vii

Preface   ix


Introduction   1

1. The Regional Foods of Florence and Tuscany   15

2. A Primer on Tuscan Wine   25

3. Restaurants and Trattorias   41

4. Pizzerias   95

5. Sandwiches, Snacks, and Light Meals   107

6. International Food   123

7. Wine Bars and Wine Shops   131

8. Markets and Shops   149

9. Coffee, Pastries, and Chocolate   183

10. Gelaterias   205

11. Cooking Classes   213

12. Culinary Excursions in Tuscany   225


Glossary   257

Index   263

# ACKNOWLEDGMENTS

First, thanks to Aaron Wehner at Ten Speed Press for igniting this idea and facilitating the book in every way. Thanks also to Nancy Austin for her excellent design work, and to Windy Ferges and Sharon Silva for their conscientous editing and proofreading. Thank you to everyone who gave me their suggestions for places to eat in Florence and Tuscany and to all the friends who came out to explore and eat with me: Maurizio, Lola, and the regulars at Chicco di Caffè; Paolo Carandini; Cristina and Gabriella at Cordon Bleu; Gianni and Marie at Millesimi; Francesca dell'Acqua; Florence Moly; Federica Armiraglio; Allie Terry; Alexandra Korey and Tommaso Oliviero; Gina and Howard Parr; Mary Quinn and Richard Savino; Marikka Malm; Sean Clegg; Melissa Clegg and Todd Frizzelle; Bill and Adair Langston; Luigi Bernas; cook extraordinaire Lila Brown; Antonia Daluiso; Nadia Zonis; and Andy Kanter and Karen Rosen. Thanks also to Judy Witts Francini, Faith Willinger, Tiziana Frescobaldi, and Leonardo Romanelli. Special thanks to the Craft. I'm grateful to my parents, Susan and Joseph Miller, for all of their enthusiastic support (especially to my father for allowing me access to his archive of *Wine Spectator* and *Art of Eating* back issues), and to my sister, Joanne Miller. Thank you infinitely to Mark Rosen, who accompanied me to most of these meals even when he wasn't hungry.

# PREFACE

Perfectly preserved Florence, with its embarrassment of late-medieval and Rennaissance riches, is one of the most visited places in the world. Like the prettiest girl in school, Florence's only problem may be overwhelming popularity. The city has never fallen off the short list of destinations on the Grand Tour, and is a highlight on the itinerary of backpackers and mass bus tours alike. They come to see the towering *David*, the treasure-packed Uffizi, and the multicolored Duomo, and to experience the jolt of pleasure you get from crossing the Ponte Santa Trinità at any time of day or night. The glory of this medium-sized city crystallized over a period of three hundred years, roughly from the end of the thirteenth to the end of the sixteenth centuries. A lucky confluence of wealth from banking and textiles, a politically tolerant and artistically minded ruling family—the Medicis—and the ineffable and impossible-to-predict outcropping of genius embodied in the likes of Donatello, Brunelleschi, Leonardo da Vinci, and Michelangelo ensured Florence's place as the center and apogee of the Renaissance, represented in its architecture, painting, and sculpture.

In addition to the city's artistic splendors, visitors increasingly descend on Florence for its food. Tuscan cooking has become the best known of Italian regional cuisines, famous for its peppery extra virgin olive oil, hearty pastas and bean soups, and succulent *bistecca*. Here you'll find mobile stands hawking the workingman's lunch of a hot tripe sandwich; the famous *finocchiona salame*, and fresh Pecorino Toscano cheese. You can dart into an *enoteca* for a quick shot of Vino Nobile on your way home from the museum, or grab a slice of rich *torta della nonna*, filled with custard and topped with almonds or pine nuts. And in the last twenty years, Tuscan wines have gone from watery slosh in bulbous bottles to award-winning boutique labels that fetch top dollar on the international market.

■ ■ ■

When I first moved to Florence from San Francisco, I thought I must be experiencing a kind of cosmic coincidence—I am a food writer; everywhere I go, people are talking about food. The house painter who sits down next to me at lunch wants to tell me the correct way to cook fish. I overhear the cell phone conversation of a young woman on the bus: "Just a few slices of tomato and a dash of vinegar," she says, "we're going vegetarian tonight." At the beach in nearby Viareggio, the women under the *ombrellone* next to ours are comparing recipes for *ragù*. One argues strenuously for the inclusion of chopped prosciutto while the other insists it's much more important to add chicken livers. "What," she says, "you don't put in any milk?" At this she shrugs her shoulders and makes a face as if to say, in that case the conversation is over and I can't help you since you were obviously raised by wolves. Men walking down the street discuss last night's *bistecca:* Was it too well done? They cook it better at Mario's? Actually his wife can make it better than any restaurant.

Finally it became clear (as any local could have told me from the beginning) there was no cosmic coincidence; the truth is that Florentines are obsessed with food. This is not a class-specific Dean & Deluca chichi kind of thing; it's an across-the-board cultural priority: Family, Friends, Food—not necessarily in that order (and wine is understood as included under Food). When I lived in San Francisco, I sometimes felt guilty that I was employed as a restaurant critic and was not doing "important work" like covering politics or writing scathing articles about the electric company. As it turns out, in Italy, politics are pretty much a joke and food is dead serious. It's an absolutely integral part of life here, as it should be everywhere. We all need to eat, and in the long run what we eat, where we eat it, and who we eat with affects the quality of our lives. Italians are acutely aware of this.

One of the most exciting things about living here is absorbing the Italian way of thinking about food. You go to the open market, you buy what's in season and what looks good. Whether you're buying fresh porcini, Mediterranean sea bass, or radicchio from Treviso, if you ask the vendor how to prepare it, he or she will always rattle off a recipe on the spot. Not a "Well you might want to . . ." but rather, "This is what you must do—no, no cream [you American cretin]—olive oil, garlic, etc." At which point the other buyers around you will pipe in with either agreement or disagreement and you feel particularly happy to be living in Florence at that moment. And the recipes are always good.

I have a friend who moved to Los Angeles and always complains about the lack of good fresh produce and meats there. I like to torment her with tales of my food shopping in Florence. When I buy my fresh ricotta, the vendor asks if I want cow's or sheep's milk; when I buy veal, I can choose between milk-fed or grass-fed. Prosciutto? How aged? Sweet or Tuscan style? Fresh sardines? Not only can I buy them, I can have them cleaned and deboned for the same price.

■ ■ ■

Italy has always been linked with great food in my mind. I came here for the first time with my family as an aesthetically challenged teenager with vertical hair, more interested in Benetton than Botticelli. However, the country, with its incredibly thin pizzas and sunny piazzas, had a huge effect on me. I vowed to come back later. In college I studied Italian language for several years just to make sure I would be accepted

into the junior year exchange program, which I spent in Venice. When I arrived there I couldn't even cook an egg, but I left knowing the difference between Parmigiano-Reggiano and Grana Padano, and how to make about a dozen delicious pasta sauces from memory. Later I would take classes in Perugia and explore the Umbrian hill towns and finally as an adult I came to Florence.

Like any food fetishist who moves to Italy, I arrived with a slew of books and several folders of clipped articles. I had excellent guidebooks covering eating in Italy, in northern Italy, and even in Tuscany, but nothing that gave more than a dozen or so pages to Florence itself—an insider's guide to the restaurants, the markets, the gelato, the wine. Someone once said that his friend gave him these directions to the best restaurant in Florence: "Drive into the city. Park your car. The first restaurant you see, go eat there." This is a great story, and in many ways very true; the average trattoria that you walk into in Florence is bound to be quite good. On the other hand, if you stumble blindly off the Ponte Vecchio into the nearest trattoria you also might end up in a place that is touristy, over-priced, and producing lazy and mediocre food because the proprietors know they can get away with it. I wanted to write a book that would lead travelers to the best restaurants—the ones that use only fresh ingredients, cooking both traditional and innovative dishes, in the Center and off the beaten path. I also wanted to go much deeper into the Florentine food scene as a whole, looking at where the locals go for pizza and beer on a Friday night; where you can get a quick lunch between sights without being caught in a tourist trap; where to buy fresh fish when the Central Market closes; and who sells the best selection of Tuscan and Italian wines.

In order to find the best places to eat, I talked to many Florentines and other longtime residents of the city—cooking teachers, bar owners, and ordinary *golosi* (food lovers)—who gave me incredibly valuable advice. I also consulted other guidebooks, both old and new in English and Italian, and finally scoured the city, keeping an eye out for new restaurants, *pasticcerie,* good-looking *enoteche,* and other points of interest.

I made an effort to search out restaurants and shops off the radar, some so far out that only dedicated food fiends will bother to track them down. I also tried to find that ever-elusive thing that Florentines love to talk about, the *buon rapporto prezzo/qualità* (a just relationship between price and quality). It is not so important whether something is inexpensive, but whether you truly get what you pay for, whether it is a Sangiovese wine or a three-course meal.

When I visited the restaurants I went incognito (though not in wig and funny glasses), without announcing myself to the owners beforehand, and without being served gratis. (The one exception to this occurred before I started working on the book, when I was served a complimentary meal on someone else's behalf.)

No doubt, some people will look at this book and find to their dismay that their favorite restaurant was not included, an unavoidable hazard of the trade. It may be that I never ate there, or it may be that I ate there several times and decided not to include it for any number of reasons. In any case, I've tried to include a broad variety of restaurants in every price range. I hope this volume will be helpful and insightful for both travelers and residents, leading to many excellent meals.

*Buon appetito.*

*A local paper announces, "Salumi vendor condemned for selling a different prosciutto than the one requested."*

# Introduction

## Restaurant Basics

*Ristorante, trattoria, enoteca* . . . trying to unscramble the code words for "place to eat" will only make you hungrier. Luckily, the semantics of eating in Florence matter less and less. There was once a time when the hierarchy of differentiation between *ristorante, trattoria, osteria,* and the like was paramount, but the lines have definitely blurred. A brief rundown of the remaining distinctions between these various names follows.

**Ristorante:** The term *ristorante* generally implies that this is a serious place to eat, with linen tablecloths, stem wineglasses, and the usual fripperies of fine dining. It also implies a more expensive bill.

**Osteria:** *Osteria* is a tricky one. It used to indicate a place to drink wine as well as eat a casual meal, much like an *enoteca,* but is now usually interchangeable with trattoria, though less common and sometimes a little smarter and/or more expensive.

**Trattoria:** Over time, the word *trattoria* has been gentrified. It once meant—and still implies—a casual place to drink wine and eat a home-style meal, the kind of place with bare wooden tables and a flask of Chianti on each one. This is often still the case, but the word has also been co-opted by restaurateurs who want to charge twenty dollars for a plate of pasta. Or sometimes a place has simply evolved over the years into a more formal, expensive restaurant but retained the original trattoria name. In any case, trattorias tend to be simpler, more down-to-earth, and cheaper places serving local and regional cooking. This is not the place to look for fusion Italian-Japanese sashimi or nouvelle Californian takes on Tuscan cooking. Instead these kitchens usually churn out hearty, satisfying dishes like soups and pastas as *primi* and roasted or grilled meats as *secondi.*

**Enoteca:** The classification *enoteca* is used in three diverse ways around town: it can be a wine store, a wine bar, or a restaurant that prides itself on its special wine list. This would be confusing except for the fact that a cursory glance inside or at the menu will tip you to the type. For example, Enoteca Alessi on Via dell'Oche is a wine shop with a tiny tasting bar for clients; Enoteca Baldovino, next to Santa Croce, is a casual place to sip wines by the glass (or share a bottle), but mainly a restaurant that happens to have a big wine list. Adding fuel to the enoteca fire is Enoteca Pinchiorri, the most famous and expensive restaurant in town. All the evidence shows that this place should rightly be called a ristorante, but as a Florentine native explained to me, Pinchiorri calls itself an enoteca not to fool people into thinking of it as a casual bar (god forbid), but rather to inform the public that this place is devoted to wine.

**Mescita, fiaschetteria:** *Mescita* and *fiaschetteria* both once meant "place to buy and drink wine," or some combination thereof, but are now often used in the same way as trattoria.

**Tavola calda:** A *tavola calda* is often a lot what it sounds like: a "hot table"—a place where cauldrons of pasta, soup, or rice are already stewing and you're likely to be served a quick, cheap, hot meal. *Tavole calde* do not have a great reputation for quality, but I recommend a couple as good lunch stops.

### Reservations

Reservations are big in Florence. It struck me as bizarre the first time I walked into a casual local trattoria for a Tuesday night dinner and was asked, "Have you reserved?" The answer was no, and I got a table anyway, but I learned a lesson: It's always better to call ahead. In high season, this city is so engorged with tourists that restaurants have become extremely reservation-savvy. Even in winter I've been stuck either waiting or wandering around looking for a place to eat because I had failed to reserve on a Friday or Saturday night. It just makes sense to either call ahead yourself or have your hotel concierge do it for you to avoid possible disappointment later. When you call to reserve, you'll find that many restaurateurs will speak a little English.

## Prime-Time Dining

You've just arrived in Florence, you know of a hot restaurant in town, so you call and make a reservation for 8 PM—prime time in most cities. When you get there, you find the place quiet and empty until you're eating dessert, when suddenly the crowd rushes in. Barcelona it's not, but people like to eat late here. In fact the dining times are surprisingly circumscribed—basically from 9 to 10:30 PM. Before that you might be lonely, and after you could have trouble finding a meal. For lunch, timing is a little more standard; most people eat between 12:30 and 2:30 (with a concentrated rush between 1 and 2), but luckily, even later in the afternoon you can always find a good snack or *panino*.

### *Days Off and Holidays*

Most restaurants close either Sunday or Monday; I have indicated closing days as accurately as possible.

If you ever go to an Italian city in August you'll witness a strange phenomenon: The tourists have the place to themselves, as almost all locals head to a beach somewhere, anywhere, for their August vacation. In Italy, the August beach vacation is more than a privilege, it's a right (and a rite). They would no sooner give it up than start eating ham out of a can.

In August, you're lucky if you get your mail delivered let alone have access to markets and shops. That's why it's better, if possible, to plan a trip to Italy for any other time of year, when restaurants will be open and the Uffizi guards are on duty instead of lying on the beach in Elba. The city government is aware of the August desertion problem and has tried to organize things so that not every single service in a given neighborhood goes on vacation at the exact same time. August 15 is Ferragosto, a national Italian holiday, so expect pretty much everything to be closed on that day. Circling out from there, many shops close for either one or two weeks around the fifteenth; others take the whole month quite literally from the first to the thirty-first, and still others have taken to expanding things to include the end of July and beginning of September.

Since most restaurants and shops are family run, the owners often decide at the last minute whether to close or for how long, so it's difficult to pin down an exact closing date from year to year. In any case, August tends to be extremely hot and sticky in Florence and you can't blame Florentines for fleeing to their beautiful coastlines. On the other hand, if you stay behind you'll have the uncrowded city almost to yourself. Now if only you could get something to eat. . . .

Many businesses also close for a week or two weeks around Christmas (until January 6, the Epiphany), but this is not usually true for restaurants.

## The Menu

With few variations, Florentine menus follow a standard order: *antipasti* (appetizers), *primi* (first courses), *secondi* (second courses), *contorni* (vegetable side dishes), *insalate* (salads), *formaggi* (cheeses), *dolci* (desserts), *caffè*, and *digestivo* (after-dinner drink), all accompanied by *una bottliglia di acqua* (bottled water), which comes either *frizzante/con gas/gassata* (sparkling) or *naturale* (still); and of course *vino*, whether it's *della casa* (house wine) or from the wine list (see chapter 2 for more information on ordering wine).

Enough foreigners tromp through here that it no longer seems bizarre when a customer orders a salad first or coffee at the same time as dessert—just as it's no longer a huge faux pas to drink a cappuccino after noon. At some trattorias, you might still feel pressure to order several courses, but it's on the decline. I've noticed both Italians and foreigners getting creative with the menu by sharing a primo and each ordering a secondo; taking a salad as a secondo; or mixing and matching any of the above. No one should feel compelled to eat more than they want to; to paraphrase Tony Soprano when confronted with the meals in his homeland, "Plowing through the full five or six courses at every sitting is enough to clog a woodchipper."

### ANTIPASTI

A few traditional antipasti appear on nearly every menu in town: *crostini toscani* (toasted bread slices topped with chopped liver pâté) and *anti-pasto toscano*, usually a mix of prosciutto and salami plus the aforementioned *crostini*; it will sometimes include *fettunta*, slices of

Tuscan bread grilled over a flame and covered with olive oil and garlic. *Crostini misti* is usually an assortment of four toasts, topped with liver pâté, chopped tomato, artichoke spread, and sometimes *lardo* (see page 17). The excellent local prosciutto is available year-round, but only comes draped over melon in summer when the fruit is in season.

## PRIMI

Though it is now synonymous with Italian cooking, pasta is not always the preeminent first course in Tuscany. Before the twentieth century, on farms and in towns, Tuscans mostly lived on soups made of simple ingredients like beans, bread, and cabbage. This *cucina povera,* or peasant cooking, is the backbone of Tuscan cuisine. The quintessential Florentine primo is *ribollita,* a thick soup made from beans, bread, and *cavolo nero* (a kind of kale), though the bread and tomato soup called *pappa al pomodoro* and soups made from chickpeas, called *ceci,* and the grain called *farro* are also common—and delicious. In summer, instead of *ribollita* you'll often see *panzanella,* a salad made of bread, cucumber, peppers, and tomatoes, all tossed with local olive oil. In addition to these standards, you'll usually find a good selection of pastas—sometimes sauced with artichokes, tomatoes, or porcini mushrooms, depending on the season—as well as a gnocchi dish or two. Polenta and risotto make infrequent appearances on Florentine menus partly because they are more popular up north in Lombardy and the Veneto, and partly because they are simply so time- and labor-consuming, requiring a half hour or so of dedicated stirring. Often when you order risotto in a restaurant what you are actually getting is more like a rice pilaf—it might taste great, but technically shouldn't be called risotto.

## Useful Phrases

*Vorrei prenotare per stasera.* = I'd like to make a reservation for tonight.

*Devo cancellare la prenotazione.* = I have to cancel the reservation.

*Siamo in due/tre/quattro.* = We are a party of two/three/four.

*Si puo sedere fuori?* = Can we sit outside?

*Vorrei un bicchiere di acqua.* = I would like a glass of water.

*Vorremmo ordinare una bottiglia di vino.* = We'd like to order a bottle of wine.

*Vorremmo condividere un antipasto.* = We'd like to share an antipasto.

*Ci porta la lista dei vini, per piacere?* = Will you bring us the wine list, please?

*Ci porta il conto per favore?* = Will you bring us the check, please?

*Ci farebbe due caffè, per favore?* = Would you make us two coffees, please?

*Ci porta un menu, per favore?* = Could you bring us a menu, please?

*Vorrei un etto di pancetta.* = I'd like an etto (100 grams, about 1/4 pound) of pancetta.

*Vorrei un mezzo kilo di cipolle rosse.* = I'd like a half kilo (about a pound) of red onions.

*Basta così.* = That's enough.

*Scusi, dov'è questa ristorante?* = Excuse me, where is this restaurant?

*È qui vicino?* = Is it nearby?

*Come si arriva in questo posto?* = How do I get to this place?

*Sono allergico/a, non posso mangiare X.* = I am allergic, I can't eat X.

*C'è carne dentro?* = Does it have meat in it?

*E buonissima, questa zuppa!* = This soup is delicious!

## SECONDI

Tuscan cooking, with its emphasis on soups, pastas, and olive oil, has gained a reputation as a light and healthful way to eat. But Tuscans love heavy meat dishes as much if not more so than Italians from any other region. (Many people forget that although it's hot and humid here during the summer and most of the high tourist season, it can get very cold in winter—down in the twenties and thirties—which helps explain the prevalence of meats and stews, as well as all those puffy jackets. You need to keep your strength up!) The high-quality meats here tend to be cooked simply, often grilled or roasted, and can sometimes be overly salted.

The secondo sine qua non is the *bistecca alla fiorentina* (see page 15), a thick slab of T-bone steak that is grilled until barely rare and served with just salt and olive oil as condiments. Other secondi to try: *arista* (pork loin roast) and *vitello arrosto* (roast veal), often sliced thin and served with a bit of their cooking juice. If you keep an eye out, you'll find things like duck a l'orange (*anatra con salsa di arancia*), which Tuscans claim Marie de' Medici took with her from Florence to the French court; *coniglio* (rabbit), cooked in white wine, roasted, or fried; and other poultry and game, like *cinghiale* (wild boar) and *lepre* (hare). Fish isn't so common on Florentine menus but some restaurants make a point of featuring it, in which case they might offer a *baccalà alla livornese* (salt cod cooked in tomato sauce), or sometimes a simple grilled gilt-head bream (*orata*) or sea bass (*branzino*). Only the new wave of chic restaurants offers true vegetarian entrées, but many vegetarians will be more than satisfied with a combination of primi, contorni, and salad—no one need worry about going hungry here.

## CONTORNI

Most of us are used to main dishes that come with meat and a side vegetable or two. In Italy you need to order the sides separately, hence the *contorno* (side dish), brought at the same time as your secondo. Contorni tend to be no-nonsense to the point of neglect, but they do go well with Tuscan meats. The most common are *patate arrosto* (roast potatoes); *fagioli* (beans), usually white beans cooked with garlic and sage; *spinaci* (spinach) or any other green that often comes *saltati* (blanched and sautéed, usually with plenty of salt and oil); or sometimes a summery *peperonata* (sautéed peppers).

## INSALATE AND INSALATONE

Small and simple *insalate* are usually served as a contorno along with the secondo, though they can also take the place of a secondo, or the primo, if you're not feeling very hungry. The most common insalata is *mista*, a small bowl of lettuce, tomato, red radicchio, and some shredded carrot. Many trattorias also serve salads of artichoke, arugula, or radicchio, sometimes mixed with shaved Parmesan, or sometimes just by themselves, along with olive oil and vinegar.

You can tell how sensitive a restaurant is to its tourist clientele by whether they feature a list of decidedly nontraditional *insalatone* on the menu. These "big salads" of shrimp, avocado, celery, grapes, cheeses—you name it—cater to Western dietary tastes but have also become popular with some Italians. They can take the place of either a primo or secondo and often have names like Californiana or Mediterranea. (I was saved by these creations when my mother-in-law came to town and announced that she was no longer eating carbohydrates.) Two good places to try an *insalatone* are Enoteca Baldovino (see page 132) and Coquinarius (see page 117).

## FORMAGGI

If your menu has a cheese section, the choice will likely include one or two Pecorini Toscani (see page 19), Gorgonzola (soft blue cheese), or caprino (goat cheese). The cheeses often come drizzled with honey or accompanied by a confiture or tart fruit *mostarda* (a kind of chutney). You might also run across a nice stinky Taleggio, an aged grana from the north of Italy, or one of the mild and creamy mozzarella or caciocavallo cheeses from down south.

## DOLCI

Many Florentines have a sweet tooth—apparent in the bustling *pasticcerie* in town and the many spoonfuls of sugar locals can squeeze into a thimbleful of coffee—but they are not so enthusiastic about restaurant desserts. A lot of diners opt for the very simple *biscottini* and *vin santo*, or just a plate of pineapple. Keep an eye out for *torta della nonna,* a local recipe of custard pie topped with pine nuts or almonds, or the more exotic *zuccotto,* a sponge cake and sweet ricotta concoction. *Castagnaccio,* a thin cake made of chestnut flour, sometimes puts in an appearance on local menus around Christmastime, but this un-sweet dessert is an acquired taste.

The sweets list at most trattorias consists of basic but delicious Italian standards: crème caramel, *panna cotta* (literally "cooked cream," usually a flavored custard made firm with gelatin and topped with chocolate, caramel, or berries), tiramisù, and *torta al cioccolato* (usually a low, dense chocolate cake). If you're at a casual trattoria or pizzeria, ask if the desserts are *fatti in casa* (made in-house); you can assume they are at a more high-end place, which makes the prospect of a delicious tiramisù or fresh *panna cotta* that much more secure.

## DESSERT WINES

Florence is the spiritual home of *vin santo* (see page 38), the sweet wine made from first drying white grapes and then aging the wine in small barrels. However, you would miss out if you only stuck with the tried and true *vin santo*. Other excellent dessert wines, which pair with sharp cheeses and sweet cakes alike, are the Moscadello from Montalcino and the well-respected Muffato from Antinori.

## CAFFÈ

It took me a while to figure out that coffee is ordered *after* the dessert and not during, but I have come to anticipate the small, strong shot of *caffè* at the end of a long (or short) meal. When taken in small doses, it seems to help digestion without keeping you awake, plus it's a good way to counteract some of the wine you've just consumed. (For a primer on coffee vocabulary, see page 187.)

## DIGESTIVI

Just when you thought your marathon meal was coming to an end and the bill was in sight, the waiter arrives to offer you a *digestivo*. Italians often refer to this as the *ammazzacaffe*—the "coffee killer" (funny because once the coffee has cleared your head of all the wine, you start the cycle all over again). Clear-but-deadly grappa served in elegant little cylindrical glasses is the traditional choice, though sometimes you can also get a whisky or cognac, if you still have room. In summer, a *limoncello,* delicious lemon liqueur from the Amalfi coast served ice cold, can be just the thing.

## The Check

In polar opposition to the New York or Los Angeles hot spot that wants to rush you out and "re-monetize" your table, Italian restaurants will rarely rush you to finish your meal. You could sit there all night wondering what you have to do to get out of there. It turns out the magic word is *conto* and you have to ask for it, since to bring it without your okay would be rude. To rush a meal is antithetical to Italian culture, and hopefully belonging to the EU, the G8, and all the rest won't be able to take that traditional courtesy away.

At many pizza places and casual trattorias, you can bring your bill up to the *cassa* (cash register) at the bar or the front of the restaurant and pay there; sometimes, if there's a serious rush or the restaurant is short-handed, it will be easiest and faster for you to go straight to the cash register and have them make up your check while you wait. This is not considered rude or unusual.

### COPERTO

What is this *coperto,* and why is it on all of my bills? The coperto is a cover charge. It used to cover bread, but I see it as a kind of a pretip tip that gets added onto most restaurant bills; it usually comes to no more than one or two euros per person.

### EUROFLATION

In January 2002 the European Union introduced into use its spanking new pan-European currency, the euro. Unencumbered by national boundaries or a long and troubled history, the euro symbolized a new beginning of cooperation and unity in Europe. Unfortunately it also ushered in a wave of inflation that—at least in Italy—was overwhelming to locals and visitors alike. The Italian state was supposed to enforce tight restrictions on raising prices or even rounding up, but somehow businesses, restaurants prominent among them, found a way. A drink or a plate of food that once cost 10,000 lire (about five dollars) suddenly cost 10 euros (around ten dollars). Instead of rounding up, it seemed like some vendors were taking the opportunity and doubling up.

Things have leveled off a bit since the beginning, but Americans who travel to Florence may be surprised to see that a nice meal here costs the same or sometimes even more than a meal back home. A dinner for two plus wine at a casual trattoria can run about fifty euros. A meal for two at a high-end restaurant can cost around 125 euros—not a pretty sight, but that's reality in the new, financially united Europe.

## Tipping

Tipping is one of those Italian mysteries for which it's difficult to get a straight answer. Some bills will say *servizio incluso,* in which case they've made the decision for you, but most don't. Do you need to leave a tip? "No, but . . . you can, if you want to," an Italian will tell you. If you are at a nice restaurant, you liked the service, and you don't see service included on the bill, I would recommend leaving 10 percent in cash on the table, though it really is up to the diner's discretion.

Don't be surprised or offended by the occasional surly waiter or diffident salesperson—they do it to everyone, local and foreigner alike, particularly in the center of town. Remember, no one is working toward a tip, which makes a *big* difference in the quality in service. Of course, you will nearly as often encounter a shopkeeper or server so friendly, so helpful, that you'll forgive the Florentines their foibles, and their sometimes frosty attitude.

## GETTING AROUND AND USING THIS BOOK

The center of Florence is blissfully walkable; you can reach most sites and businesses in the narrow alleyways of the Center more easily on foot (or bike) than by any kind of motorized transport. But when you're out and about, or want to explore the periphery and perhaps aren't in the mood for an hour-long walk, there are a few things you should know.

## Florentine Addresses

With a few exceptions, residential addresses in Florence are big and blue and business addresses are smaller and red. When an address reads "Via della Condotta 26r," the *r* refers to red. This causes confusion because streets will have two of each address number, one blue, one red.

## Taking the Bus

Florence has two systems of buses, the small lettered electric buses (A through D) that cover the center of town, and the bigger buses, numbered 1 through 80-something, that spread out and cover an impressive area in every direction from the Center, from Scandicci to Sesto Fiorentino. The first thing you want to do is get yourself a handy bus map, either from the ATAF (the bus company) office in front of the train station or from a tourist office. These maps not only show you all the bus routes, they are also just plain good maps of the city and very useful to have. Before you get on a bus you'll need to buy a ticket, which you can do at any *tabaccheria* or any bar displaying the ATAF sticker on its window. The cost is currently one euro, though if you plan to use the bus at all regularly you should consider buying a *biglietto multiplo*, which gives you four rides at a slight discount. Once you get on a bus, validate your ticket by sticking it in one of the yellow machines; once you've validated, your ticket is good for another hour. The buses work on an honor system and most of the time no one will check your ticket, but if you get caught without one, or with a ticket that hasn't been validated, the fine is hefty.

Most bus lines lead to and from the central train station and branch out from there. Piazza San Marco and Piazza Antinori are two other hubs. You may find yourself using the station as either a starting point or transfer point for many of your voyages.

Make sure to consult the map in addition to the bus designations in this book, as in some cases the bus goes right to the restaurant door and in others you'll need to walk a block or two. Also, ATAF has a habit of frequently changing its routes, just to keep us all on our toes. If in doubt you can also ask the driver. Bus service becomes *much* less frequent after about 9 PM, so if you take a bus to dinner at a restaurant, you might find yourself taking a taxi home. Service on Sunday is also much less frequent than during the week. At most bus stops you'll find little schedules for the various buses that are more or less accurate and will tell you when they stop running.

## Taking a Taxi

Taxi drivers in Florence prefer to be called rather than hailed. If you see a taxi stand, then by all means go for it, but otherwise your best bet is to call. Your hotel, if you have one, can of course call for you, as will any restaurant. The main taxi line is **Radio Taxi: 055/4242**, and the beautiful thing is, once you call them, they come immediately. Taxis here tend to be clean and new, and the drivers are often knowledgable and sometimes even friendly. Taxi rides become more expensive after 9 PM, if you have baggage, and if your party has more than two people. However, this is by far the best way to travel when you are dressed up and going out for a nice dinner, and sometimes the only choice of travel at night when the buses run infrequently. Tipping is not expected, though you can round up if you feel like it. Most cabs will only take four people max, but if you tell them you are five when you call, they will send a larger taxi for you.

### The Listings in This Book

The Restaurants and Trattorias chapter is organized by price (and then alphabetically within a given price range), while other sections are arranged alphabetically, with pricing indicated where relevant. Please note that prices will change and are also extremely variable depending on what you order. The pricing key for the book is as follows:

Inexpensive, € = Under € 20 per person including wine and coperto

Moderately priced, €€ = From € 20 to € 40

Expensive, €€€ = From € 40 to € 75

Very expensive, €€€€ = € 75 and up

For several reasons, alphabetizing in Italian is tricky, as a glance through the phonebook bears out. Trattoria Mario might be listed under T, under M, neither, or both. I have tried to alphabetize in a way that is both loyal to Italian grammar and rational to an English-speaking user. To this end, I have omitted the nominal designation of a place (trattoria, gelateria, ristorante) in the listing unless it is an integral part of the name.

In noting the hours of operation, I have done my best to indicate when a venue closes for August and/or Christmas. If there is no such indication, then there is no extended closing period.

Most listings include a map designation (for example, D4) that refers to the map on pages 272 and 273. When a location falls outside the map, I have indicated the neighborhood or town.

A star (✳) next to a listing means that the spot is truly exceptional—a personal favorite.

*A butcher stall inside the Sant'Ambrogio market.*

# 1

# THE REGIONAL FOODS OF FLORENCE AND TUSCANY

Like the light gray *pietra serena* marble from the outlying hills that makes up the backbone of distinctive Florentine architecture, the abundant raw ingredients of Tuscany form an ideal foundation for its hearty traditional dishes. The regional gastronomy is identifiable by its simplicity and quality, with a clear distaste for anything too fussy and fancy. Here is a brief list of ingredients and dishes that are unmistakably Tuscan.

## BISTECCA ALLA FIORENTINA

A few years ago, a dark pall fell over the city of Florence. No, it was not a sequel to the black plague that drove Boccaccio to flee the city in the Middle Ages, though not so far off. Fears about a more modern scorge, mad cow disease (called *mucca pazza* in Italian) led the European Union to outlaw the sale and consumption of beef on the bone, including the beloved premier dish of Florence, the *bistecca alla fiorentina.* (At press time the ban was still in effect, but cows slaughtered before twelve months of age are exempt. That loophole, and the assurance that strict controls are in place for all meat, account for why you still see so many Florentine steaks around town, though they might be a bit smaller than they once were.)

For a couple of months before it was outlawed, rumors of mad cow in Italy were already circulating, and foreigners in Florence were being decidedly finicky at restaurants, ordering pork, duck, rabbit . . . in short, anything that wasn't likely to go mad. But Italians were not nearly as squeamish. Despite alarmist headlines, Florentines could be seen at trattorias throughout town quite happily gnawing near-raw beef right off the bone. In short, no modern plague was going to get between a Florentine and his Chianina beef!

Chianina is a species of white-coated grass-fed cattle raised in the Val di Chiana area around Siena and Arezzo, and also in the Mugello area, believed by locals to produce the most flavorful, tender beef in all of Europe. The origins of the *bistecca alla fiorentina* are a bit murky, but the name was supposedly coined by traveling Englishmen happy to see a juicy, familiar "beefsteak" on their table. A *fiorentina* is simply the T-bone cut (often enormous, enough to serve two), about one and a half inches thick, grilled over charcoal or wood, and always served rare, with just olive oil, salt and sometimes lemon or rosemary as flavoring. (Asking for a *fiorentina* well done is like asking a sushi chef to microwave your tuna roll.) When a *fiorentina* is cooked properly and rested before being served, it tastes tender and juicy without being offensively raw. This is truly Florentine cooking at its simple and flavorful best.

Some of the best places in town to sample *bistecca alla fiorentina*:

**Al Antica Ristoro di Cambi,** page 59

**Trattoria Mario,** page 81

**Omero,** page 87

**Osvaldo,** page 88

## CAVOLO NERO

Along with beans, bread, wine, and oil, *cavolo nero*—a dark crinkly winter green on a long stalk—is a staple of the Florentine kitchen. Literally "black cabbage", and outside of Italy commonly called Tuscan black cabbage, *cavolo nero* is in fact most similar to a variety of kale known as dinosaur kale. Like the oblong radicchio of Treviso, *cavolo nero* is the signature vegetable of Tuscany; it can be grown elsewhere but flourishes in the Tuscan hillsides. Don't confuse it with the more banal *cavolo,* plain round cabbage, or *verza,* another cabbage with dark crinkly outer leaves.

*Cavolo nero* makes up the backbone of Tuscan *ribollita* soup (see page 20), but it's also satisfying when boiled in salted water and then sautéed with garlic and oil. I've had it as a simple side dish and also as a topping for *crostini* over melted pecorino cheese (sublime). The long, glorious culinary life that Florentines have given their *cavolo nero* illustrates their pluck; where others would see a bitter, funny looking plant, they uncovered vegetal gold.

## LARDO DI COLONNATA

Most of us associate lard with mushy white stuff that grandmothers once used to make pie crust before the substance was basically outlawed by the artery police. But on a Florentine menu or in a shop, when you see something called *lardo* or *lardo di Colonnata*, it's not rendered fat for baking, but is instead a prized regional delicacy. The town of Colonnata, close to Carrara, is famous for its beautiful white marble—as well as its *lardo*. Here a small number of dedicated producers cure unrendered pork fat with salt and herbs and then age it in special marble tubs. Don't shy away from *lardo* when you see it as an antipasto; when sliced thin and served warm on *crostini,* the *lardo* simply melts in your mouth, giving you a whole new perspective on pork fat.

## OLIO DI OLIVA EXTRAVIRGINE

In Tuscany, where oil production goes back to the Etruscans, extra virgin olive oil greases the gears of life. The region's ubiquitous olive trees with their thin silverish leaves provide about 20 percent of the country's oil. The greenish-gold peppery oil is the Tuscan universal solvent, as appreciated and venerated as fine wine. It gets tossed with wild greens, poured over hot soups and pastas, and dripped on hot bread to make the regional version of *bruschetta,* called *fettunta* (roughly translated as "oiled slice"). Tuscans are so fond of their strong-flavored oil that they even deep-fry in it, and occasionally use it for baking and desserts. As Cristina Blasi of Florence's Cordon Bleu cooking school put it, "For us Tuscans, other oils simply don't exist." They even use it to cure a baby's diaper rash.

In late October and November, the olives are either painstakingly picked by hand, or harvested by a more mechanical method (some growers use a machine that shakes or vibrates the trees and sends the olives falling into large nets). Once the olives get to the mill, which must happen immediately after they're picked, they are cleaned and then the whole fruit—pit, meat, and skin—is crushed to a pulp between large stones. The pulp is either spread on nylon mats interspersed with stainless steel disks (the traditional method) or, much more common now, centrifuged to separate the oil from the water. The oil is kept for up to a month in large steel containers where the debris settles to the bottom, and then the oil is clarified and ready for the final stage, filtration. The result is green-tinted, fresh-tasting extra virgin olive oil.

Tuscans consume so much oil that they actually import olives from other countries, usually Spain and Greece, in order to meet local demand. If you want to insure the olives are local, look for estate-bottled oils that say *prodotto e imbottigliato nel . . .* and then give the name of the estate. You can expect to pay about ten to twenty-five euros for an estate-grown and bottled liter. It's not cheap, but makes sense when you consider that it takes five kilograms (about ten pounds) of olives to make one liter of extra virgin oil. However, you can also buy less fancy and still utterly delicious extra virgin oil for much cheaper if you don't need to have a name-brand estate on your label.

Extra virgin legally means that the oil has less than 1 percent acidity, and has also been officially tasted to assure the best flavor. There is really no reason to buy anything other than extra virgin, though some people believe it's better to fry in regular olive oil so as not to waste money. The finest estate-bottled oils are best used raw, drizzled on top of vegetables and soups, to grasp their flavor fully, though you can certainly cook with them, too. I like to keep one bottle of inexpensive extra virgin and one smaller bottle of really fine oil in the house so that I'm prepared for any oil eventuality.

Cultivation of grape vines and olive trees often goes hand in hand, not to mention the extensive know-how intrinsic in the making of both; therefore it's not surprising that some of the best oils come from estates known for their wines: Badia a Coltibuono, Querciabella, Castello di Ama, and Capezzana to name a few.

## PANE TOSCANO

You'd never know how important a touch of salt is for the taste of bread until you eat bread without salt, otherwise known as *pane toscano*, Tuscan bread. As far as I know, Tuscans are the only people anywhere who make bread without salt, and they will defend it to the end. This is peasant bread traditionally made with coarse flour and wild natural yeast and baked in a wood-fired oven, though you will rarely find it in its original form these days. The lack of salt causes the bread to have a thicker crust with a dusty pale-brown color. Tuscans claim that the organic yeastlike organisms trapped inside the usually large (one kilogram or more) loaves make the bread easier to digest and also make it last longer, which was important back when the method was first invented.

By itself, Tuscan bread tastes dry and dull to a foreign palate, but there are times when it is just the thing—for sopping up the salty sauce of a meat dish (the act of which locals call *fare la scarpetta,* or "doing the slipper") or adding to a flavorful soup. Bread is a key ingredient in several ubiquitous Tuscan dishes, including *ribollita, pappa al pomodoro,* and *panzanella.*

If you want to order bread with salt in a bakery, you can ask either for *pane salato* or *pane pugliese.* I am trying to develop the taste for Tuscan bread, though I admit it's tough going. And then I have to wonder, if Tuscans love their traditional bread so much, why is the salted bread at the bakery always sold out?

Some places to find good Tuscan and other breads:

**Forno Galli,** Via S. Agostino 8r, 055/219-703 (Map C6)

**Forno Pagnotti,** Borgo La Croce 109r, 055/247-9362 (Map H4)

**Forno Sartoni,** page 109

**Cantinetta dei Verrazzano,** page 115

## PECORINO TOSCANO

Outside of Italy, when people think of pecorino they usually think of hard, aged Pecorino Romano, which is often grated onto pasta as a substitute for the more expensive Parmesan. It's a shame that Pecorino Toscano in its various forms has not yet made serious inroads into the export market. Pecorino is made from sheep's milk and aged for varying amounts of time, from twenty days for soft and mild *pecorino fresco* to several months for the deliciously tart, medium-density, semi-aged (*mezzo-stagionato*) version, which goes well with pears, green apples, and local Chianti wines. Experts claim the fine taste is due to the especially good grassy areas for sheep in the region. The making of Tuscan pecorino was already regulated as far back as the nineteenth century, but it didn't receive the prestigious DOP (protected designation of origin) until 1986; it's still one of only about two dozen cheeses to be labeled DOP. The skin is usually a soft yellow, unless it has been tinted with ash or dried tomato, and the inside should be buttery white. The rounds usually weigh between one and three kilograms (two to six pounds). Pecorino from Pienza Province is especially prized (you'll sometimes see it named on menus); it usually comes in smaller rounds and is aged anywhere from 60 to 180 days. The results range from a soft and fairly mild "eating cheese" to a semi-aged product with a definite kick.

## RIBOLLITA

What began life as a peasant soup made from leftovers has become one of the signature dishes of Florence. *Ribollita,* a thick and delicious mix of beans, bread, and *cavolo nero,* will warm you up in winter more effectively than a down parka. It is made from a *soffritto* of carrot, celery, and onion to which you add beans (sometimes pureed), stale bread, and the local leafy *cavolo nero.* You can make it at home, but it somehow is not quite the same as sampling it at the local trattoria, where *ribollita* is often served in a thick ceramic bowl to retain the heat, accompanied with a nice glass of Chianti or Morellino di Scansano. Some of the best places to try *ribollita*:

Osteria Antica Mescita di San Niccolò, page 77

Trattoria Mario, page 81

Da Ruggiero, page 82

Vecchia Bettola, page 75

*Lina Mazzetti serves up a hearty portion of* ribollita *to cooking school students.*

## Salumi Toscani

Tuscan *salumi* are known and appreciated throughout Italy, and they turn up as a specialty on menus from Venice to Palermo. The prosciutto, salami, and other cured meats of this area tend to be salty and strongly flavored. Tuscans love their cold cuts and often eat prosciutto and pancetta plain, with no need for bread as an intermediary.

**Prosciutto toscano:** Perhaps not as famous as its counterpart from Parma, Tuscan prosciutto—a cured leg of raw ham, aged for at least a year—is salty, delicious, and subtly flavored with a mix of rosemary, garlic, pepper, and juniper berries. Production of prosciutto in Tuscany is limited, which means you'll be hard-pressed to find this delicacy in gourmet shops abroad.

**Pancetta:** Italian-style bacon that is salt-cured instead of smoked, pancetta isn't truly a specialty of Tuscany, but it's certainly prevalent here. You usually see it in a wide bricklike piece topped with lots of pepper.

**Salame toscano:** This is an all-pork *salame* made with lots of pepper, spices, and a fair amount of fat—an excellent all-around *salame* that is great in sandwiches.

**Finocchiona:** Larger than a *salame toscano*, *finocchiona* is made of coarsely chopped pork, pork fat, and fennel seeds, stuffed in a natural casing. It's a specialty of the area around Prato.

**Soppressata:** This headcheese, or pig's head sausage, is made with left-over pieces of meat and cartilage and flavored with salt, pepper, garlic, and lemon peel. Often gray, it's not to everyone's liking, but it can be very good when made by an artisanal producer and sliced very thin.

**Cinta Senese salumi:** Cinta Senese refers to a rare breed of free-range pig—named for the white pelt that encircles the animal's front quarters and looks like a belt, or *cinta*—raised in the hills outside Siena. These special swine get to roam through the forest and eat twigs and leaves and acorns instead of the banal slop fed to their penned brethren. This results in an especially dark, fatty, and flavorful meat, made into pancetta, pro-sciutto, *salame,* and *guanciale* (cheek meat). Because the breed is feisty and hard to raise, production is tiny and the meat is extremely costly, up to fifty euros per kilogram.

**Prosciutto e salame di cinghiale:** Wild boar, called *cinghiale*, make a grotesque and oddly hilarious appearance in the movie *Hannibal* (filmed in Florence), but rest assured these big, hairy, snouty beasts are more often eaten by people than the other way around. They roam primarily in the Maremma area in southern Tuscany as well as near Arezzo, and are a favorite catch for hunters. The dark gamey meat can be made into *salame*, prosciutto, and sausage. They have a very strong particular flavor, are a bit greasy, and go better with cheese and bread than on their own.

## SCHIACCIATA

*Schiacciata* is one of those words not limited to a particular sphere of life. When a friend broke her hand and went to the hospital, the doctor's diagnosis: *schiacciata*. How do you want your nuts from the store, whole or *schiacciata?* Michael Jordan makes a slam dunk at the all-star game; what do the announcers yell: *Schiacciataaaaa!! Schiacciata*, pronounced skee-ah-cha-ta, essentially means crushed, broken, squashed, or slammed, though when you're hungry, the most important definition is a perfect rectangle of salty golden focaccialike bread. *Schiacciata* is Florence's answer to Ligurian focaccia, which is higher and less dense. To make it, the bakers take the dough for *pane toscano*, flatten it on a sheet, poke it with their fingers, and top it with a hefty dose of salt and oil before baking. The result is a delicious snack, often topped with onions, anchovies, or various other savories. Florentine babies and kids cry out for it, though sometimes they can only get out "cha cha"; it's okay, their parents know what they want. To get good *schiacciata*, stop at **Pugi** (see page 113), or any reliable *forno* (bakery) in town.

*Wines by the glass at Fratellini.*

# 2

# A Primer on Tuscan Wine

## From Fiasco to Forerunner

For most people, Tuscan wine means Chianti, but this fertile region produces an impressive and sometimes overwhelming list of wines, from very light whites that go down easily to full-bodied Brunello di Montalcino, which requires a heavy meal to counter its strong personality. Even so, multifaceted and highly drinkable Chianti is number one here, and the traditional Sangiovese grape still reigns as *magnum uva*.

In the 1970s and early 1980s, Chianti wine hit a low point in its long history. Coasting on the appellation's name, the producers put out more and more wine of a decreasing quality, much of it diluted by a large percentage of white grapes. Chianti's reputation suffered, and its wines became synonymous with the cheap, watery stuff usually served in the traditional bulbous straw-laced bottle, ironically called a *fiasco*.

Fortunately, a group of dedicated winegrowers, with the Antinori and Frescobaldi families in the lead (see pages 30 and 33), decided to take matters into their own hands and raise standards of Tuscan wine to compete in international markets with France and the New World. Taking cues from the French in particular, these forward-thinking winery owners and their hardworking oenologists began experimenting with growing Cabernet Sauvignon and Merlot grapes to add to their reds, Chardonnay and Sauvignon Blanc to spice up the whites, and importing French oak barriques—smaller than the more traditional large Slavic barrels—to impart an oakier flavor to the wines as they age. Even more important, the winemakers put enormous resources into their core product by improving the quality of their Sangiovese grapes. The result of all this work, which often fell outside the DOC and DOCG regulations (see box opposite), was the advent of the Supertuscan.

The first Supertuscans were Sassicaia, made by Tenuta San Guido in Bolgheri, and soon after, the groundbreaking Tignanello, a heady concoction of Sangiovese and Cabernet grapes made by the Antinori family. These wines caused a sensation both with Italian and foreign wine cognoscenti, and have spawned a multitude of Supertuscans, as well as IGT wines of all stripes from other regions: everything from a sharp all-Sangiovese bottle to those mixed with Merlot, Syrah, Pinot Noir. At this point the possibilities seem endless.

Just as military and NASA research eventually leads to your younger cousin getting a handheld Global Positioning Device for Christmas, the lessons of the Supertuscans trickled down into Tuscan winemaking in general. Eventually the winemakers brought this new expertise to bear on the bread and butter of the vineyards: the everyday and *riserva* Chiantis, which have improved markedly over the past fifteen years. Supertuscans also gave way to the current wave of IGT wines that mix French grapes, are often aged in wood, and go outside the DOC regulations, but are not necessarily as hyped and price-inflated as their famous forebearers. (Some people call these the baby Tuscans.) At this point, there are those who would argue that the one-hundred-dollar bottles of Supertuscan wine are pure marketing hype, and that you will do much better with a bottle of Chianti Riserva from Castello di Ama or a Bolgheri Rosso from Michele Satta. However, going "outside the system" and the strict guidelines of DOC and DOCG still allows winemakers to experiment and be creative, and thus Supertuscans can be considered the research and development departments of the top wineries.

## DECIPHERING THE WINE LIST

Florence is not only the capital of Tuscany, but also the seat of some of its finest winemakers. So it's no surprise that wine lists in this city can be thrilling and sometimes overwhelming. Below is a brief rundown of the major choices you're likely to find on Florentine wine lists, which should offer a few signposts along the way.

## What's Up, DOC?

You may have already attempted to unscramble the acronyms adorning your bottle of Chianti or Vernaccia. Many flaunt the DOC or DOCG labels, which stand for *Denominazione d'Origine Controllata* and—even better—*Denominazione d'Origine Controllata e Garantita,* respectively. (The DOCG is simply a stricter version of DOC, with tighter guidelines and higher standards.) The DOC system (pronounced "doc," not "d.o.c.") is Italy's answer to the French appellation system, in which wines are regulated under strict guidelines by the government. DOC regulations affect everything from the grape varietals allowed (including specific percentages) to yield and aging, all pegged to a specific geographical winegrowing area. In order to earn their DOC stripes in Tuscany, wines must follow the regulations and then be tasted and approved by elected officials in Florence and Siena.

Most of all, as the name implies, the DOC label is a guarantee that your Chianti Rufina really comes from the Rufina area. This is important, since Italian wines are known primarily by geographical origin—tied in intrinsically with their *terroir*—instead of by the grape (for example, Chianti is called Chianti, not Sangiovese). What can you take away from all of this? Essentially, these acronyms are an assurance of consistency and quality. They don't promise that you'll like the wine, but they are a decent indication that someone knew what they were doing when they made it. In other words, it's not necessary to have the DOC label, but as an authoritative marker in the vast sea of wines, it helps.

Vino Nobile, Brunello di Montalcino, and Vernaccia of San Gimigniano were among the first DOC wines in Italy. In the mid-1980s, the central Chianti Classico region was raised from DOC to DOCG, tightening guidelines, eliminating some of the shoddy practices previously in place, and generally helping raise the status of Chianti wines. Recently, not only Chianti Classico and the other traditional leaders, but also Colli Senesi, Colli Aretini, Rufina, Colli Fiorentini, and a fistful of other Tuscan wines have been graced with the DOCG denomination.

Most non-DOC wines are now marked IGT, for *Indicazione Geografica Tipica*. The IGT label is a way of identifying that someone is experimenting outside the DOC system—often a good thing. It is a more egalitarian and in fact more accurate way to identify non-DOC wines than the name Supertuscan, which at this point refers to a small number of very expensive wines. Though it is becoming less common, you will occasionally see a bottle marked simply *vino da tavola* (table wine). This not only means that the wine is made outside the DOC system, but implies it uses grapes grown outside its own geographic area—for example, cheaper "blending" grapes from Puglia or Sicily.

## Chianti Classico

Chianti Classico refers to the heart of the Chianti region, the rolling hills between Florence and Siena, which comprise the towns of Greve, Radda, Castellina, Gaiole, and bits of other territories. There is no doubt that some of Tuscany's finest and certainly most characteristic wines—epitomizing the Tuscan *terroir*, somewhat dry as far as red wines go, with hints of raspberry and cherry and a slight kick—come from this area. Chianti Classico wine is made primarily from Sangiovese grapes, with a small addition of Canaiolo, Colorino, or other complementary grapes. Despite leaps and bounds in quality, Chianti continues to be a relatively affordable, drinkable wine, perfect for everyday meals.

Chianti Classico *riserve* are aged longer—some in oak barrels—with a higher alcohol content, and tend to have smoother texture and deeper flavors; they also cost a bit more. Some of the names to look out for in both the *riserva* and regular Classico categories are Fonterutoli, Fontodi, Querciabella, Castello di Brolio, and Castell'in Villa. Castello di Ama and Felsina also turn out top-quality, special occasion *riserve*, while Castello Aiola and Villa Vistarenni make some good low-priced bottles.

On some bottles of Chianti Classico, in addition to the DOCG appellation you'll see a logo of a black rooster called Gallo Nero. This consortium of Chianti Classico winemakers is purely voluntary and promotional, so again, it's not a guarantee of anything in particular, but it's a stamp of peer approval.

## Other Chiantis

The greater Chianti winemaking region comprises the provinces of Florence, Arezzo, Siena, Pisa, and Pistoia. Don't be afraid of venturing outside Chianti Classico for your bottle of wine; vintages from Chianti Rufina, Colli Senesi, and Colli Fiorentini have also improved over the past few years (Rufina is generally agreed to yield the finest wines), and tend to be very economical. They can be drunk quite young but are at their best when aged one to four years. Names to look for include Frescobaldi, Colognole, Lanciola, and La Querce.

## Carmignano

Carmignano winemakers started adding Cabernet Sauvignon to their Sangiovese red wines before it was even a trend, and thus set themselves apart from the Chianti region. This area west of Florence encompasses Artimino, Carmignano, and Poggio a Caiano (for more on this area, see page 230). Current DOCG regulations now stipulate nearly two years of aging, and 45 to 70 percent Sangiovese, with the rest a mix of Cabernet and other white grapes, at the discretion of the individual maker. The name that comes up most often in respect to Carmignano is Tenuta di Capezzana, though other good wines come from Villa Artimino, Fattoria Baccheretto, and Fattoria Il Poggiolo. Capezzana and other producers also put out a lighter, less expensive DOC red called Barco Reale and a popular rosé called Vin Ruspo.

## Bolgheri and the Maremma

This region on the Maremma coast of Tuscany, south of Pisa, is *the* current winemaking hot spot. Word is, if you owned a corner of land in Bolgheri, you'd be rich right now, as every producer from Piedmont to Puglia wants to stake a claim in this fertile coastal soil. The area's reputation as prime grape-growing territory can be traced to Tenuta San Guido's introduction of Sassicaia in 1968. In 2001, *Wine Spectator* chose Tenuta dell'Ornellaia's Bolgheri Superiore Ornellaia as its wine of the year, and in 2002 Ornellaia was sold to a partnership including the Frescobaldi family and Robert Mondavi of California.

As this one-time boggy mosquito zone has become widely acknowledged as a winemaking paradise, Bolgheri has been given several DOC

# Big Names, Big Wines

Antinori is one of the biggest names in the Florence wine world—and growing. An archival document shows that Giovanni di Piero Antinori joined the vintner's guild in 1385, giving the current Marchese Piero Antinori a real claim to having the longest-running wine dynasty in the area. In 1506 the family bought the majestic Florentine palace (originally called the Palazzo Boni, later renamed Palazzo Antinori) that still holds their offices and the restaurant and wine bar Cantinetta Antinori.

The Antinori family and their master oenologist, Giacomo Tachis, made an enormous contribution to the improvements in Tuscan and Chianti wines in the 1980s, and their large stable of wines continues to receive high praise among experts. The reliable everyday and *riserva* Chiantis simply labeled Villa Antinori, and the low-priced Santa Cristina brand make frequent appearances in wine shops and on menus around town. In addition, the family now counts among its Tuscan estates Badia a Passignano, Pèppoli, and Tignanello, which turn out Supertuscans Tignanello and the award-winning Solaia wine. In addition they have acquired La Braccesca in Montepulciano, which produces a Vino Nobile and an affordable Rosso; Pian delle Vigne in Montalcino, a specialist in Brunello; Tenuto Guado al Tasso in Bolgheri (not to be confused with Tenuta San Guido, owned by an Antinori relative), an award-winning maker of DOC reds and a white of that distinctive region; Fattoria Aldobrandesca, producer of a red wine called Aleatico; and finally Castello della Sala, actually in Umbria, a specialist in white wines such as the Orvieto Classico. And that's not even getting into their grappa, *vin santo,* olive oil, or investments in foreign wineries in California and Hungary. The family also runs the Cantinetta (see page 46) on the ground floor; the very traditional Tuscan eatery Bucca Lappi, downstairs in the basement; and the *tartufo*-oriented snack and wine bar Procacci (see page 163) across the street—truly a little gourmet cul-de-sac.

## Antinori Offices
*Palazzo Antinori, Piazza Antinori 3, D4, by appointment only, 055/292-234.*

denominations, including Bolgheri Rosso and Bolgheri Bianco; plus Sassicaia became the first single-vineyard DOC in all of Italy. The Bolgheri reds tend to include a hefty dose of Cabernet Sauvignon and Merlot grapes, which give all the wines from this region a bit of Supertuscan oomph. With popularity and hype come high prices, however, and the name Bolgheri on a bottle sometimes entails a steep price especially for the top wines of San Guido and Ornellaia. (For more information on this region and its wines, see page 247.)

In addition to the big names like Guado al Tasso and Ornellaia, several small producers are creating excellent wines that are accessible and complex even when quite young. Among the smaller, less expensive but eminently drinkable wines of this area are those made by Enrico Santini: an excellent low-priced red called Poggio al Moro, a more sophisticated Bolgheri Superiore, and a light *bianco* made mostly of Trebbiano grapes. And producer Michele Satta is gaining popularity for his drinkable reds and whites.

*Bottles on display at Millesimi.*

In an ever-expanding wave of wine appreciation, the nearby region of Val di Cornia and even the island of Elba have been granted their own DOC status. The Val di Cornia includes the area around Suvereto, where some of the labels to look for are Tua Rita, which makes a good—if very dry—all-Sangiovese Supertuscan as well as other wines; Le Pinacce; and Jacopo Banti.

### Morellino di Scansano

This up-and-coming red hails from Scansano in the Maremma region, just southeast of Bolgheri. Morellino is a variant of the Sangiovese grape and is sometimes blended with Malvasia Nera, Canaiolo, or Grenache. Like Chianti, Morellino di Scansano is an excellent everyday wine with a bright ruby color and plenty of body, but not so much as to overpower your meal. Some good choices in this category are Moris Farms, Il Boscheto, and Erik Banti, who is often credited with spearheading the comeback of this wine region. Plenty of estates such as Fonterutoli and Rocca delle Macie, better known for their Chianti Classicos, have also staked a claim here and begun to make their own Morellino.

*All'Antico Vinaio.*

## What's New with Frescobaldi, a Tuscan Wine Dynasty

The Frescobaldi family is obsessed with land. "We have really concentrated on the *terroir*, on the land. We come from a long line of landowners, and this has always been the Frescobaldi philosophy," explains Tiziana Frescobaldi, head of communications for the Marchesi de Frescobaldi wine company, one of the largest in Tuscany and Italy as a whole. The Frescobaldis have been on a bit of a land-buying spree recently, consolidating their holdings in Tuscany and farther afield. In 2002 they bought the famed Ornellaia estate in Bolgheri in partnership with Robert Mondavi of California. They are, however, adhering to the "not broke, don't fix it" rule of thumb and are not planning to make any immediate drastic changes to the wildly successful Ornellaia.

Frescobaldi first partnered with Mondavi in 1995, when they started a company called Luce della Vite. The joint venture bought prime land in the Brunello-growing Montalcino area and first produced Luce, then Lucente, then another line called Danzante. The two companies were able to play on each others' strengths. "The Mondavis are very careful about respecting the land, the soil," says Tiziana. "Of course we've learned a lot about marketing from them, and perhaps in terms of production in Tuscany we were able to share our knowledge with them."

In addition to Ornellaia, the Frescobaldi family purchased another estate, near Livorno, called Nugola, as a joint venture with the Florentine Marchi family, where they are also doing new planting. In 2002 they engaged noted Italian architect Piero Santolo to design a new cellar at the Castelgiocondo estate. At their main Chianti estate in Nipozzano they've opened a little enoteca where you can visit the cellars and have a tour. Asked about the lack of organized wine tourism in Tuscany, Tiziana explains, "The Italian wine industry here has been very traditional and not so marketing oriented, so there has been resistance to this kind of thing. But recently producers have discovered that this is a very good publicity tool and so it is finally changing a little bit." The best thing to do, she says, is go to a *consorzio* and ask for a map and brochure of wineries that are open for visits in that area. Nipozzano, for example, is part of the Chianti Rufina consortium, which comprises lots of little makers. (The *consorzi* are part of the Strada del Vino, a wine tourism initiative in the works all over Tuscany, which is still in its start-up phase.)

### Changes in Tuscan Wine?

When asked about the seemingly inexorable trend toward the "international style" of wine, including the use of French barriques and foreign grapes, Tiziana is adamant that, while the Supertuscan has been a huge benefit to Italian wine in general, growers need to be careful not to make mistakes now; "we need to defend our *tipicità*," what is typical of Tuscany. "Sangiovese is actually a difficult vine to grow, but it has always been the basis of all our wines and I think it is worth the trouble." Frescobaldi does make wines that are pure Cabernet and pure Merlot, but for the most part they use Sangiovese; Luce, for example, is Sangiovese with a little bit of Merlot. Sangiovese and Tuscany go hand in hand, according to Tiziana. "There are few places where Sangiovese gives excellent results, and here we have the right climate, the right *terroir*." Cabernet and Merlot are much easier to grow, she says, but the use of Sangiovese will certainly continue.

On the other hand, she says, "In our experience, the native Tuscan white grape Trebbiano is dying out." Part of the problem is that it was used in Chianti but now it isn't anymore. In addition, tastes have changed. "Little by little we have taken out the Trebbiano and planted Sangiovese or Cabernet. But we think there is a little area in Tuscany called Pomino that is good for producing white wines," she explains, "owing to its historical background, the climate, the soil, and the Chardonnay and the Pinot Grigio that have always been in Pomino." Frescobaldi has also recently purchased a company in the Collio region of Friuli in northern Italy called Attems, where it produces Pinot Grigio, Tocai, and Cabernet Sauvignon. "That is our strategy," she says, "to take away all the Trebbiano in the places like Chianti where we can have better results with reds and concentrate our whites in Pomino and in Friuli."

## Brunello and Rosso di Montalcino

The sloping hillsides around Montalcino capture the postcard fantasy of green and sunny Tuscany. The Brunello grape, also called Sangiovese Grosso, has grown here for more than a century, giving local winemakers plenty of time to perfect their craft. To be considered Brunello di Montalcino, among other requirements, the wine must be made from 100 percent Sangiovese Grosso, and it must age for a minimum of four years (two years in oak)—five years for a *riserva*—after which it is vigorously taste-tested. Usually the wine ages in a combination of Slavic *botti*, or large barrels, and smaller barriques, until just the right flavor is achieved. The Brunello is a robust wine, and needs to be paired with strong dishes such as hearty winter roasts, lest it overpower your dinner. To get some of the taste of Brunello without the punch—or the price, which is always high—try a Rosso di Montalcino, made from the same grape but with less stringent requirements and aged for a much shorter time. Poggio di Sotto, La Poderina, Siro Pacenti, and Col d'Orcia all produce award-winning Brunellos. Villa Banfi, Castelgiocondo, Fattoria Barbi, and Biondi-Santi are some of the best-known producers in the region, consistently making excellent wines.

## Vino Nobile and Rosso di Montepulciano

Vino Nobile is like Brunello's younger brother: the same prestigious pedigree, the same depth of flavor, but literally younger—made from a minimum of 70 percent Sangiovese grapes and aged for three years instead of four—so it is usually a touch lighter and less expensive. Also like Brunello, Vino Nobile's grapes enjoy prime real estate on southern Tuscany's sun-drenched hillsides. Swept up in the tide of Tuscan wine's renewal, Nobile has undergone major improvements in the past ten years, helped by dedicated vintners such as Poliziano and Avignonesi. Nobile also has its own more accessible line of Rossos, priced for everyday consumption and extremely satisfying on their own merits. (Don't confuse these wines with Montepulciano d'Abruzzo, a completely unrelated wine from the Abruzzo region.) In addition to Poliziano and Avignonesi, look for excellent Nobiles from Fattoria del Cerro, Tenuta Valdipiatta, and Villa Sant'Anna.

## Supertuscans and IGT Wines

Tenuta San Guido's Sassicaia and Antinori's Tignanello launched a revolution in Tuscan winemaking in the 1970s and early 1980s that continues to flourish. The term Supertuscan was coined in the 1980s by American wine writers who were bowled over by the new Tuscan *vini da tavola;* they didn't want these top wines to be confused with regular table wine, hence the superlative new name, which was eagerly embraced by Italians (who pronounce it "Soopertooscan"). These wines, which were originally made outside the DOC and DOCG restrictions, were distinguished mainly by two things: their use of international grapes such as Cabernet Sauvignon, Cabernet Franc, and Merlot, either alone or mixed with native Sangiovese; and the aging in small French oak barrels (barriques). Every rule has an exception, however, and now you will find several Supertuscans made with all Sangiovese (which I see as a Tuscan assertion of pride in the face of impending French grape domination). The most esteemed output of the estate from which they come, Supertuscan bottles often display elegantly designed labels and strange and nonsensical names. Some very good Supertuscans to look for include Fontalloro, Solaia, Siepi, and Brancaia.

The name Supertuscan has come to mean any top boutique Tuscan wine that is expensive and made according to the parameters described above, whether within or outside the DOC system. For example, the original Super, Sassicaia, is now a DOC in and of itself, while other Supertuscans are classed under the recently designated DOCs of Bolgheri Rosso or even of Chianti. Many others are now labeled IGT, an increasingly popular designation that you'll see on bottles and on wine lists all over Florence in place of the old *vino da tavola*. An IGT mark indicates that a wine is typical of the zone from which it comes and adheres to many, but not all, of the DOC regulations from said zone. This classification allows for a certain amount of creativity in the winemaking process, but is not a license to adulterate wine with cheap grapes. The designation is being used increasingly as a descriptive name for any alternative wine that is non-DOC, be it a pricey Supertuscan or other, more affordable wine.

In sum, the question "What is a Supertuscan?" has become a more confusing semantic game, and the wine rules and regulations continue to change.

### Vino Novello

It was inevitable that winemakers looking north toward France would also want to try their hand at *vini novelli* (new wines), an Italian version of Beaujolais Nouveau. The trend began in the northern regions of the Veneto and Friuli, but Tuscans are also getting in on it. Like Beaujolais, the *vini novelli* are made using the carbonic maceration process, which ferments the just-pressed grapes in such a way that the wine can forgo traditional aging; conveniently, it also allows the wineries to off-load some of the wine they would normally age in expensive barrels and earn some cash in what is usually a down time of year.

Every November come the clamorous announcements of the arrival of the *novello*, with bottles often costing less than five euros. In my opinion, the Tuscan *novelli* have yet to hit their stride. Instead of a light and fruity drinkable red, many of the Tuscan *novelli* fall flat. Compared to traditional winemaking, *novelli* are still in the nascent stage, and so it's not surprising to find a few kinks. As star oenologist Giacomo Tachis explains on the National Institute for Vino Novello website, "In general the Italian *novelli* have a stronger taste of carbonic acid [than the French], which is almost always pleasing to an Italian palate, but not so for foreigners." This may be true, but I've met many Italians who won't drink the stuff. It's likely, given their track record for success, that the dogged Tuscan winemakers will soon produce bright red and fruity *novelli* that are pleasing to everyone, so we can look forward to that time. Some producers making *vini novelli* are Antinori, Villa Banfi, and Rocca della Macie.

### Whites Wines

Though Tuscany is best known for its cherry red wines, local winemakers, eyes turned toward California and France, have been creating some internationally acclaimed whites, increasingly by using tried-and-true grapes like Chardonnay and Sauvignon Blanc instead of the local white grapes, the less exciting Trebbiano and Malvasia. These refined, sometimes oak-aged bottles are the present and, it seems, the future of white wine in Tuscany, competing with the traditional proud whites from farther north in Piedmont and Friuli. A typical producer, Castello di Ama makes an extremely aromatic Chardonnay that is so oak-y it might not be to everyone's liking. Bolgheri winemakers such as Ornellaia, Enrico Santini, and Michele Satta all turn out decidedly lighter whites that go well with light meals.

San Gimignano's Vernaccia was one of the first wines in Italy to be acknowledged with DOC status. The Vernaccia grape creates a dry, full-bodied white, and is sometimes mixed with a small amount of other grapes, usually Malvasia or Trebbiano. The storied wine has had its ups and downs, but has come back fairly strong, thanks to the confident care of several key makers, including Tenuta Le Calcinaie, La Lastra, and Giovanni Panizzi. Vernaccia is one of the only traditional whites to retain its popularity in today's market, while everyone else is going Chardonnay. Other whites have evolved over the past ten years, including Bianco di Pitigliano, Bianco Vergine Valdichiana, and refined whites from the Montecarlo region.

## Vin Santo

Instead of dessert, many Florentines will opt for a plate of crunchy *cantucci* (also called biscotti or *biscottini*) and a dipping glass of amber *vin santo* (literally, "holy wine"). *Vin santo* is usually made from Malvasia and/or Trebbiano grapes which, instead of rotting on the trees à la Sauternes, are either dried out on mats or hung from a ceiling for a period of weeks (a process called *passito*) before spending the next six to ten years (or less for lower-priced bottles) in small oak barrels. The process is lengthy and expensive, resulting in a small output of delicious dessert wine that can be either sweet or dry depending on small variances in its creation. This prized drink is usually quite expensive. You'll find many a bottle labeled *vin santo* on sale for under ten euros per liter, but this is not the true *vin santo;* it is fortified sweet wine, labeled *vino liquoroso.* I happen to like the cheap stuff, especially for cooking or dunking, but it's worth seeking out the true aged *vin santo* either for yourself or as a gift for someone you really like. Some of the best *vin santo* is made by Avignonese, Isole e Olena, and Badia a Coltibuono.

## Grappa

Grappa, the remarkably strong after-dinner brandy made from the skins and seeds (pomace) of wine grapes left over in the fermenting tanks, was once associated primarily with the north, particularly the Veneto, where the town of Bassano del Grappa is famous for its hard liquor as much as for its covered bridge designed by Andrea Palladio. But as with almost every other possible area of wine and wine-related production, Tuscan producers have made serious inroads. You'll now see the elegantly designed bottles containing pure, clear grappa from Brunello, Chianti, Vernaccia, and almost every type of Tuscan wine. Some producers to look for, in addition to Antinori and Frescobaldi, are Ornellaia, Il Poggiolo of Carmignano, and San Giorgio of Montalcino.

*One of the friendly waiters at Osteria de' Benci.*

# 3
# RESTAURANTS
# AND TRATTORIAS

Florentines love and appreciate well-cooked Florentine food. And who can blame them? They are heirs to one of the most hearty and satisfying, simple yet influential of all cuisines, made with a bounty of local ingredients. This means that any visitor to Florence need only walk down the street to find innumerable restaurants serving *ribollita, pappa al pomodoro, bistecca alla fiorentina,* and *arista,* and these standards are almost always quite good. The drawback to this obsessive adherence to tradition is a highly reluctant attitude toward innovation. Fabio Picchi and Benedetta Vitali shook up the Florentine food scene when they opened Cibreo in the 1980s; here was a place cooking up long-forgotten Tuscan dishes, but with a modern sensibility.

The best restaurants in Florence today vary among the tried-and-true outposts of *pappa* and *bistecca,* and a growing number of "international style" restaurants where the chef may have spent time in London or New York and knows his or her way around a tuna tartare or beet and goat cheese salad, but still makes a true *ribollita.* Such places often have architect-designed bars, open kitchens, ochre walls, and a multi-lingual staff. Some may lament this new wave, but I see it as a necessary injection of fresh air in terms of both the cooking and the ambience. Now you can have the best of both, the old school and the new cool, all in one place.

## Ristorante Cibreo

**Via del Verrocchio 8r, 055/234-1100**
**Open Tuesday through Saturday 1 PM to 2:30 PM and 7 PM to 11:15 PM;**
**closed August**
**Map H4, Buses A, C, 14**
**Credit cards accepted**
**€€€€**

Cibreo's fame and fortune can be measured in part by its international clientele—diners come from far and wide to sample owner Fabio Picchi's legendary fare. Cibreo began in 1979 when Picchi and then-wife Benedetta Vitali (see page 92) decided to open a restaurant that was at once innovative and traditionally Tuscan, dedicated to bringing back long-forgotten peasant cooking of the region. *Cibreo*, a rich soup made of cockscombs and assorted variety meats, is an old, traditional Tuscan dish of the sort perfected in Picchi's kitchen—a fitting emblem for the restaurant.

Picchi is known for his eccentricities, which shine through in the unusual dining experience. Japanese businessmen and American honeymooners alike may be surprised when they are shown to their table and find others sitting there. In this bizarre scenario, both solo and coupled diners smile at one another a little uncomfortably across large round tables decked out in linens and crystal goblets. The empty seat between each group is used by the server who sits down with you to recite a long list of primi and secondi, in Italian or English as you prefer. The menu is surprisingly long, so be prepared for a challenging game of memorization.

Possibly the best part of dinner is the assortment of little antipasti that are brought to the table to be nibbled alongside a glass of fruity white wine. Local pecorino and walnuts come bathed in a strong garlicky olive oil; also full of garlic and spice is the house's famous tomato parfait, which tastes like a gazpacho mousse. Other bites include a delectable slice of prosciutto, a delicate ricotta *sformato* (mousse), and marinated slices of tripe, for many an acquired taste. The tuna tartare and celery dish is also excellent. For a primo you can choose from among an assortment of Tuscan soups or stews made with *farro,* polenta, *cavolo nero,* or other rustic ingredients. At some point during the meal each diner is handed an elongated bone-shaped baguette—awkward to handle, but I have to say this is some of the best bread I have tasted in Florence.

When it comes to secondi, you can almost picture the devilish Picchi, with his wizardlike gray beard, giggling with glee as he imagines what tricks he can pull on the unsuspecting tourists flocking to his restaurant. Not that he wants to treat diners badly; on the contrary, he wants to challenge and possibly even shock them out of culinary complacence. Whereas any American chef knows he or she must stack the entrée deck with steaks and chicken dishes because that's what people want, Picchi will not be limited by mob rule. The secondi menu is made up almost entirely of preparations rarely found on an American menu: calves' brains, pig's hooves . . . it begins to sound a bit like the witches brew from *Macbeth.* Have culinary hang-ups? Get over them. The most "normal" dishes on the menu might be something like a delicious white fish baked in tomato sauce or roast pigeon with sweet-and-sour *mostarda*—itself a haute Tuscan classic.

Navigating the expensive wine list can be tricky, but you can make out well without spending a lot by choosing a Chianti from the Leonardo da Vinci collective, recently voted one of the best bargain wines by Italian food magazine *Gambero Rosso.* The desserts, on the other hand, are not at all difficult to navigate: just think chocolate. The flourless chocolate torte dusted with powdered sugar will expand your mind; I'm also quite partial to the chocolate *budino,* essentially really, really good chocolate pudding. Not everyone is a chocolate fiend, however, and all of the desserts here are delicious.

(For more on Cibreo, see the review of the trattoria, page 66.)

## Enoteca Pinchiorri

**Via Ghibellina 87, 055/242-777; fax: 055/244-983 (best to reserve at least two weeks in advance)**

**Open Tuesday and Wednesday 7:30 PM to 10 PM; Thursday through Saturday 12:30 PM to 2 PM and 7:30 PM to 10 PM; closed August and Christmas Day**

**Map G5, Bus 14**

**Credit cards accepted**

**€€€€**

First, money must be no object. Second, you should be excited by the kind of old-world elegance—sterling silver water pitchers, Murano glass chandeliers, pale pink table linens, liveried waiters—that is a dying breed in this new world of sharp designer lighting and square plates. Third, you should be very interested in wine. If all this sounds enticing, Enoteca Pinchiorri opens its Renaissance palazzo doors to you.

Today Pinchiorri is known in turn by some as the best restaurant in Florence (it was even voted best in Italy by the Touring Club Italiano guide), certainly the most expensive restaurant in town with a price of about €250 per head (depending largely on your wine choice), and the only Florentine eatery to earn two Michelin stars. The restaurant has been part of the prestigious Relais & Chateaux chain since 1984, but owners Giorgio Pinchiorri and Annie Féolde—he an expert in wine, she a top haute chef—opened it back in 1973. Now the kitchen is run by executive chefs Italo Bassi and Riccardo Monco.

You can choose between à la carte dishes or two extensive tasting menus. Among the à la carte appetizers is a goose liver terrine served with figs and star anise and a dish of sea scallops with celery and caviar in a basil vinaigrette. The limited primi on offer, all pastas, include handmade *trofie* pasta with chopped scampi, fresh tomato, and *bottarga* (dried mullet roe). Among the meat and fish secondi you might find a lobster with asparagus tips and pear and ginger sauce or monkfish with potatoes, as well as baked baby lamb with its deep-fried brain and roasted potatoes flavored with lard. One tasting menu is done according to the chefs' inspiration (€160) and the other according to season (€145); both include eight small-sized tasting plates of rich and creative fare.

Though the food is certainly over the top, it may take a backseat to the wine. Giorgio Pinchiorri's famed cellar is said to hold 180,000 bottles from Italy, France, and California—one of the finest collections in the world. Expert sommeliers, including Giorgio himself on occasion, will come to your table and suggest wines to accompany your meal. If you wish, they will suggest wines by the glass that can accompany each course.

Details like nineteenth-century antique furniture and huge bouquets of white lilies (the official flower of Florence) may even go unnoticed amid all the serious eating and drinking happening here. In the end, Pinchiorri's brand of gold-plated opulence is not to everyone's taste, but for those who would like excellent wines and haute Tuscan food in a setting of hushed elegance, look no further.

## EXPENSIVE

---

## Beccofino

**Piazza Scarlatti 1, Lungarno Guicciardini, 055/290-076**
**Open Monday through Saturday 7:30 PM to 11:30 PM; Sunday 12:30 PM to**
**   2:30 PM and 7:30 PM to 11:30 PM**
**Map C5, Buses 6, D**
**Credit cards accepted**
**€€€**

Leading the charge among elegant and contemporary new restaurants in Florence, Beccofino attracts a mix of visitors and adventurous Florentines to its prime location along the Arno. This was one of the first restaurants in town with a sleek architectural interior—blond woods, bold geometric shapes, flatteringly dim lighting, and the coolest bathroom in the city (check out the lighted floorboards). The cooking is also architectonic; chef Francesco Berardinelli creates dishes that arrive beautifully displayed on unusually shaped chargers, with the colorful food strategically laid out to resemble modern art.

The menu is a modern mix of styles and flavors; pastas, soups, meat, and fish dishes are made with an Italian slant but in a way that is slave neither to tradition nor fashion. Primi might include a hearty ravioli stuffed with a beet and potato purée and sprinkled with roasted artichoke bits or a carpaccio of *baccalà* with *haricots verts*. The delicious second courses are so vertical they look like mysterious rock piles on the plate, whether a turbot stacked on top of chard, nicely rare salmon on a bed of cauliflower, or roast lamb with garbanzo bean and chard mash. For dessert don't miss the *torta al cioccolato,* actually more of a mousse, up-ended in the shape of a ramekin and surrounded by more chocolate sauce. Beccofino doubles as a stylish wine bar (see page 132), and the wine list is heavy on Supertuscans, but roomy enough to satisfy both those looking for a reasonably priced Chianti or a more refined bottle of either red or white.

---

## Cantinetta Antinori

**Palazzo Antinori, Piazza Antinori 3, 055/292-234**
**Open Monday through Friday 12 PM to 2:30 PM and 7 PM to 10:30 PM;**
   **closed most of August and from Christmas Day to January 6**
**Map D4, Buses A, 6, 11, 36, 37**
**Credit cards accepted**
**€€€**

Cantinetta Antinori was conceived as a quiet and elegant oasis in the center of Florence's designer shopping district, very near both physically and spiritually to Ferragamo and Armani. Double glass doors keep out the extremes of weather on both ends of the Florentine spectrum; crisp white tablecloths, fine stemware, and trained wait staff make this place as popular with upscale travelers as with the local elite.

The Cantinetta is both a showcase for the Antinori family's roster of wines and a font of traditional Tuscan cooking taken seriously. *Ribollita* and *panzanella* (served in winter and summer, respectively) are made according to stringent traditional recipes and with the freshest ingredients, including oil culled from Antinori properties. Other antipasti and primi might include simple dishes like prosciutto and melon or fresh porcini bathed in olive oil. For secondi you can choose among lighter fare like *bresaola* with *rucola* and Parmigiano or something as meaty as classic osso buco. In addition to the regular menu there are daily specials, where the chef gets a little more creative, conjuring up such delights as an original and excellent swordfish fillet sandwiched between thin slices of puff pastry, a refreshing cold soup made from zucchini and mint, and a seafood and bean salad. The wine list—all Antinori of course—includes casual everyday fare like Santa Cristina on up to Tignanello, with plenty of very drinkable whites and reds in between. The price of a meal here is on the high end for *ribollita* but not unfathomable—about what you'd expect to pay for dining in style in one of central Florence's famed Renaissance palazzi.

## The Fuss about Fish

Florentines have a strange relationship with fish. The Mediterranean Sea is only an hour away, but fish plays almost no part in the traditional cuisine of the city. The one dish that shows up most regularly on local menus is *baccalà alla livornese,* salt cod cooked in garlic and tomato sauce; sometimes a swordfish carpaccio might make an appearance on menus, but otherwise you'll be hard-pressed to find many fish secondi at your local trattoria, despite the fine fresh fish on sale daily at the Central Market.

Instead, in Florence you'll find specialized "fish restaurants," usually expensive, sometimes chichi places that have fish shipped over daily from the ports of Livorno and Viareggio. Most of these places prepare fish in the simplest of ways—grilled, roasted, sautéed—and offer a smorgasbord of shellfish such as oysters, clams, mussels, and crayfish, seasoned with parsley and hot pepper and tossed with spaghetti or linguine. The problem with seafood is that it must be served extremely fresh, which explains why this mostly simple fare ends up being so expensive.

Florentines often rave about these places, telling visitors from around the world that there's a great new fish restaurant on the outskirts that they simply must try. But for people who are more accustomed to seeing fish on everyday menus, the concept of trudging a great distance and paying an inflated price to eat fresh fish will seem considerably less appealing. Generally people don't come to Florence to eat fish; they'd rather sample the famed *bistecca, ribollita,* and other meaty fare. But if you do crave seafood, here are the main choices in town. Just know that the fish will be fresh, the atmosphere pretentious, the preparation probably not too exciting, and the bill quite high.

### Da Stefano

*Via Senese 271, Porta Romana, 055/204-9105; open Monday through Saturday 8 PM to 11 PM, closed August; Buses 36, 37; credit cards accepted; €€€.*

"Only fish, only fresh, only in the evenings" is this restaurant's not-so-catchy motto, plastered on the business cards and the back of every server's T-shirt. Da Stefano has been around for a long time and has developed a reputation as one of the best fish restaurants in the city—a short taxi or bus ride south of the Porta Romana. The fish is indeed fresh, and the spaghetti with clams, shrimp, and crayfish especially flavorful, but the service is almost comically inept. Still, the garden in back is a fun and vibrant place for a date. The wine list, designed by the Millesimi enoteca in town (see page 145), is excellent, full of reasonably priced Sauvignon Blancs, Chardonnays, and white blends from all over Italy and Burgundy.

### Fuor D'Acqua

*Via Pisana 37r, 055/222-299; open Monday through Saturday 8 PM to 10:30 PM, closed August; Map A5, Bus 6; credit cards accepted; €€€.*

The elegant, minimalist dining room has a semi-oceanic feel, with cloth-covered chairs and a sleek look. The menu includes primi such as *tagliolini freschi con zucchini e calamari* and *penne alle astice* (a kind of lobster). Secondi are equally mouthwatering to fish lovers, including *orata* (gilt-head bream) or *branzino* (sea bass) cooked in various ways, a mixed seafood grill, *zuppa di pesce* (fish soup), or *aragosta alla catalana* (lobster cooked in the Catalan style). Many of the secondi are priced by weight, according to season.

### Lo Scoglietto

*Borgo Ognissanti 68r, 055/280-264; open Monday through Saturday 8 PM to 10 PM, closed most of August; Map C4, Bus A; credit cards accepted; €€€.*

Lo Scoglietto touts itself as an elite private club, but all you need to be a member is an appetite and possibly an American Express gold card, as a meal here is certainly pricey. The menu changes depending on what fresh fish are available that day, but might include entrées such as wild rice with crabmeat, lobster, and truffle pulp or John Dory with green pepper. The interior is elegantly appointed and air-conditioned.

## Cavolo Nero

**Via dell'Ardiglione 22r, 055/294-744**
**Open Monday through Sunday 8 PM to 11 PM; closed August**
**Map B6, Buses 11, 36, 37, D**
**Credit cards accepted**
€€€

This midsized restaurant, hidden in one of the more picturesque lanes between the Santo Spirito and San Frediano neighborhoods, underwent a major restoration with impressive results. The new interior is a modern and sophisticated study in white, orange, and black. Black wooden moldings and doors frame muted orange walls. Large evocative black-and-white photos of the eponymous *cavolo nero* and other vegetables (raw vegetables never looked so good) are framed in black. Tables are covered with crisp white linen, and even the chairs have been canvased in white. Off-white cylindrical lamps hang discreetly from the ceiling.

The kitchen is clearly trying to concoct some unusual dishes, and for the most part succeeding. It's nice to see a menu that offers antipasti other than the usual prosciutto and *crostini,* and here the choice ranges from calamari salad to phyllo-wrapped goat cheese with an excellent caviarlike *tapenade* of black olives sweetened with honey. The equally adventurous primi run the gamut from standards like spaghetti with clams and *farro* soup with a leek cake in the middle to the unholy alliance of gnocchi with broccoli and clams (in my opinion, broccoli and clams are two foods that should never meet). The buckwheat *crespelle* (crepes) stuffed with artichokes are a little too heavy on the béchamel and light on the salt.

Secondi diverge from the usual Tuscan chops and meats, offering instead a nice selection of fish (turbot and sea bass), fowl (duck breast with orange sauce, chicken breast with mushrooms, pigeon stuffed with foie gras), and other meats. The one false note was a plate of chicken livers cooked in sage, a traditional dish that would have been fine as an appetizer, but perhaps because it was overcooked, was too tough and dry to be eaten as an entire entrée, even when accompanied with a superb miniature spinach soufflé. The wine list features a number of expensive Supertuscans, but also plenty of well-chosen lower priced bottles, such as a 2000 Morellino di Scansano from Moris Farms and a 1999 Capezzana Borgo Reale—both a bargain for the quality. For dessert, the not-too-heavy chocolate torte is a highlight.

---

## Cento Poveri

**Via Palazzuolo 31 r, 055/218-846**
**Open Wednesday through Monday 7:30 PM to 10:30 PM; Sunday lunch**
**(noon to 3 PM) from October to May; closed two weeks in August**
**Map C4, Buses 11, 36, 37**
**Credit cards accepted**
**€€€**

It seems ironic that although many Florentines recommend Cento Poveri as one of the city's best restaurants, it is often filled with foreigners. Nonetheless, the recommendations are apt; Cento Poveri (which translates as "one hundred poor people") serves excellent, interesting food in a warm and inviting atmosphere, with country decor and knickknacks hanging from the ceiling.

Delicious, slightly unusual primi like *tortellaci* (big pasta pockets) filled with potato puree in a mushroom and garbanzo bean sauce and lobster pasta with tomato sauce come in surprisingly large portions. The tender and flavorful *bistecca alla fiorentina* is excellent. The grilled duck breast with a sweet brown sauce is also good but a bit too heavy on the sauce, which threatens to drown delicate raw arugula leaves. Service here is friendly and the wine list is priced to drink, with plenty of appealing Chiantis and Rossos from Montalcino and Montepulciano on offer.

# Divinus

Via dell'Orto 35r, 055/224-148
Open Tuesday through Sunday 7:30 PM to 11 PM; closed two weeks in August
Map A5, Buses 6, D
Credit cards accepted
€€€

Divinus is a classy operation, with professional, friendly service, large dining rooms brightened by flickering candles, and an alluring bamboo-covered patio for warmer nights. The restaurant is owned by the same savvy group of partners that operates Quattro Leoni (see page 71), but here the food is a bit more adventurous. The rather strange menu makes some silly tongue-in-cheek references to the two chefs, one Italian, the other Japanese, as well as waxing hyperbolic about some of the appetizers: "Taste these cheeses and lose yourself in an ecstasy of the palate."

The appetizers are in fact the best part of the menu, and I would mainly recommend Divinus as a place to taste wines from the cellar along with a selection of delicious and unusual antipasti. In the *"spaghetti" di peperoni e seppie alla puttanesca,* roasted marinated peppers are sliced into squiggly lines like spaghetti and topped with gracefully thin slices of squid. Other unusual combinations? How about a mound of marinated octopus wrapped in escarole and topped with a fresh tomato sauce. For more familiar fare, order a mixed plate of Cinta Senese *salumi* (see page 22), or the aforementioned tasting plate of ecstatic cheeses.

The experimentation and strange combinations of ingredients take a less successful turn when it comes to the primi. Little squid-ink gnocchi mixed with more squid and topped by sliced aged pecorino with truffle oil is a clash of flavors, and homemade *pici* (thick spaghettilike pasta) with a version of *amatriciana* made with peas instead of tomatoes has a pleasant savory taste, but the peas used are either frozen or canned. Secondi are more classic, including fresh salmon with a mustard-fennel sauce, a *bistecca alla fiorentina* served with white beans, and the "sushi di Chianti" carpaccio made by butcher Dario Cecchini (see page 236).

The wine list focuses on Tuscany, but also offers some interesting choices, such as a Falanghina from Campania and several Sicilian reds. Wines are stylishly served in large tasting glasses.

## Frescobaldi Wine Bar

**Via dei Magazzini 2–4r, 055/284-724**
**Open Monday noon to 2:30 PM, Tuesday through Sunday 7 PM to 11:30 PM**
**(midnight for cold plates); closed August**
**Map F5, Buses A, 23**
**Credit cards accepted**
**€€€**

I was wondering when the Frescobaldi winemaking family (see page 33) would catch up to the Antinori and open up a glamorous restaurant and wine bar, until one day there it was, dead center, next to the Palazzo Vecchio. This is a major undertaking, a sprawling, multiroom restaurant with cool stone floors and walls elegantly painted in burnt ochre to look like draperies. Tables are covered in white cloth and topped with candles. The staff is multilingual, as is the menu.

The kitchen, headed by chef Giuseppe Fabretti, formerly of Cibreo (see page 42), is attempting some interesting and well-conceived dishes. Start with *arancine di riso,* little fried balls of rice stuffed with goodies, a

*The casual side of Frescobaldi Wine Bar.*

Sicilian specialty. They also serve a distinguished ricotta and vegetable flan and a plate of disappointing boiled pearl onions from the southern town of Tropea (famous for their sweet onions). Primi are kept pretty simple; spaghetti with *bottarga* is just as it sounds, with plenty of Laudemio oil and some thin-sliced mullet roe on top. Risotto with porcini is excellent, brimming with Parmesan cheese.

For a secondo you can choose from standards like roast beef with potatoes or more imaginative cooking such as a rabbit terrine with Vin Santo di Pomino (dessert wine made from white grapes of Pomino). The chocolate cake is a little dry and disappointing, which seems a shame in the city of Dolci & Dolcezze.

Of course the restaurant was conceived in large part as a showcase for the Frescobaldi wines. The wine list is made up entirely of Frescobaldi offerings, including wines from their holdings in Chile, and those of their partners such as Mondavi. Because Frescobaldi makes so many wines, the choices don't come across as terribly limited. You can order bottles from Luce and Lucente (including older vintages), Ornellaia, Castelgiocondo, and several others. They have also set up a very cute, casual little wine bar with a wooden counter and stools. The entrance to Frescobaldini, as the smaller wine bar is called, is on Via della Condotta.

---

## GustaVino

**Via della Condotta 37r, 055/239-9806**
**Open Monday through Saturday 11 AM to 3 PM and 6 PM to 11 PM;**
   **closed one week in August**
**Map F5, Buses A, 23**
**Credit cards accepted**
€€€

A few ambitious Florentine partners with a passion for food and wine recently opened this extremely stylish wine bar and restaurant in the center of town. Taking a cue from the success of places like Beccofino, GustaVino is ultramodern, with an open kitchen, glass-walled wine cantina, chrome tables and chairs, and minimalist Japanese-style dishware. They did a nice job with the space; it feels contemporary without being too cold. They even preserved little glass-covered peepholes in the floor through which you can get a vertiginous look down into the building's medieval foundations.

There are a couple of different ways to enjoy GustaVino. You can think of it as a wine bar, where you can order from a large choice of white and red wines by the glass that go well with the tasting plates of delicious local *salumi* and cheeses. Wines by the glass are mostly Tuscan, with a choice ranging from an inexpensive Chianti or Morellino di Scansano all the way up to Sassicaia (€30 per glass), but you'll also find a Barbera d'Alba among the reds, and several whites from Piedmont and Alto Adige. The list of wines by the bottle is extremely broad, representing choices from all over Italy with very reasonable markups.

You can also come here for an equally satisfying meal. Things start off on adventurous footing (for Florence) with appetizers such as a foie gras salad and a tuna tartare. Primi—all stuffed pastas—are equally appealing, especially the seasonal lemon ravioli with saffron and pecorino ravioli topped with fava bean pesto. For a secondo I recommend the rack of lamb if it is on the menu. The small but able kitchen also turns out a savory duck dish and the occasional salmon. For dessert indulge in the soufflé-like chocolate cake, soft and saucy in the middle, and very addictive.

---

## Pandemonio

**Via del Leone 50r, 055/224-002**
**Open Monday through Saturday 12:30 PM to 2:30 PM and 7:30 PM to 10:30 PM;**
**closed August, Christmas Day, and New Year's Day**
**Map B6, Bus D**
**Credit cards accepted**
**€€€**

Pandemonio skirts the line between classic trattoria and elegant restaurant. The menu is basic Tuscan trattoria cooking, with *ribollita* and *pappa al po-modoro* as well as some more inventive primi such as fresh pastas *al ragù,* spaghetti with *bottarga* (dried mullet roe), and house-made *tortellaci* (large pasta pockets) with a Gorgonzola and radicchio sauce. Secondi tend to be on the heavy side, with the classic Florentine steak served either whole, for two people, or in slices (called a *tagliata*) with either arugula and balsamic vinegar or artichokes and Parmesan cheese. Other secondi on offer are

# Bagels, Lox, and Buffalo Mozzarella

The concept of brunch only arrived in Florence about two years ago as part of a marketing campaign by Nescafé. Why a country overflowing with outstanding coffee would want to start drinking Nescafé is beyond me, but the scheme did have some positive side effects: you can now find several places in town that serve a tasty hangover-killing brunch.

### Capocaccia
*Lungarno Corsini 12–14r, 055/210-751; open Tuesday through Sunday noon to 2 AM, closed August; Map D5; Bus B; credit cards accepted.*
Capocaccia, in addition to being perhaps the most popular *aperitivo* bar in Florence (see page 137), serves a buffet brunch on Saturdays and Sundays. The menu is more or less standard American fare: pancakes, waffles, eggs, fruit, and some changing specials. The cost is about €15 per head. Call in advance to reserve.

### Fusion Bar at Gallery Hotel Art
*Vicolo dell' Oro 5, 055/272-63; open daily 11 AM to midnight; Map G5, Bus B; credit cards accepted.*
There is nothing standard about the brunch menu at this incredibly cool minimalist hotel bar. The prix fixe menu, which costs €21, includes miso soup, salmon tartare, vegetable tempura, sautéed beef sukiyaki, and other Japanese fare that most people would not consider brunch food; but since they serve brunch on Saturday and Sunday from noon to 3 PM, you can also consider it lunch.

### Hemingway
*Piazza Piattellina 9r, 055/284-781; open Tuesday through Saturday 4:30 PM to 1 AM; Sunday 11 AM to 8 PM (brunch 11:30 to 2:30), closed August; Map B5, Bus D; credit cards accepted.*
This bar/hangout is known mostly for its gourmet chocolates, but on Sundays they open at 11 AM to serve brunch. The menu always includes American-style items like pancakes and eggs, but also features a changing menu of international entrées, such as Thai- and Indian-influenced dishes. You'll pay about €20 per person.

more classic Tuscan dishes like fried chicken with fried artichokes, a classic *peposo* (a kind of pot roast), and a fish soup. One of the best reasons to come here: the chocolate and cheese cakes are rated tops in the city, tied with those at Cibreo (see page 42)—not bad company.

Whereas the menu is basic and unassuming, the atmosphere and prices aspire to greater things. Hushed conversation (largely in foreign languages) fills the dining room, soothingly decorated in yellow linens and lit by candles. The wine list offers a respectable choice of *spumanti*, Champagne, and local vintages. You won't go wrong with one of the Chianti Classicos, such as Badia a Coltibuono, or a similarly priced bottle of Morellino di Scansano. The prices here are high for these familiar menu items, but you are essentially paying for the smooth atmosphere, as well as small nods toward elegance, such as a gratis glass of *spumante* to start and *limoncello* and grappa to top off the meal.

## Pane e Vino ✳

**Via di San Niccolò 7or, 055/247-6956**
**Open Monday through Saturday 8 PM to 11:30 PM; closed August**
**Map F7, Buses D, 23**
**Credit cards accepted**
**€€€**

The assorted wine bottles arranged on shelves at this elegant enoteca-restaurant make the perfect casual decor, much like bookshelves in a house. I was immediately taken with the simple and intimate candlelit dining rooms; with interesting art on the walls and fine linens and professional wine-tasting glasses on each table, this is a place to come for an anniversary or quiet dinner with friends. The murmur of conversation is pleasant without ever becoming a din.

The chef's tasting menu is an appealing deal: for about €30 it includes bites of two antipasti, two primi, one secondo, and a sampling of sweets. I like the idea, in principle, of being able to sample dishes at the chef's discretion, but in practice you should know that the chef's discretion might be different from what appeals to you most on the menu. I enjoyed the antipasti of leek tart and cannellini beans with *soppressata salame*, and the primi, which made traditional Tuscan ingredients and dishes seem inventive and new: *cavolo nero* pasta sprinkled with salty *bottarga* (dried mullet roe), and fava bean soup topped with puree of bitter chicory. But I couldn't help looking with envy at the slightly more sumptuous à la carte dishes at nearby tables, like my neighbor's chicken liver mousse pâté antipasto and duck ravioli with duck sauce.

On another visit, the primi were absolutely stellar: a *strozzapreti* (more like gnocchi really) flavored with fresh porcini was unforgettable, and the delicately flavored *taglierini* with *baccalà* and *peperoncini* was equally good. One of the best secondi is a plate of tender lamb chops served with mashed fennel and fried sage, a feast for both the eyes and palate. The eggplant timbale, a rarity as a vegetarian entrée in Florence, is fortified with béchamel. Desserts from the kitchen are on the airy side. A tasty *biancomangiare* (a kind of half-frozen mousse) had the texture of marshmallow fluff and the flavor of toasted almonds, while an orange *bavarese* (like pudding) came with small bites of house-made pine nut brittle.

The service is very low-key, which is perfect as long as you're not in any hurry. The vast wine list, with five or six pages of Tuscan reds alone, is as extraordinary as you might expect from a former enoteca. You'll find high-flying bottles of Supertuscans such as the Sassicaia and Tignanello, as well as more affordable wines from all regions of Italy and abroad. A 1999 Chianti Classico from Querciabella combines very well with the restaurant's innovative Tuscan cooking, as do very reasonable wines from small producers in Carmignano. The staff are quite knowledgable about wines and are more than happy to suggest bottles in any price range.

---

## Parione

Via del Parione 74–76r, 055/214-005
Open Wednesday through Monday 8 PM to 11 PM; closed part of August
Map D5, Buses A, B, 6, 11
Credit cards accepted
€€€

Walking into Parione, you might think you've come in the wrong door as you practically step on the chef's toes and need to be careful of plates flying off the stainless steel kitchen counters. It is definitely an unusual entrance for a high-end restaurant, but then again, this early peek at what's happening in the kitchen, where the bustle of activity, good-looking slabs of meat, and nicely presented plates are clearly visible, will make you confident about what's coming your way.

Both of Parione's dining rooms are tastefully outfitted with wine-bottle-filled shelves and crisp white table linens. As customers arrive, the place fills up with happy chatter (almost all in Italian) and clinking wineglasses, while candles cast a warm light over the whole scene. One of the dining rooms is dominated by a gaudy, almost psychedelic modern wall painting, but other than that, the atmosphere is perfect for a sophisticated, celebratory night out.

Antipasti range from the classic combination of *crostini* and thin-sliced *salumi* to a more complex *sformatino di verdure,* a tasty mound of chopped spinach and chard accompanied with frothy hollandaise. The choice of primi is likewise a mix of the usual and the chef's *fantasia:* you can have a classic *ribollita,* a beautiful plate of *taglierini* with artichokes and herbs, or a plate of *"caramelle,"* actually stuffed pasta shaped like little candies, filled with spinach and ricotta, and topped by a peppery pork *ragù.*

Parione is known for its fish, but the secondi offer a selection of meat dishes, too. The beef fillet *en croute* is an incredibly rich concoction of steak, chopped liver, and pastry crust. The fillet of *spigola* (sea bass) instead is delicately sauced with a creamy shrimp broth. Desserts might include a ricotta soufflé or an extremely dense and delicious slice of flourless ganache. Unlike the menu, the wine list is a bit disappointing, filled with ridiculously expensive Supertuscans (strange given how untouristy this place is) and very slim on bottles for under €30.

# Al Antico Ristoro di Cambi

**Via Sant'Onofrio 1r, 055/217-134**
**Open Monday through Saturday noon to 2:30 PM and 7:30 PM to 10:30 PM;**
   **closed August 15**
**Map B5, Buses D, 6**
**Credit cards accepted**
**€€**

At Cambi, you'll find the very model of a classic trattoria in the up-and-coming San Frediano neighborhood. It has all the ingredients necessary for success: a crowded clutch of uncovered wooden tables and stools, vaulted brick ceiling, the right noise level for eating and chatting with friends, warm lighting, and a drop-dead amazing *bistecca alla fiorentina.* The fact that *every single person* seems to be eating the *bistecca* in lieu of the other attractive secondi is the tip-off that this is no ordinary steak. The primi here are fine—a very Tuscan bean-laden *farro* soup, or a more unusual dish of *pennette* with fresh ricotta and arugula—but basically serve as time-killers leading up to the main event. The enormous T-bone steaks are perfectly cooked (rare but not raw) and served no-nonsense on wooden platters. A side of roast potatoes and refreshing mixed salad goes well with the beef. Other salads here are good but can be a little DIY for my taste; one time I ordered fava beans with pecorino cheese, only to be served a basket of unshelled beans and a hunk of cheese. (I later learned this is a special dish for May Day.) The only negative about this place is that the house wine is undrinkable grape-juice moonshine; I would recommend ordering a real bottle of red from the bar, even though you might be the only customer in the place to do so.

## Trattoria Baldovino

**Via San Giuseppe 22r (Piazza Santa Croce), 055/241-773**
**Open daily 11:30 PM to 2:30 PM and 7 PM to 11:30 PM**
**Map G5, Buses C, 14**
**Credit cards accepted**
**€€**

Noisy, popular Baldovino is the creation of Scottish restaurateur David Gardner, who is also responsible for the Baldovino wine bar next-door (see page 132) and Beccofino (see page 45) across the Arno. The menu is broad enough to please everyone in a group (in fact, this is one of the best places in the city to come with picky eaters), with a wine list to match. Start with *crostini* and prosciutto antipasti or something more unusual like swordfish carpaccio with arugula and radicchio. From there, you can pick and choose from focaccias, which aren't sandwiches but more like giant no-cheese pizzas, big salads for the diet crowd, and a wide choice of primi and secondi. The pizzas here are fantastic—try the Baldovino, with prosciutto, arugula, and Parmesan; or the *crudaiola* with fresh ricotta and chopped tomatoes on top. I've had excellent gnocchi and pastas here— heavy in the winter with black truffles or porcini and rabbit *ragù*. Secondi lean toward the hearty, with lots of beef and wild boar. If you still have room, finish off with one of the delicious house-made cheesecakes or chocolate cakes. The wine list offers plenty of choices, mainly Tuscan but also from other regions. At one meal we ordered a 1998 Carmignano from Villa di Capezzana that was fantastic. This is also an excellent place to try some unusual dessert wines by the glass.

My one complaint about Baldovino is the extremely uneven service. Because it is so crowded, diners are sometimes herded through the meal without the usual Italian-style lingering time; the harried staff can seem so overworked that it's no surprise when service is slow or slapdash. The vestibule-like front room has been improved, but I still prefer to sit in the main dining room, with its open kitchen, country French–style wooden tables and chairs, and colorful paintings on the walls.

## Enoteca le Barrique

**Via del Leone 40r, 055/224-192**
**Open Tuesday through Sunday 8 PM to midnight**
**Map B5, Buses D, 6**
**Credit cards accepted**
**€€**

Owners Paolo Raspa and Roberto Meucci have put together a small but interesting menu at this little place in the neighborhood of San Frediano. Their culinary philosophy is, as they put it, "No *ribollita,* no *pappa,* no *bistecca*!" Instead the tiny kitchen turns out creative and beautifully presented dishes that have a nouvelle twist. On one night we began with a warm porcini soufflé, and two fingers of herbed *baccalà* pâté on *crostini.* All of the primi feature homemade pastas, many with seafood, including a colorful plate of ravioli filled with sea bass topped with diced vegetables, and a heartier plate of *maltagliati* ("badly cut" pasta) with a *ragù* made from rabbit. Secondi often take a backseat at Tuscan restaurants but not here: The duck breast with figs, balsamic vinegar, and *toscanelli* (white beans) ranks as one the best meat dishes I've had in Florence. The fillet of *cernia* (grouper) in an olive crust with tomato sauce and white beans is also top quality.

Don't be put off by the unattractive bamboo shade in the front window. Once inside, you'll find a small, bright trattoria with wooden tables and chairs, green and white tile trim, and the daily menu scribbled on a blackboard. Things start out slowly in the evenings, but by 10 PM the place is booming with Florentines on dates and out for a night. The restaurant also has a pretty vine-covered garden in back, a tempting option for summer months.

The owners seek out smaller interesting producers to fill out their impressive wine list, with many bottles from Tuscany and Sicily under €20. On a given night you might find a Chianti Classico from Palazzino or a Cabernet-Sangiovese mix from Vigliano on offer by the glass. Those who only want to taste wines and not eat a full meal should come either early or late, at nonpeak hours.

## Osteria de' Benci

**Via dei Benci 13r, 055/234-4923**
**Open Monday through Sunday 1 PM to 2:45 PM and 8 PM to 11 PM;**
**closed two weeks in August and Christmas Day**
**Map F6, Bus 23**
**Credit cards accepted**
€€

Reading the long, esoteric menu at Osteria de' Benci is like trying to enter into the brain of a sometimes lucid, sometimes mad chef—capricious, hard to fathom, but with moments of brilliance along with the incomprehensible. I recommend sticking to the more traditional Tuscan fare and forgiving the chef his trespasses as he forgives those who ask him to cook the *bistecca* well done.

The signature dish—extremely popular with some diners but off-putting to others—is the *spaghetti dell'ubriacone* (drunken spaghetti), pasta boiled in wine so that it turns a bright burgundy, and then tossed with garlic, olive oil, red pepper flakes, and parsley. Other selections change monthly to reflect the seasons, but there is always a focus on meat. You can't go wrong with a steak or slices of Chianina beef with arugula and Parmesan. The restaurant also serves a fair number of rabbit, chicken, and pork dishes, often oven-roasted or grilled with small sides. One secondo I didn't particularly like was the *carpaccio di Chianina* braised quickly with aromatic oil (my feeling is that a carpaccio is best kept raw). The most successful primi are simple pastas: fresh tagliatelle with *ragù*, or a summery *tagliolini* with cherry tomatoes and grated Parmesan. Some desserts are made in-house, but I would actually recommend those brought in from Dolce & Dolcezze (see page 190), including the raspberry tart and chocolate tart.

In winter Benci is a cozy outpost with warm art-covered walls, brick-vaulted ceiling, and a big basement room for overflow. In summer, one entire wall opens onto the street and the shrub-enclosed patio outside bustles until the wee hours. The restaurant's young owner and friendly, energetic staff keep things hopping, if not always efficient.

## Boccadama ✳

**Piazza Santa Croce 25–26r, 055/243-640**
**Open daily 8:30 AM to midnight; closed Monday afternoon**
**Map G5, Buses C, 14**
**Credit cards accepted**
**€€**

It took a few visits to Boccadama before I figured out what this place is really about. At first it struck me as an exceedingly pleasant casual restaurant with a small menu of slightly unusual takes on Tuscan cuisine and some very good wines. But when I went with a wine-expert friend, I experienced a Copernican moment as it dawned on me that the cooking is focused around the wines and not the other way around. This is a great place to match exceptional Italian wines by the glass with various flavors from the adept kitchen.

Start your meal with white wine—a Chardonnay from Tuscany or Piedmont, or a Tuscan Sauvignon Blanc—accompanied with a plate of French cheeses with white wine confiture, a plate of salty mixed Tuscan *salumi,* and some thin-sliced *lardo di Colonnata* on toasts. The kitchen also makes an excellent *bruschetta* with fresh tomato and basil. For the main course you might move to a red wine, such as a Tuscan IGT blend of Cabernet Sauvignon with Cabernet Franc, or Sangiovese blended with Merlot, both of which go well with the roast lamb or potato ravioli topped with wild boar *ragù.* If you like chocolate, try the incredibly dense, unadulterated slice of *torta al cioccolato,* which pairs well with some of the sharper red dessert wines. The Moscato from Piedmont is a light and bubbly accompaniment to the all-American carrot cake with white chocolate frosting. Service here is friendly, informative, and multilingual. There's a nonsmoking room in back and outdoor seating in summer months.

---

## Borgo Antico

**Piazza Santo Spirito 6r, 055/210-437**
**Open daily noon to 3 PM and 7 PM to 11 PM**
**Map C6, Buses D, 11, 36, 37**
**Credit cards accepted**
€€

Borgo Antico has redone its interior, but it's the large shaded patio out on tree-filled Piazza Santo Spirito where the main action takes place. The restaurant does incredible business all summer and on Sundays when Italians like to have a big family lunch together. Big is apt, as the portions here are unusually generous: mounds of gnocchi with tomato sauce, acres of pizza, seafood coming out of your ears. The pizzas from the wood-fired oven, including the *Margherita* and choices like spicy sausage with eggplant, are good if not always memorable; the linguine with abundant clams is great; and I've seen diners get ecstatic over their huge platter of risotto with stracchino cheese and zucchini flowers. The place has a young, fun atmosphere; a big black-and-white mural depicting cyclists by a local artist covers one wall and the open kitchen lets you spy on the raucous dancing *pizzaiolo* hamming it up in the back. I also like the fact that the servers don't try to rush you with your meal or always push you to order secondi—a good thing since the primi are so huge. If you are thinking of ordering a secondo, try the tender, succulent lamb chops on a bed of arugula.

The same partners who own Borgo Antico also run Osteria di Santo Spirito across the piazza, as well as Osteria dell'Olio in Piazza dell'Olio right near the Duomo.

---

## Osteria Caffè Italiano
**Via Isola delle Stinche 11–13r, 055/289-368**
**Open Tuesday through Sunday 12:30 PM to 3 PM and 5:30 PM to 11 PM;**
    **wine bar open Tuesday through Sunday 3 PM to 5 PM**
**Map F5, Buses A, 14, 23**
**Credit cards accepted**
**€€**

Osteria Caffè Italiano has two faces. On weekdays they serve an inexpensive light lunch of soups and pizzas that is the balm of weary travelers seeking refuge after ogling Giotto's frescoes in the Santa Croce church; by night (and weekend days) the dining room (and patio in summer) is elegantly turned out with white linen tablecloths and candlelight. The food is traditional Tuscan. You're wise to order anything cooked in the wood-fired oven, especially the *arista* (roast pork) wrapped in pancetta and sage. Simple veal and lamb chops and vegetable side dishes are also served, and the wine list is extensive. Desserts here are fine, but you might pass them over in favor of a gelato from Vivoli (see page 211) just down the street.

Don't be alarmed if one of your dinner companions disappears for a stretch of time; they've probably just gone to use the bathroom, which requires descending one flight in a rickety elevator that only holds about one and a half people at a time. It can really be an annoyance in this otherwise slick operation.

The Osteria Caffè Italiano also has a a tiny but excellent authentic little pizzeria next door to the restaurant (see page 97), well worth a visit.

# Trattoria Cibreo (also called Cibreino) ✳

**Via dei Macci 122r, 055/234-1100 (no reservations)**
**Open Tuesday through Saturday 1 PM to 2:30 PM and 7 PM to 11:15 PM;**
**closed August**
**Map H4, Buses A, C, 14**
**No credit cards**
**€€**

As the more casual counterpart to the famous Ristorante Cibreo (see page 42), this small trattoria is a pleasure to experience. The two share a kitchen and many menu items, so you can taste the same innovative takes on traditional Tuscan dishes, but in a relaxed atmosphere, at a fraction of the price. Some of the standard dishes include the tomato flan appetizer; some very simple primi like the *infarinata* with *cavolo nero*, a grainy yet creamy soup with black cabbage; and homemade *passatelli* noodles floating in meat broth. The secondi are even better, if more challenging: The stuffed chicken neck sounds unappetizing, but is actually more of a delicious cold chicken mousse, sliced and served with lemony homemade mayonnaise; it does, however, arrive complete with the chicken head (albeit roasted) right on your plate. A few fish dishes are served every night, often something with *baccalà* (salt cod) or stockfish (dried but unsalted cod). The wine list has several affordable options, the best of which may be the very drinkable Barco Reale from Capezzana, though it also includes some excellent Chiantis and Brunellos as well as a few non-Tuscan choices. Whatever you do, leave room for dessert. The splendid flourless chocolate cake releases endorphins I didn't even know I had, and the chocolate *budino* (something between a pudding and a mousse) with caramel sauce is equally good.

Considering how similar the food is, the difference in price between the restaurant and the trattoria around the corner is striking. I actually prefer the trattoria's understated decor of wooden tables and wall paneling, modern art, and dried chile peppers hanging from the ceiling. The one big drawback at the trattoria is that they do not take reservations, so on a given night you might end up waiting anywhere from ten minutes to an hour. The trattoria is extremely small, so it's a good idea to arrive either very early, around 7 PM when the place opens, or very late, after 10 PM.

## Il Guscio

Via dell'Orto 49, 055/224-421
Open Tuesday through Sunday 8 PM to 11 PM; closed August
Map A5, Bus D
Credit cards accepted
€€

Il Guscio holds a position of high esteem among Florentines, a good reason to track down this San Frediano haunt. The larger-than-expected interior is unassuming, with peach walls, red tile floor, and no windows.

Your best bet is to stick with the excellent primi, such as creamy, pungent *guanciale* (pillows) of spinach and ricotta in a truffle cream sauce, or tagliatelle with meat sauce. Secondi, such as roast piglet with potatoes, are a little too heavy and salty, though many people enjoy their *bistecca* and sea bass. Solid, satisfying desserts include a disk of vanilla ice cream in a bowl of hot chocolate—a different take on the *affogato*—and a *crostatina di crema,* a delicious mini-tart filled with fluffy pastry cream and topped with fresh fruit. The wine list includes substantial choices from

Piedmont and Tuscany, as well as a couple of labels from Puglia and Sicily. Best of all I was impressed by the more than fair mark-ups; a 1999 bottle of Isole e Olena Chianti Classico costs only €17. The one sour note in this otherwise fine place is the sometimes neglectful service.

## Where the Florentines Are

Sometimes Florence can feel like the fifty-first state of the Union, with more English spoken on the street than Italian. Once in a while it's nice to go where the Florentines actually eat; what they generally look for in a restaurant is *tipicità,* traditional Tuscan recipes cooked the way they should be. They like their roasted meats salty and their wine economical. Here are places where you can mix with the locals:

**Il Guscio,** page 67

**La Piazzetta,** page 100

**Sabatino,** page 82

**Santa Lucia,** page 102

**Targa,** page 89

**Il Tranvai,** page 83

**Tre Soldi,** page 90

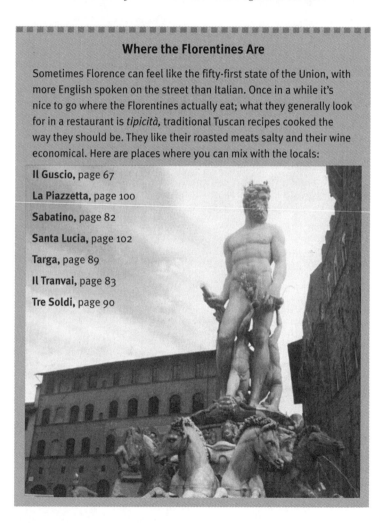

# Il Latini

**Via dei Palchetti 6r, 055/210-916**
**Open Tuesday through Sunday 12:30 PM to 2:30 PM and 7:30 PM to 10:30 PM;**
    **closed for lunch in August**
**Map D4, Buses A, 6**
**Credit cards accepted**
**€€**

Maybe you can't be too rich or too thin, but you can be too famous. The line snaking out the door at all hours of day and night lets you know that Il Latini's greatness has been hailed in every guidebook from Hong Kong to Helsinki. It's so popular because it is exactly what people want when they come to Florence: a lively, casual joint with satisfying, delicious Tuscan food. The raucous atmosphere, complete with Chianti *fiasco* bottles and hanging ham hocks, jokey staff, and classic food keep them coming. You might want to try lunch instead of dinner, when you're less likely to need riot gear in order to make it through the door, and the wait staff is less likely to sling food at you, whether you ordered it or not.

The especially good *crostini* taste like they were dipped in butter before being slathered with succulent chopped liver. Excellent roast beef and *bistecca alla fiorentina* are a better bet than the *arista* (roast pork), which is also a thick slab, but too salty for my taste. Standard-setting *ribollita* and *pappa al pomodoro* are also served. Finish it off right with *biscottini* and terrific *vin santo,* which is made from grapes from the proprietor's own vineyard.

When you stumble out of Il Latini, sated and possibly drunk on Chianti and *vin santo,* take the time to look at the rest of the Palazzo Rucellai (the Latini entrance is in the back), a classic Florentine Renaissance palace whose façade along Via della Vigna Nuova was designed by Leon Battista Alberti.

## Perseus

**Viale Don Minzoni 10r, Piazza della Libertà, 055/588-226**

**Open Monday through Saturday 12:30 PM to 2:30 PM and 7:30 PM to 11:30 PM; closed two weeks in August**

**Buses 1, 7**

**Credit cards accepted**

**€€**

The same restaurant impresarios who transformed 13 Gobbi (see page 74) into its present cheerful state also own Perseus, and their trademark style is easily recognizable: a cute and cluttered interior filled with mismatched painted chairs and tables, arts and crafts on every wall, and garlic and pepper garlands dangling from the ceiling. On the verge of being too self-consciously cute or "characteristic," it actually works well, lending an upbeat eccentric atmosphere to this big space filled with mostly local eaters (due to its north-of-center location just past Piazza Libertà).

The appealing aesthetic of abundance here extends to the way the food is arranged and served. When you first walk in you will see the proud display of fresh pasta and raw beef, a good sign that *bistecca* is served here. When an entire table orders it, the waiter rolls out a wooden butcher block holding the grilled slab of meat and slices it at the table. As at 13 Gobbi, appetizers here are unusual. You can choose from imaginative menu items such as grilled Treviso radicchio served with melted Gorgonzola, or white beans with *bottarga*. Primi include fresh pastas like a simple ravioli with butter and sage, or risotto with more red radicchio. For a secondo, most diners opt for the *bistecca,* though other roast meats are on offer. The wine list includes several interesting choices, but I usually stick with the house wine, which is a perfectly good Chianti.

## Quattro Leoni ✳

**Piazza della Passera, Via Vellutini 1r, 055/218-562**
**Open daily 11:45 AM to 2:30 PM and 7:30 PM to 11 PM**
**Map D6, Buses D, 11, 36, 37**
**Credit cards accepted**
€€

Quattro Leoni is simply one of the best all-around trattorias in Florence—the kind of place where I always feel confident taking visiting friends and family—with a comfortable atmosphere, excellent service, fair pricing, and a menu that takes an original look at the local cuisine.

You can start with a plate of traditional *crostini misti* or an *antipasto toscano,* or better yet with a fresh and satisfying *carpaccio di bresaola,* paper-thin slices of bright-red cured beef topped with shaved Parmesan, arugula, and pine nuts. Also popular is the serving of soft-pink prosciutto next to a mound of bufala mozzarella. Fresh pastas dominate the list of primi. The most original creation out of several contestants is the *fiocchetti,*

*Gnocchi with arugula pesto and fresh tomatoes at Quattro Leoni.*

little "purses" of pasta filled with a springtime bounty of pear, asparagus, and Taleggio cheese. The combination of flavors is sweet, with a little bite from the tangy Taleggio. The kitchen also serves an impressive plate of *maltagliati con fiori di zucca,* "badly cut" fresh pasta in green and white with zucchini flowers, and a gnocchi topped with a very fresh and colorful pesto of arugula with fresh tomato. All of the pastas come sprinkled with a fistful of parsley and red onion for color and flourish. The best secondi are the grilled meats, such as *tagliata* of steak, veal, or chicken, simply grilled and served with a wedge of lemon. If you've still got room at the end, try the cheesecake or the *panna cotta,* a disk of sweet cream topped with wild berries.

Quattro Leoni's interior is a sprawl of brick-walled rooms with substantial charm (one room is reserved for nonsmokers), but the best way to enjoy this place is in the warm weather months when you can sit outside in the quiet, nearly traffic-free piazza. As with all restaurants in Florence, you should call in advance to reserve.

---

## Tre Merli

**Via dei Fossi 12r, 055/287-062**
**Open daily noon to 3 PM and 7 PM to 11:30 PM**
**Map C4, Buses A, 11**
**Credit cards accepted**
**€€**

Tre Merli is a young and punchy enterprise; with its bright southwestern oranges, blues, and reds, high ceilings, and dim party lighting, it sets itself far apart from the Florentine norm.

With the menu, the owners are clearly attempting something lighter, fresher, and less traditional than other restaurants. The antipasti are dominated by a broad choice of carpaccios: smoked salmon, smoked tuna, swordfish, *bresaola* (thin-sliced cured beef), and even a vegetarian offering of zucchini with grana among them. The thin slices of smoked tuna are a particularly nice way to start, layered as they are with arugula and shavings of Parmesan. You can also begin with more traditional choices like *bruschetta* with *zolfino* beans and olive oil or with the classic tomato

# Meatless Retreats

If you or a traveling companion are determined to uphold vegetarian tenets despite being in the land of pancetta, *soppressata*, and *bistecca alla fiorentina*, you must be mad! Okay, not mad, but that's the reaction you'll get from most Italian restaurateurs. Eating vegetarian in meat-loving Florence actually isn't so difficult. Your best bet may be pizza; you know exactly what went onto or into it. Otherwise, most trattorias offer at least a couple of no-meat pastas and soups. But if you are vegan, kosher, or have specific dietary needs, several vegetarian restaurants serve particularly interesting fare.

### Ruth's Kosher Vegetarian Restaurant

*Via Farini 2a, 055/248-0888; open Sunday through Friday 12:30 PM to 2:30 PM and 8 PM to 10:30 PM (closed from sundown on Friday to sundown Saturday and Jewish holidays); Map H4, Bus C; credit cards accepted; €.*
This bright restaurant next to the synagogue serves kosher Sephardic and Middle Eastern fare like couscous and tabbouleh at very low prices.

### Sedano Allegro

*Borgo La Croce 20r, 055/234-5505; open Tuesday through Sunday 7:30 PM to 10:30 PM, closed week of August 15; Map I4, Bus A; credit cards accepted; €.*
Sedano Allegro is an unpretentious place near Piazza Beccaria whose name means "the happy celery."

### Il Vegetariano

*Via delle Ruote 30r, 055/475-030; open Tuesday through Friday 12:30 PM to 2:30 PM and 7:30 to 10:30 PM, Saturday and Sunday 7:30 PM to 10:30 PM, closed most of August; Map F1, Bus 4; no credit cards; €.*
This down-to-earth, inexpensive vegetarian restaurant with a political edge harks back to the 1970s. An inefficient self-service system makes getting food a challenge, though once you eat, the meals are generally good if a bit uneven. Save room for the homemade desserts.

**Sugar Blues**
*Via dei Serragli 57r, 055/268-378; open Monday through Saturday
9 AM to 2 PM and 5 PM to 8 PM, closed Saturday in summer; Map C6,
Buses 11, 36, 37; credit cards accepted.*
This health-food shop sells a host of whole wheat, sugar free, and
organic goods.

and basil. The primi include some hits (*spaghettini* with clams) and misses
(a *ribollita* overpowered by thyme).

The secondi are focused on the *bistecca,* with various slices and dices
of meat plus a side vegetable, or you can branch out and get a well-made
roast rabbit or chicken. A small selection of seafood dishes, such as sea
bass with roasted vegetables or shrimp with grilled vegetables, is offered,
as well as some none-too-creative but still laudable vegetarian entrées,
including an eggplant Parmesan and a big plate of mixed grilled vegetables. This place has some coltish kinks to work out, especially with the
service, but I applaud the effort to do something big, different, and fun.

## I 13 Gobbi

**Via del Porcellana 9r, 055/284-015**
**Open Tuesday through Sunday 7:30 PM to 11 PM**
**Map C4, Bus A**
**Credit cards accepted**
**€€**

I noticed 13 Gobbi while walking home from another restaurant around
the corner, and almost had a Woody Allen *Stardust Memories* moment
where I pressed my face against the glass, wishing that I, too, were laugh-
ing, eating, and drinking with all the shiny happy people inside. In fact, as
I learned later, this restaurant, whose name means the thirteen hunchbacks (hunchbacks are considered lucky in Italy), has been around for
about twenty years, but was recently remodeled to become its snappy
new self, complete with purposefully mismatched countryish wooden tables and chairs, subdued lighting, and assorted bric-a-brac (hanging

hams and garlic ropes) cluttering brick walls in the two large rooms. Little touches like checkered cloth napkins and hand-painted ceramic plates also add atmosphere. Even the house wine—a respectable Chianti—comes in a rustic little ceramic mug instead of a glass carafe. All of this Tuscan country kitsch pushes the point a little, but it still works.

The antipasto specials are pleasingly unusual here—buttered toasts with *bottarga* or a chicken salad (very rare in these parts). The specialty of the house is a dish of homemade *pici* (thick wormlike noodles) with garlic, olive oil, hot pepper flakes, and pancetta—a slight variation on the classic spaghetti *aglio olio.* The spaghetti with clams comes very al dente and lacks a bit of panache, though they are certainly generous with the clams. You can also order the Tuscan stalwarts *ribollita* and *pappa al pomodoro,* always good choices. Seconds include *bistecca alla fiorentina* as well as a savory *tagliata*—sliced steak served with arugula and drizzled with balsamic vinegar. Desserts are the usual attractive assortment of crème caramel, biscotti, and *panna cotta.* The chocolate cake strikes the right compromise between being rich but not too concentrated.

---

## Vecchia Bettola ✳

**Via Ariosto 34r (Piazza Torquato Tasso), 055/224-158**
**Open Tuesday through Saturday 12 PM to 2:30 PM and 7:30 PM to 10:30 PM;**
**closed August and Christmas week**
**Map A6, Buses 12, 13**
**No credit cards**
**€€**

Vecchia Bettola is owned by the same family that presides over Nerbone, that home of the legendary *bollito* sandwich in the Central Market (page 112), which should assuage any anxiety you might have about the quality of the food. This is one of the best old-school trattorias in the city, where you sit on wooden stools and benches, drink wine out of a giant straw-wrapped *fiasco,* and wolf down *ribollita* and *bistecca alla fiorentina* with gusto. The special pasta of the house, *penne alla Bettola,* is made with a tomato and vodka sauce that is wonderfully sweet and delicious. Other outstanding primi are the *ribollita,* rigatoni with olive and roast-tomato sauce, and creamy risotto dishes.

The secondi, sides, and salads are usually excellent as well; simple, unadorned steaks and chops of pork, beef, and veal abound. They serve a celebrated *bistecca alla fiorentina*, as well as a decadent osso buco—wintry, but served year-round. Even the simple *insalata mista* outshines similar dishes around the city. The outside seating is terrific in summer, when the bustling interior can be too hot. One caveat: save your coffee stop for after dinner; they don't have an espresso machine here and serve only Nescafé in little tin cups.

*A waiter outside Vecchia Bettola.*

## Osteria Antica Mescita di San Niccolò
**Via di San Niccolò 6or, 055/234-2836**
**Open Monday through Saturday 7:30 PM to 11 PM**
**Map G7, Buses D, 23**
**Credit cards accepted**
€

The Antica Mescita, in the heart of the San Niccolò neighborhood, is one of my favorite casual trattorias (even if it calls itself by every name except that one). The place is warm and friendly, with the usual beaten-up wooden tables, benches, and stools, and old photos and wine bottles lining the walls. The menu has all the staple comfort items, but also a few more challenging dishes. The kitchen loves *lardo*—on *crostini,* as carpaccio—as well as tripe, and they always offer some surprising dishes like carpaccio of smoked goose breast; but you can also enjoy a near-perfect *ribollita* or stunning rosemary-spiked *farro* and garbanzo bean soup. I like almost everything served here, though in general I recommend the soups more than the pastas. Secondi don't take a backseat either: I often get the thin-sliced *arista* with apple-prune compote, though I'm tempted by the various stews, like wild boar with spices or beef stew with porcini. The menu changes at least slightly every day, including featured wines and cheeses. The house wine is an eminently drinkable Chianti, but bottles are priced so reasonably that it's a good chance to try something else, and to watch them precariously pull the wine off a shelf above your head with a cherry picker. For dessert, you can get an *affogato* (a scoop of gelato doused with an espresso), a plate of assorted cheeses with honey, or other traditional sweets.

When you call to reserve or stop in, make sure to ask to sit in the charming upstairs, and not be relegated to the much-inferior downstairs, which is dark, dank, and dungeonlike. In summer they set up a pleasant little outdoor space with three or four tables, protected by bushes from scant passing traffic.

## I'Brindellone

**Piazza Piattellina 10–11r, 055/217-879**
**Open Thursday through Tuesday noon to 3 PM and 7 PM to 11 PM**
**Map B5, Bus D**
**No credit cards**
€

If you love Florence's offerings of pastas and soups but can usually pass when it comes time for the secondi (and this applies to a lot of people), you'll appreciate Brindellone. Here they've taken the basic concept of a no-frills trattoria but dispensed with the obligatory stuff-yourself-until-you-drop three or more courses, focusing instead on what is often the best part anyway: a creative and extended list of tempting primi. The choices include a simple but delicious spaghetti with *pomodorini,* sliced garlic, shredded basil, and grated shards of salty aged ricotta. The *zuppa livornese* turns out to be a large bowl brimming with mussels cooked in an aromatic mix of tomatoes, pepper, and garlic, with a sauce-soaked slice of bread at the bottom. The menu also features Parmesan and balsamic vinegar *gnocchetti* in a crispy cheese basket, as well as nettle-filled ravioli topped with basil—intriguing. The antipasto of mixed *crostini* is also quite good. This is one of the best places in town for a nonvegetarian to take a vegetarian friend or vice versa without having to worry about being trapped by a menu full of tofu and bean sprouts or *bistecca* and brains, respectively; the menu is mainly vegetarian but in such a way that you would never notice—it's just good Italian food. Though the menu lists no secondi, on a given night the server will list off a few specials, often chicken or fish. A very inexpensive prix fixe lunch with a limited menu is also served on weekdays.

## Casalinga

**Via dei Michelozzi 9r, 055/218-624**
**Open Monday through Saturday noon to 2:30 PM and 7 PM to 10 PM;**
    **closed August and Christmas week**
**Map C6, Buses 11, 36, 37**
**Credit cards accepted**
€

One definition of *casalinga* is "housewife," and since most of us will never have one, this casual neighborhood place is the next best thing. Much loved by locals, this is the kind of restaurant where people come to smoke, chat, catch up on the gossip and soccer news, and eat extremely cheap and basic good food. The large no-nonsense interior, with big communal tables and red-and-white-checkered tablecloths, is almost always full, and bubbling with life at both lunch and dinner. The best primi include lasagne, *ribollita* served in a hot ceramic pot, and simple dishes of spaghetti with piquant pesto or *aglio olio*. The secondi also hit the spot; a wonderful grilled pork chop (*braciola di maiale*) arrives adorned only with a wedge of lemon. Salads are ridiculously simple: shredded arugula or radicchio in a metal bowl. Only order the *bollito misto* if you are prepared to see a big pink tongue (along with other boiled meats) on your plate, ready to be sliced and doused with tangy green sauce. The house wine is a decent Chianti Rufina, and almost as cheap as water.

## Slow Food in Florence

"The Slow Food movement wasn't born in Florence," explains local director Leonardo Romanelli, "but the city has one of the biggest and most active *convivia* [chapters] in Italy." A friendly and slightly disheveled Florentine foodie, Romanelli organizes programs, writes books and articles for Slow Food, and teaches the Masters of Wine course in Florence.

Like any Italian movement worth its salt, Slow Food has a rousing manifesto that makes sweeping claims: "A firm defense of quiet material pleasure is the only way to oppose the universal folly of 'Fast Life.'" It makes sense that a movement born to protect traditional foods and ways of eating would take root here in Tuscany, where so many of the region's staples are painstakingly produced.

The organization began in 1986 in the town of Bra in Piedmont. Its message of defense against the depredations of fast food, agribusiness, and homogenization of cuisine spread quickly, first to the rest of

Europe and then throughout the world. There are currently 70,000 members worldwide, with *convivia* in places as far-flung as Reykjavik and Los Angeles. The organization has grown to include a prolific publishing house, an annual awards ceremony, and an arm that acts to protect traditional foods in danger of disappearing, such as the Cinta Senese pig (see page 22) or *zolfino* beans.

Every month the Florence chapter organizes a flurry of wine and food-related activities, including the Cantina del Sabato, Saturday get-togethers with wine producers; Cena con Produttori, where members dine with esteemed producers of cheese, *salumi,* or other foods; and Pranzo al Sabato, a lunch at a grand Italian restaurant hosted by a wine producer. They also occasionally organize a Caccia all'Ingredi-ente, a kind of a "name that ingredient" dinner, and a culinary treas-ure hunt in and around the center of Florence. Recently they have begun a series of educational seminars called Masters of Food, four- or five-part classes on the making and appreciation of cheese, wine, and oil—with more to come.

Florence residents who want to join the local chapter should either attend an event and join there or else go to **Antica Gastronomia** (see page 158), where you can sign up in person and immediately start receiving information via email. Visitors who would like to attend an event should check the website, www.slowfoodfirenze.it. Unfortunately, the site is monolingual at the moment, as are most of the activities. However, wine and food can act as a kind of universal language.

Every other year Slow Food Italy hosts the Salone del Gusto in Turin, a food and wine festival and conference extravaganza. Toscana Slow, a regional celebration of Tuscan food that takes place over about a week in several cities and towns, happens on the years when there is no Salone. To find out more about these regional and national events, and Slow Food in general, go to the organization's main web-site, www.slowfood.com.

## Trattoria Mario ✳

**Via Rosina 2r, 055/218-550**
**Open Monday through Saturday noon to 3:30 PM; closed most of August**
**Map E3, Bus 1**
**No credit cards**
€

My first meal in Florence was at Mario, giving me an unrealistically inflated view of what future meals had in store. Why is the food so good at Trattoria Mario? Maybe because it is right across from the Central Market, or maybe because all the energy goes into the cooking. Décor is somewhere between simple and nonexistent, service is straightforward, the menu includes the same items as most other trattorias in Florence, and only lunch is served. You sit elbow to elbow at tables with whomever you are told to, and you like it! Mario has been discovered and is now listed in some guidebooks, including the *Slow Food Osteria Guide* (in Italian), but is still extremely popular with locals, including businessmen and professors from the university, some of whom eat lunch here every day.

For primi, both the soups—*ribollita, zuppa di farro, zuppa di fagioli*—and the pastas, such as *amatriciana* (pancetta, tomato, hot pepper) or the *tagliatelle al ragù,* are consistently incredible: hearty, savory, pure in flavor. Mario is also one of the best places to try a real *bistecca alla fiorentina,* though the other veal and beef dishes, such as a plain fillet of beef or juicy *vitello arrosto,* are also perfectly cooked. The *patate fritte* are outstanding, as is the mixed salad; here is a bowl of simple lettuce and tomato dressed with olive oil, a drop of vinegar, and salt and yet somehow it always tastes especially good—it's either the freshness of the produce or some kind of Mario X factor. Friday is fish day, when practically every item on the menu has some kind of seafood: seafood pasta, salads, secondi. Dessert is usually biscotti and *vin santo,* if you have room. The house wine is drinkable, but there is also a longer wine selection that patrons rarely take advantage of since Mario only serves lunch. I don't want to hype this place out of all proportion, but when people ask me what's my favorite restaurant in Florence, I think of Mario. Then I get hungry.

## Da Ruggiero

**Via Senese 89r, Porta Romana, 055/220-542**
**Open Thursday through Monday 7:30 PM to 10:30 PM; closed August**
**Buses 36, 37**
**Credit cards accepted**
€

If you don't mind going a little bit out of your way (a few blocks past the Porta Romana), this place will satisfy your every Tuscan trattoria wish at a reasonable price. The wood-paneled walls are decorated with a clutter of old prints and photos, and even a stuffed deer's head. There's nothing fancy or experimental here, just simple, classic Florentine food, such as an excellent *ribollita* and *pappa,* memorable chopped liver *crostini,* and secondi that often include a fish or two. This is a good place to try a *pinzimonio*—a plate of raw vegetables that you cut up yourself and dip into extra virgin olive oil. The spicy *spaghetti alla carretiera* is cooked perfectly al dente and tossed with an *abbondanza* of fresh tomatoes, garlic, and *peperoncino.* Definitely call in advance to reserve, as the small place is often booked.

## Sabatino

**Via Pisana 2r, 055/225-955**
**Open Monday through Friday noon to 2:30 PM and 7:30 PM to 10:30 PM;**
   **closed August, Christmas Day, and New Year's Day**
**Map A5, Buses D, 6**
**Credit cards accepted**
€

Sabatino used to have a more ramshackle atmosphere before they moved to new digs, which are spacious and clean but still quite bare-bones, with industrial-strength fluorescent lighting and long plastic-covered tables. Anyone who gets this place confused with Sabatini, a fine-dining restaurant that's been around for years, will quickly realize the mistake, as Sabatino is probably one of the cheapest places to eat in town, with primi hovering at about €3 and secondi a mere €5 or €6. In itself this wouldn't be a recommendation, but the food is quite good. The menu is utterly basic: spaghetti with tomato, spaghetti with meat sauce, tagliatelle with tomato . . . you get the idea. I've enjoyed several meals here of *farro* soup, roast beef with potatoes or *pancetta di vitello,* and house wine. The owners are friendly, and it's not hard to get in here at the last minute, even with a large group. The location, too, is fairly convenient, just outside the Porta San Frediano in the Oltrarno.

---

## Il Tranvai

**Piazza Torquato Tasso 14r, 055/225-197**
**Open Monday through Friday noon to 2:30 PM and 7:15 PM to 10:45 PM;**
  **closed August, Christmas Day, and New Year's Day**
**Map B6, Buses 12, 13**
**Credit cards accepted**
€

Tranvai is beloved by locals, though the food can be hit-and-miss. Like other no-nonsense Florentine joints, this one is noisy, often smoke filled, and tightly packed at mealtimes. The popular mixed *crostini* plate—a cute little wooden tray of *crostini* topped with artichoke, tomato, and chicken liver—is sometimes fantastic and sometimes tastes like it's been sitting out for a while. Same with the primi: I've had delicious pasta with tomato and spicy sausage, but also a failed experiment of walnut gnocchi and one so-so vegetable soup. Secondi are very traditional: tripe, chicken, beef; I greatly enjoyed a plate of pork meatballs covered with tomato sauce. One atypical aspect of this place is the excellent selection of house-made desserts. Wine here is extremely reasonable, and the atmosphere is convivial and truly *fiorentino.*

*Wild mushrooms at the Sant'Ambrogio market.*

Trattorias whose main attraction is often the extraordinary view or a garden circle Florence and form a kind of gustatory ring road, connecting the dots from Arcetri to Careggi and other peripheral towns in between. Some make a very pleasant walk from the Center if you don't mind a long or uphill climb to build up your appetite, while others can be reached easily on a bus, or in a car or taxi, since buses can be unreliable at night.

---

## Bibe ✻

**Via delle Bagnese 1r, about four miles outside town near Scandicci,**
**055/204-9085**
**Open Friday through Tuesday 12:30 PM to 2 PM and 7:30 PM to 10:30 PM;**
**Thursday 7:30 PM to 10:30 PM**
**Bus 16**
**Credit cards accepted**
€€

When the birds are singing, the sun is shining, and the stone streets of Florence feel narrow and stifling, I can think of nothing better than lunch at Bibe, a short ride from town. Make sure to ask to sit in the leafy, tree-shaded garden if it's sunny. (In winter you'll sit inside the charming farmhouse, so either way you're set).

Like most of the restaurants around Florence, Bibe is a family-run operation that hasn't changed much over the years, nor does it have reason to. The menu consists mainly of Tuscan standards, but also includes a few unusual and expertly done specials and unusual seasonal dishes. The old-school waiter might assume you want the house red, but take the time to look over the wine list, which offers a number of excellent whites and reds at prices barely higher than retail. On a summer day, you might start with a chilled bottle of Chardonnay from Alto Adige, and then move on to a local red such as a superb Chianti Classico from Fontodi.

Meals start off soundly, especially if you order the fried zucchini flowers—in season in spring and summer—stuffed with mozzarella cheese and fried in a light but luscious batter. Another antipasto features a fava bean salad with creamy goat cheese. For a primo, you might try the *papardelle al ragù di lepre,* fresh pasta with a savory wild hare *ragù.* Secondi include a range of roasted and grilled meats. I found the duck a bit tough though tasty; alternatively, the kitchen will grill any piece of chicken you like. The lamb roasted with potatoes comes as a petite but succulent portion wrapped in aluminum foil. Though the food is excellent here, the true beauty of this place is the magic atmosphere outdoors, where the sun glitters off pink tablecloths and sparkling wine goblets.

One final note: Even if you're feeling energetic, I don't recommend walking to Bibe; the road is sans sidewalk and full of homicidal traffic. The cab from town only costs about €8 (more after 9 PM), and it's worth it.

## Insider Spaghetti

If you want to boldly go where no tourist has gone before, hoof it (or bus or taxi it) out to **Fratelli Briganti,** a busy no-frills restaurant on the outskirts of town near the Fortezza da Basso. The reason to come here is a platter-sized serving of thin, al dente spaghetti topped with a simple but so-good sauce of fresh tomatoes, Parmesan cheese, and cayenne pepper. The ingredients are basic, but there's something extra in there that makes it a treat. Most Florentines know about the spaghetti at Briganti, but they keep it to themselves. The dish isn't even on the menu, but if you ask for the *spaghetti della casa,* or *gli spaghetti speciali,* the waiter will know what you mean. Briganti also serves pizzas and other pastas and secondi, but the reason to come here is for the secret spaghetti.

### Fratelli Briganti

*Piazza Giorgini 12r, Fortezza da Basso, 055/475-255; open Friday through Wednesday noon to 3 PM and 6:30 PM to 1 AM, closed Friday lunch and for two weeks in August; Bus 4; no credit cards; €.*

## Cent'Anni

**Via di Cent'Anni 7, Bagno a Ripoli, 055/630-122**
**Open Monday through Saturday 6 PM to midnight; closed one week in August**
**Bus 33**
**Credit cards accepted**
€€

The first thing to know about Cent'Anni is that it's best enjoyed at lunchtime when you can take full advantage of the hilltop location and resulting stunning view of the surrounding countryside. The second thing to know is that the restaurant was probably at its prime about fifteen years ago; the vast interior of wood paneling and fluorescent lighting seems a little dated and can feel quite empty if you go off-season. The third thing to know is that it still serves excellent basic Tuscan cuisine, highly esteemed by chefs and foodies around town, and has one of the most sophisticated wine lists and sommeliers in the area. A bit contradictory, yes, but there you have it.

The Burgassi family who own Cent'Anni are also importers of salt cod and other cured fish; it's no surprise, then, that the best way to start a meal here is with a platter of the family's delicious wares arranged atop toasts. For a primo, the kitchen mainly sticks with the classics—*ribollita* and hearty pastas that will not disappoint. For a secondo, the grilled meats are excellent: I still think about the delicious and simply prepared *lombatina di vitello* (veal chop) that I ate here. As a bonus, the younger Burgassi, son Silvano, is glad to discuss the extensive wine list in either Italian or fluent English.

## Omero  ✳

**Via Pian dei Giullari 11r, Arcetri, 055/220-053**
**Open Tuesday through Sunday noon to 2:30 PM and 7:30 PM to 10:30 PM**
**Buses 12, 13**
**Credit cards accepted**
**€€**

Galileo's house arrest doesn't seem so cruel when you approach the gilded hilltop area where he was confined, southwest of town in a place called Arcetri. It's about a ten-minute cab ride or forty-five-minute walk uphill from the Ponte Vecchio to get up to Omero, and well worth the trip.

If it were down in the Center, Omero would still be an elegant restaurant serving classic Tuscan fare of a very high quality, but the reason to trek up here is not so much for the food as for the blockbuster view and tranquil country atmosphere. I would highly recommend coming at lunchtime to experience the full spectacle. Omero's upstairs and downstairs dining rooms have tall windows on three sides overlooking a picture-perfect valley and old stone farmhouse across the way. In winter, double panes let in the light without the cold, and in summer, this place really shines, with a large outdoor seating area and breezes blowing gently through.

Start with an outstanding mixed antipasto plate, some of the best *crostini* and *salumi* I've tasted, sliced paper-thin and arranged in the little "shop" in the front entryway. For a primo you can choose from classics, *ribollita* and *pappa,* but the *pappardelle* with wild boar is also rich and satisfying. As a second you might opt for the *bistecca alla fiorentina,* sliced beef with arugula, or a grilled veal chop. The kitchen likes to fry, and specialties of the house include a surprisingly succulent fried pigeon, fried chicken, and fried rabbit. They never veer from Tuscan favorites, but since they do it all so well this isn't a problem. The accompanying wine list includes plenty of extraordinary, expensive reds, as well as many reasonably priced choices (Chianti Classico, Carmignano, and other local wines). I was particularly pleased with a 1999 Rocca delle Maccie.

Not only does Omero offer *casalinga* (home-style) cooking that is a cut (or two) above average, but also an elegant, refined atmosphere complete with Richard Ginori china and professional, if sometimes chilly, service. And finally, there's the stupendous view.

# Osvaldo

**Via Gabriele D'Annunzio 51r, on the way to Settignano, 055/602-168**

**Open Thursday through Monday noon to 2 PM and 8 PM to 10 PM;**

   **Wednesday noon to 2 PM; closed August**

**Bus 10**

**Credit cards accepted**

**€**

We should all be so lucky to have a place like Osvaldo as our neighborhood restaurant. Run by the Righi family since 1978, Osvaldo is an old-school Florentine trattoria in the best sense: casual, welcoming, inexpensive, and full of regulars. The interior looks like a sprawling country house, and many of the rooms are decorated with portraits, bric-a-brac, and yes, even red-and-white-checkered tablecloths. In summer they open up a big covered patio for semi-alfresco dining. You're likely to see mostly Florentines here, plus some scholars from Harvard's Villa I Tatti, which is right up the road.

Osvaldo sticks to the standards, and with great success. The *tagliatelle al ragù, tagliatelle con porcini freschi,* and homemade *pici alla carrettiera* (essentially tomato sauce with a little kick) are all terrific, though the best primo here is the *gnocchi della casa:* rotund potato gnocchi in a tangy mushroom-tomato cream sauce. Seconds were equally uplifting: the *bistecca* here is supreme, served rare and on the bone (you'll be dreaming about this one for weeks to come). The fried rabbit, which can be extremely dry and disappointing at other places, is also a standout, dipped in a thick savory batter and fried golden brown—crunchy outside with tender and juicy white meat inside. Another secondo worth mentioning is the delicious stuffed zucchini, filled with a combination of meat, zucchini, bread crumbs, and herbs. The wine list is almost nonexistent—just a scant page of Chianti and Morellino di Scansano—and most diners opt for a liter of the house red, which is a quite good Chianti. In any case, a no-frills carafe of ruby red house wine is appropriate to the traditional *casalinga* cooking.

# Targa

**Lungarno Cristofero Colombo 7, near Piazza Alberti, 055/677-377**
**Open Monday through Saturday. 12:30 PM to 2:30 PM and 8 PM to 10:45 PM**
**Buses 31, 32**
**Credit cards accepted**
€€€

Targa, formerly called Caffè Concerto, overlooks the Arno just east of town. Neither a reliquary of hanging hams and country knickknacks like many trattorias, nor a paragon of contemporary architectural virtues, Gabriele Tarchiani's twenty-year-old mainstay has a kind of laid-back West Coast ambience; a little Steely Dan playing softly in the background wouldn't be entirely out of place. But to do justice, the restaurant—despite an incongruous entryway that looks like a disco—is actually extremely inviting and romantic. (Due to its out-of-center location, it's said to be a popular assignation with Florentines on romantic dates with partners other than their spouses.) The whole place feels immersed in warm cherrywood—tables, chairs, even the ceiling. Picture windows overlook the river, and there are plants everywhere: little plants on each table, bigger plants placed advantageously throughout the two dining rooms.

The menu has a welcome focus on seafood, and though rooted in Italian traditional cooking, the chef is not afraid to look abroad for successful new ideas. The antipasti are complex creations; you can begin your meal with a crepe of smoked salmon and salmon egg with a side of *finocchio* salad, or *culatello* (a prized form of prosciutto) served with braised marinated scallions. Your best bets among the primi are the various pastas with shellfish, such as an incredibly delicate and flavorful linguine dish cooked in shellfish broth and sauced with shrimp, scallops, and parsley; or a *pasta alla chitarra* (thick, square-cut homemade spaghetti) with a spicy calamari sauce. The *orecchiette* with lamb and fresh favas was less successful, its sauce lacking depth.

Fish also dominate the secondi, such as a fresh and tender baked turbot served with fingerling potatoes, and a more unusual dish of red mullet fillets served on a bed of Tuscan white beans. The beef cheeks braised in a sauce of Armagnac and basil is intensely satisfying, an upscale bourguignon with the tenderest of beef that melts in your mouth. The menu also has a section called "third courses," which is essentially devoted to a cheese plate, a specialty of the house. The selection of French and Italian cheeses is proudly displayed front and center in the dining room. If you still have room, desserts are an appealing mix of the usual (tiramisù) and the bizarre (strawberries with basil and black olives in a confection of white chocolate gelato).

Be careful not to drop the wine list on your foot as you could really hurt yourself. The offerings are truly encyclopedic, perhaps due to the fact that Tarchiani also owns an enoteca at a separate location (Via Nigra 11, 055/674-496). The wine list has a decent markup (though nothing compared to what you'd see in the States), yet the dessert wines such as Muffato di Antinori and Moscato di Asti are quite reasonable. You can order wines from all over the map, but the focus on fish means that whites take on more importance here. We were very happy with a bottle of 1998 Chardonnay from Felsina (better known for their Chianti Classico).

The staff here speak English, and English-language menus are available, yet I was pleased to notice that most of the diners here are Italian. Perhaps because it's been around for a long time and is a little farther from the Center, Targa is not as crowded as many lesser restaurants, yet it is well worth the long walk or bus or taxi ride to get here.

---

## Tre Soldi
**Via Gabriele D'Annunzio 4r, Campo di Marte, 055/679-366**
**Open Sunday through Thursday noon to 2:30 PM and 8 PM to 10:30 PM;**
**Friday noon to 2:30 PM**
**Bus 10**
**Credit cards accepted**
**€€**

Tre Soldi is extremely popular with Florentines, who come here both for the Tuscan classics and also to try a little something different. It's in a nondescript part of town past the stadium, on the road toward Settignano, reachable by bus or by a long but-not-so-picturesque walk from the Center. In winter diners eat in the pleasant indoor rooms with white tablecloths and simply decorated white walls. In summer the action moves outside to the spacious covered patio, where the dive-bombing mosquitoes can sometimes get in the way of full enjoyment of the otherwise fun atmosphere, which feels almost like an elegant picnic.

For an antipasto, you can choose delicious *crostini* with liver, or be a bit more daring: the *mocetta d'agnello*—cured slices of lean meat taken from the tail of a lamb and paired with a feta-like cheese—is an unusual treat that I had never seen before on a menu. The primi are uneven; the *fiochetti* (pasta pockets) with caciocavallo cheese and pear was good but paled in comparison to the similar dish at Quattro Leoni (see page 71). You might stick to something classic like the *tortellini al ragù.* The specialty of the house among secondi is the *tagliata,* and this platter of succulent sliced Chianina beef, perfectly cooked (rare) and served either with arugula or *lardo* and herbs, is indeed delicious. On the other hand, the thin-sliced *arista alla porchetta* soaked up too much oil for my taste. The dessert list is more extensive than at most trattorias, with a choice of wildly intriguing sorbets (lemon and sage, green apple and Calvados, melon and hot pepper) and equally odd gelati (pistachio with gin and pepper, cinnamon with balsamic vinegar). Chiantis, Nobiles, and other mainly Tuscan choices fill out the conventional list of wines. One thing I find slightly annoying: they include a coperto and automatic *servizio* of 10 percent although the service can be less than stellar.

---

## Zibibbo ✳

**Via di Terzollina 3r, Careggi, 055/433-383**
**Open Monday through Saturday 12:30 PM to 3:30 PM and 7:30 PM to midnight; closed August**
**Bus 14C (Capolinea, end of the line)**
**Credit cards accepted**
**€€€**

The colorful, sun-filled dining room at Zibibbo is presided over by Benedetta Vitali, an energetic Florentine woman who has dedicated her life to Tuscan cooking. Together with ex-husband Fabio Picchi she helped create Cibreo (see page 42), perhaps the best-known restaurant in Florence, where she was the pastry chef as well as partner. In 1999 she opened her own restaurant in the suburb of Careggi. The short drive

## Benedetta Vitali's Culinary Philosophy

In September 2002, I spoke with Benedetta Vitali, cofounder of Cibreo and chef-owner of Zibibbo, about recent changes in the Florentine food scene.

"Recently I've seen lots of new ethnic restaurants—African, Greek, Japanese. Certainly the Japanese food here is nothing like the food I ate when I was in Tokyo or Kyoto, but in general I think all of these new places are great for the city. I always try to go to the new restaurants that open, and in general I think all these new ethnic restaurants are great because they are opening the horizons for both Florentines and visitors. Fusion has also become very popular. It can be a good thing or not-so-good, all depending on the quality of the ingredients and how it's done.

"I am not at all ideologically against integrating the cuisines of other cultures; on the contrary, I firmly believe you need to experiment in the kitchen, and that some of the great cuisines of the world are a mix of outside influences and different ideas and ingredients. However, cooking this way poses risks for chefs, as things have the potential to go very wrong. If someone has a desire to shock instead of satisfy, this I don't like.

"With Zibibbo I wanted to create a restaurant where Florentines could come and find some familiar dishes, but also some more unusual ones, like *spaghetti alle sarde* from Sicily. I love southern Italian cooking—I love the sea, the sun, the fish—and it was a natural progression that here at Zibibbo we began to integrate more Mediterannean dishes and even some Middle Eastern ones. Our philosophy was always to cook with the best ingredients: great quality and great simplicity."

or bus ride from the Center does not deter Vitali's admirers; the modern dining room with skylights and contemporary Tuscan landscapes is bustling with locals and foreigners at both lunch and dinner.

One of the most memorable primi at Zibibbo is also probably the simplest: a *ceci* soup flavored perfectly with rosemary and a little tomato. You might also try the *crostini al fegato,* which here is a plate of homemade cakelike bread served with two luscious fingers of fine liver paté, rather than the more rustic chopped-liver version you usually see. Other excellent primi are a mix of pastas and Tuscan and Sicilian dishes, as well as some with a Middle Eastern influence. On a given day you might be able to choose among a southern Italian *spaghetti alle sarde* made with sardines, raisins, and pine nuts, or a more Tuscan tagliatelle with duck sauce. The secondi always include a choice of fish dishes—unusual for Florence— as well as several interesting meat offerings, such as roast pork with a purée of apples, and duck with a grape sauce. Save room for dessert, as they are Vitali's claim to fame. The all-Italian wine list includes Tuscan leaders like Felsina and Ama as well as up-and-coming makers from the South, all with very reasonable markups.

A word about getting here: If you take the bus, it will drop you almost in front of the restaurant, but you need to give yourself a good forty minutes of waiting-plus-riding time. Also, make sure to take the 14C, not B, all the way to its final stop. Or you can just call a cab, which should cost about €10 from the center of town.

*Working the wood-fired oven at Il Pizzaiuolo.*

# 4

# PIZZERIAS

Italians consume 56 million pizzas per week, 3 billion per year, and that's not even counting pizzas sold by the slice. Pizza is just so simple, cheap, and delicious—a perfectly balanced combination of carbohydrate, vegetable, and protein—that it's easy to understand why from north to south, the pie is perennially popular.

The origins of pizza are a little murky, but Naples lays claim to the first *pizza Margherita*. In nineteenth-century colonial Naples, pizza maker Rafaelle Esposito invented the *Margherita* when he served a perfect round of crust topped with tomato sauce, mozzarella cheese, and basil to the visiting Queen Margherita of Savoy. Pizzerias in Naples still serve it simply and expertly, molded by hand and cooked in wood-fired ovens, and usually accompanied by a beer or a Coke.

In Florence, many pizzerias are also full-service restaurants serving pastas and sometimes even meats, plus a choice of wine (though beer and Coke are still the most popular pizza accompaniments). Two styles of pizza battle it out for the hearts and stomachs of Florentines: *napoletana* and *romana*. Naples-style pizza has a somewhat thick, undulating crust that is formed by hand, while the Roman style is flattened to a thin crisp disk using a wooden dowel. The thinnest pizzas in town can be found at Antica Porta, while the thickest without doubt (said to weigh twice as much as a normal crust) are served at Spera, where a pizza often sits unfinished on the vanquished diner's plate. The most common pizzas, usually listed at the top of the menu, are the *Margherita* and the marinara, a thin crust topped with only tomato sauce, garlic, parsley, and oregano. Some pizzerias keep it simple and offer those two plus slight variations, while others list pages and pages of topping combos, including bizarre additions like broccoli and clams. Some of the most popular local toppings are spicy sausage, grana cheese, and *prosciutto crudo* or arugula, both added after the pizza comes out of the oven.

To find Florence's best and busiest pizzerias, it's often necessary to leave the confines of the city walls. This is partly a question of real estate: pizzerias should be big and bustling, with room for the hot oven and a maximum number of customers paying a modest amount for their favorite food. Any direction you go out to the periphery, you'll find an unpretentious pizzeria filled with locals; in fact, you almost always have to reserve in advance to get into even the most casual place, but for true pizza lovers it's worth the walk or ride and the effort.

## Antica Porta ✳

**Via Senese 23r, Porta Romana, 055/220-527**
**Open Tuesday through Sunday 7:30 PM to 1 AM**
**Buses 36, 37**
**Credit cards accepted**

I lived up the hill from this pizzeria for three or four months before really noticing it and then finally eating here. When I think back on the pizzas I could have consumed during those ignorant months, I quiver with regret. I no longer live in the neighborhood, just outside the Porta Romana on the southern tip of town, but Antica Porta is still my favorite pizzeria. Curly haired, gravelly voiced Nello answers the phone and acts as host and cashier. He and his partners, who have been running this place for ten years, come from Salerno, which explains the obsession with burrata (a soft cheese that combines mozzarella and caciocavallo cheeses) and bufala mozzarella.

Barely noticeable from the street, the front room—its window always steamed up in winter—has just a couple of tables; but beyond you'll follow a skinny hallway to the back where the place opens up into a busy, boisterous dining room painted a pleasant ochre. The back rooms have no windows, which gives them a cavernous feel, but this is actually the choice seating area: warmer in the winter months (farther from the drafty door) and cooler in summer when the blessed air-conditioning is turned on.

You can't help but notice the roaring wood-fired oven up front where they make pizzas with the thinnest Roman-style crust in town: delicate, crunchy, crackerlike. The pizza menu is daunting; the first few times I came here I was so overwhelmed by the choices—a page and a half just on vegetables, a whole page of different cheeses, even a page of seafood pizzas—that I ended up retreating to a *Margherita,* only later to branch out. Some of the best on the list are the *Margherita* with grana and basil; the pizza with *bresaola* and arugula; the specials with fresh tomatoes and bufala mozzarella; and the *fiori di zucca* with mixed cheeses. In summer they serve a delicious and beautifully presented *prosciutto e melone* and an equally artistic *bruschetta,* with the sliced tomato spread out like petals of a flower. The pastas here are also surprisingly good, especially the *gran scoglio,* a platter of linguine tossed with mussels and clams cooked with garlic, parsley, and olive oil (an obsessed friend back in the States is still talking about it). *Tiramisù al caffè,* with amaretti instead of ladyfingers, is astonishingly good. I couldn't get over the fact that people were leaving it half uneaten on the plate while my husband and I dueled over the last spoonfuls. And even the service is usually great—in addition to Nello, we find the same hardworking staff here time after time, always attentive, friendly, ready to translate a menu item or recommend a favorite dish.

---

## Pizzeria Caffè Italiano
**Via Isola delle Stinche 11r, 055/289-368**
**Open Tuesday through Sunday 7 PM to 1 AM**
**Map F5, Buses A, 14, 23**
**No credit cards**

Caffè Italiano is expanding its reach. The owners have a reliable osteria and charm-filled café under their auspices (see pages 65 and 195), and attached to the osteria is this little bare-bones pizzeria. Essentially just a huge wood-fired oven and about four wooden tables, the pizzeria is used mainly as a take-out stop for savvy Florentines, but you can also eat here, as I have several times. It's not the kind of place where you want to spend hours chatting with old friends, but more of a quick stop before a movie, where you can usually get a table pretty easily before 8 PM.

Like at real Naples pizzerias, there are only three choices here: *Margherita,* marinara, and *napoletana* (with capers and anchovies), plus Coke and beer. I've had all three, and they are thick, a little chewy, and very authentic. Recently the owners set up a separate dining room for pizzeria overflow so you now have a better chance of getting a table at busy times.

## EDI House
**Piazza Savonarola 8r, 055/588-886**
**Open daily 7 PM to 1:30 AM; closed August**
**Map H1, Buses 10, 11, 13, 33**
**Credit cards accepted**

Most pizzerias on the outskirts of town flaunt their divey, down-and-dirty atmosphere—part of the whole pizza-and-a-beer experience—or else might look like a *napoletana* version of elegance circa 1965. But EDI House on Piazza Savonarola is more chic and modern, fitted with black fabric and polished wood. Amazingly, it's been around for fourteen years, though it looks as if it opened yesterday. Bright and clean, with widely spaced tables and discreet plants here and there, it almost lulls you into thinking you're in the States, until the friendly old Italian waiter comes to take your order.

The menu includes a full lineup of primi and secondi in addition to the pizzas. As an antipasto, the *crostini toscani* are especially good, as is the mix of Tuscan and Milanese salami. If you are with a group, and some people want pasta, some pizza, and some otherwise, this place will satisfy all comers. The *penne alla crema di olive e rucola* with a creamy, tomatoey sauce and raw leaves of arugula spread on top is terrific. The kitchen also prepares stock favorites like *spaghetti alla carbonara* and *alle vongole* (with clams). The secondi favor skewered meats, a range of veal scallopini, and also one of the only hamburgers I've seen on a Florentine menu. However, potential burger eaters should know that while the meat is succulent high-quality ground beef, this burger comes bunless.

The thin-crust pizzas come with a wide choice of toppings. In addition to the predictable favorites, they offer some interesting house specials: one with *prosciutto cotto* (cooked ham) and porcini, another with capers, *prosciutto crudo,* and mozzarella. I always love arugula on pizza, and the *Margherita* with arugula and shaved grana cheese tastes great washed down with a cold stein of Tuborg beer. The house wine is a surprisingly good *vino sfuso* (from a big vat instead of a bottle).

---

## Firenze Nova
### Via Benedetto Dei 122, Firenze Nuova, 055/411-937
### Open Monday through Saturday 7:30 PM to 11 PM; closed August
### Credit cards accepted

Another one of Florence's best pizzerias, Firenze Nova is a decent cab ride from the city center, out in an unattractive commercial zone near the airport. But if you can make the trip, your persistence will be rewarded. I entered Firenze Nova the first time as a jaded pizza connoisseur, unsure of what new twist this place could possibly show me. I had already tasted Florence's wood-fired offerings, from cracker-thin crust that wobbled under the weight of cheese and sauce to thick *napoletana*-style pies with a lake of buffalo mozzarella across the middle that would be better served by a canoe and paddle than knife and fork.

The interior has been upgraded, but unfortunately the recessed lighting is a little too bright. In the end it doesn't really matter; the décor is entirely secondary in this comfortable spot full of Florentine couples and families. Though there is nary a tourist in sight, you'll need to reserve in advance because Firenze Nova is beloved by locals for its truly excellent and slightly unusual pizzas. Naples-style crusts are just the right thickness and not too heavy (easily digestible, as Italians would put it). The *sorpresa* (surprise) in the *pizza Margherita* is smoked mozzarella and perfectly flavored tomato sauce, while the *melanzane a sorpresa* includes mounds of fresh ricotta, smoked mozzarella, thin-sliced sausage, and bits of roast eggplant on top—absolutely delicious.

Pizzas are the main event here, but the restaurant also offers a full menu of primi and secondi. Once I noticed many happy diners with steaming plates of fresh mussels and could not resist. When the waiter asked me how I wanted them cooked, I simply replied "I'll have whatever he's having," pointing to the man wolfing down a big plate of mussels across from me. The mussels, cooked in white wine and pepper flakes, were as excellent as they looked.

---

## La Piazzetta

**Piazza del Bandino 43r, corner of Viale Europa, Gavinana, 055/680-0253**
**Open Wednesday through Monday noon to 3 PM and 7 PM to 1 AM**
**Bus 23**
**Credit cards accepted**

The one problem with most pizzerias in Florence is that a hot oven in a tight enclosed space does not always make for a tranquil dining experience, especially in summer. One exception to this rule is La Piazzetta, which is east of the city center in the residential neighborhood of Gavinana. The pride of La Piazzetta is a big outdoor patio with retractable ceiling and enclosing shrubbery. The overall design has been executed with care and taste: brass trim on the roof, dark wood matching tables and chairs, blue place mats, wood-fired oven blazing away in the open kitchen. It's a family place in every sense: family-run, friendly vibe, kids running amok in between gobbling down their pizzas and calzone.

La Piazzetta is also a full-fledged restaurant, offering classic antipasti such as delicious liver-topped *crostini* and prosciutto with melon. If you don't want a pizza, you might choose ravioli stuffed with pecorino and pear topped with walnut sauce, or *trofie* (fresh pasta shaped in triangles) with shrimp, tomato, and arugula. For secondi, La Piazzetta specializes in grilled meats: veal, lamb, and *bistecca alla fiorentina*. But most people come here for the pizzas, which are in the Naples style, with a hefty, crunchy crust. You'll find all the standards (*Margherita,* marinara, *funghi*) plus some unusual picks, and a wide choice of calzone, focaccias, and great-looking *covaccini* (pizza dough with oil, garlic, and choice of topping— essentially a pizza without the sauce and cheese). The Napoli DOC is a good choice, with melt-in-your-mouth anchovies and capers, and the Gorgonzola pizza is quite piquant. The wine list focuses almost entirely on big-name Tuscan producers like Antinori, Ricasoli, and Frescobaldi, but most people opt for the beer (Nastro Azzurro from the tap). In all, it's an excellent destination for escaping the tourists and dining *all'aperto* on wood-fired pizza, especially if you have a car or some means to get out here. The final bonus: This is some of the best service I've had in the area.

## Il Pizzaiuolo

**Via dei Macci 113r, 055/241-171**
**Open Monday through Saturday 7:30 PM to midnight; closed August**
**and Christmas**
**Map H4, Bus 14**
**No credit cards**

This appealing little pizzeria in pole position, right across the street from the Cibreo complex and the Sant'Ambrogio market, makes some of the best pizza you can get within the city limits. The atmosphere is nicer than at most pizza places; it looks more like an updated trattoria, crowded with weathered wooden chairs and marble-topped tables, white walls decorated with the occasional tchotchke, and a pretty green sign out front.

The pizzas here are so deep and wide, I often have trouble eating the whole thing, not a common occurrence. When they say Naples style, they mean it, so be prepared for some lumps and bumps in your crust, as well as a potential puddle of bufala mozzarella cheese. The basic *Margherita* is quite tasty, as is the *quattro formaggi* (four cheeses), a veritable lake of *latte* barely kept in check by the encircling crust. Be sure to call for a reservation, since Il Pizzaiuolo is a popular spot.

## Santa Lucia

**Via Ponte alle Mosse 102r, 055/353-255**
**Open Thursday through Tuesday 7:30 PM to 1 am; closed August**
**Map A1, Buses 2, 17**
**No credit cards**

If I were to wax metaphoric about Santa Lucia's pizza, I might say that the tomato sauce laps against the white sandy beach of crust like the Bay of Naples, while puddles of mozzarella—added midway through baking so as not to burn—float about like lily pads.

Santa Lucia is another out-of-the-way pizza pilgrimage, about three or four blocks outside the Porta al Prato on the west side of town. You can get here by bus or taxi, or you can walk, though this busy road is not particularly attractive. The pizzeria's big, noisy interior is a bit smoky (a hilarious sign on the wall hints that it *might* not be such a great thing if clients smoked, but looking around you'll see they've put the ashtrays out on all tables just to be on the safe side), and, as many Florentine friends have described it, *squallida* (bleak). Not that it's a dive—on the contrary, here the tables are clothed and the walls adorned with fantasy images of Naples—it's just a tiny bit dated, a little rough around the edges, much like an authentic Naples pizzeria.

Santa Lucia is one of the most popular pizzerias among locals, which means you should definitely reserve. The menu, perhaps also as a nod to all things *napoletana,* is heavy on seafood, and an appetizer of mussels in butter and garlic is outstanding. Many patrons partake of good-looking primi like spaghetti with clams and *rigatoni alla puttanesca* (spicy tomato sauce), as well as meat and fish secondi.

The pizzas come either in thin Roman style *(basso)* or thicker Naples style *(alto),* so diners have a choice. The eponymous Santa Lucia pizza is especially good, topped with *prosciutto cotto,* ricotta, and mozzarella. I also like the pizza topped with tomato, cheese, onion, and spicy sausage, and the marinaras are equally enticing. Both the *alto* and *basso* pizzas are very tasty—good crust, quality topping ingredients—and best of all, this place is truly cheap, as pizza and a beer should be.

*A typical Roman-style flat-crusted pizza.*

## Pizzeria Spera
**Via della Cernaia 9r, Fortezza da Basso, 055/495-286**
**Open Tuesday through Friday noon to 2:30 PM and 7 PM to 11 PM; Saturday**
**and Sunday 7 PM to 11 PM; closed August, Christmas, and New Year's Day**
**Buses 4, 8, 20**
**No credit cards**

Salvatore Spera, the ex-boxer who runs this place, missed his calling as a heavy on *The Sopranos,* but you can still watch him, resplendent in white baseball cap and tanktop, muscles covered with tattoos, as he arranges pizzas for the oven behind a sliding glass window. You just don't see too many men like him around Florence anymore, where everyone is meticulously aftershaved and well-shod (or else just as meticulously dreadlocked in carefully ripped jeans). Spera is from Naples originally, and he and daughter Elena serve *napoletana*-style pizza to the madding crowds. Newspaper clippings on the walls proudly announce that Elena won an international competition in which she was voted the world's best pizza maker; she even appeared on Jay Leno and showed the audience how to make real Naples pizza. Now she can be seen beside her father loading her award-winning disks into the blazing pizza oven on any given night.

You can call in advance to put your name down, but they don't seem to quite get the reservation concept. As Seinfeld put it, they can *take* the reservation, but they cannot *hold* the reservation, and you are just as well off if you show up unannounced since the system is essentially first come, first served. This place is very popular with the locals, mainly young Florentines whom you'll see spilling out of the tiny take-out section. Downstairs, luckily, is much calmer, with two rooms of wood-bench tables and 1950s movie posters adorning otherwise plain walls. Unlike most Florentine pizzerias, Spera only serves pizza—no salads, no pastas, just pizza. The offerings are a mix of tomato and *bianco* (white) pizzas, but your best bet is to stick with the tomato-based pizzas like a nice *Margherita* or a pizza with tomato and spicy sausage. The no-tomato versions such as potato and mozzarella, which I normally like, just don't seem to work as well with Naples-style thickness.

Spera has achieved cult status, but the pizza is worthy of hoopla—you can taste the quality of the ingredients in the crust, the tomato sauce, and the fresh mozzarella cheese. What really makes it stand out is the crust, which is a hefty inch and a half thick around the outside. If you manage to finish your plate here, I'll be impressed. The pizzas are also incredibly cheap; you can easily get out of here for less than €10. On the way out, have a look at the photo of Spera in boxing mode and his old gloves hanging from the ceiling.

---

## I Tarocchi
**Via de' Renai 12–14, 055/234-3912**
**Open Tuesday through Sunday 12:30 PM to 2:30 PM and 7 PM to 1 AM**
**Map F7, Bus 23**
**Credit cards accepted**

I Tarocchi has been around for ages, initiating American students abroad and others to the ways of good thin-crust pizza year after year. The quality of the pizzas may have gone down a bit lately, but I still think of this as a reliable place to go for a casual dinner. In addition to pizza, they serve some very good pastas such as linguine with clams and alternating specials. You can often get in at the spur of the moment, which is a bonus.

The main dining room has a laid-back feel with long wooden benches and posters of tarot cards (hence the name). I usually get a pizza with Gorgonzola cheese or else a *Margherita* with arugula, along with a good lager from the tap and a nice big mixed salad of lettuce, tomato, and carrot. I Tarocchi is about a ten-minute walk from Piazza Santa Croce across the Ponte alle Grazie in the San Niccolò neighborhood, where afterward you have a host of bars to try out if you so choose.

*Grabbing a snack at All'Antico Vinaio.*

# 5
# SANDWICHES, SNACKS, AND LIGHT MEALS

Eventually anyone who visits Florence finds him- or herself stuck in the middle of town, hungry, but not necessarily interested in sitting down and having a big, heavy meal. Maybe you just need a snack to refuel between museums, or you've made a reservation for dinner and don't want to spoil it by having a big lunch. This chapter mainly lists spots in the center of town because that's often where a light bite can be the most useful.

Several of the new wave of Florentine *enoteche* and quite a few *pasticcerie* also offer light savory meals, so check chapters 7 and 9 for other possibilities.

## Sight–Light Meal Index

**Accademia:** Oliandolo

**Duomo:** Coquinarius, Forno Sartoni, I Fratellini, Cantinetta dei Verrazzano

**Palazzo Pitti:** La Mangiatoia

**Palazzo Vecchio:** I Fratellini, All'Antico Vinaio, Forno Sartoni, Cantinetta dei Verrazzano

**San Lorenzo:** Nerbone, Stenio

**San Marco:** Pugi, Oliandolo

**Santa Croce:** Balducci, Osteria Caffè Italiano (weekdays), Enoteca Baldovino

**Santa Maria Novella:** Amon, Capocaccia

**Uffizi:** Caffè Italiano, I Fratellini, Forno Sartoni, All'Antico Vinaio

## All'Antico Vinaio

**Via dei Neri 65r, 055/238-2723**
**Open daily 9 AM to 3 PM and 5 PM to 7 PM; closed Sunday afternoons**
**and Monday mornings; closed August**
**Map F5, Bus B**
**No credit cards**

Around noontime this little wine bar overflows onto the street with happy snackers. It's a good choice for a light bite, especially if you don't mind standing, as the few barstools go quickly. The draws are great-looking *crostini* topped with artichoke, tomato, and liver pâté, and the attractive platters of cooked pasta, as well as little sandwiches, all meant to be downed quickly with a cheap glass of wine.

## Amon

**Via Palazzuolo 26–28r, 055/293-146**
**Open Tuesday through Sunday noon to 3 PM and 6 PM to 11 PM;**
**closed August**
**Map C4, Buses 36, 37**
**No credit cards**

If you don't mind eating on your feet, Amon is a terrific quick stop for lunch or snack. Get in line, choose among kebab, gyro, or *shwarma,* all delicious variations on the same theme: pita bread filled with meat sliced off a rotisserie and topped with eggplant salad, tahini sauce, lettuce and tomato, feta cheese, and optional spicy sauce. (You can also get a felafel, made of deep-fried spiced chickpea patties.) You then stand in the adjacent room with several other eaters, and down your food with water or a soda. The sandwiches are satisfying without being too heavy. Arabic music in the background and nice people serving you doesn't hurt, either. The sandwiches here go for about €2 to €3 each.

## Tripe Sellers: The Offal Truth

The freewheeling tripe sellers who hawk their hot sandwiches from little mobile carts are a Florentine tradition, and for a long time these sandwiches were the favorite quick lunch of the working class. Today the *trippai* are an endangered species, but you can still find a few die-hard vendors offering both tripe and *lampredotto* (fatty intestine), their carts usually surrounded by a crowd of delighted eaters—everyone from art students to carpenters to university professors. Choose from *paniabili,* served on a round roll with *salsa verde* (green sauce), or a *fiorentina* with tomato sauce and Parmesan. You'll find some of the best *trippai* outside the Porta Romana, next to the Boboli Gardens' south entrance; at the corner of Via dei Macci and Borgo la Croce, right near the Sant'Ambrogio market; and in Piazza dei Cimatori, in front of the American Express office.

## Forno Sartoni

**Via dei Cerchi 34r, 055/212-570**
**Open Monday through Saturday 7:45 AM to 8 PM; closed part of August**
**Map E4, Bus A**
**No credit cards**

Forno Sartoni serves several important purposes: It is an excellent bakery, selling baguettes, rounds, and all kinds of breads with and without salt; it's a place to pick up fresh sweets like *papatacci,* a flat sweet breakfast roll filled with raisins that I particularly like; and it is one of the best places in the Center to eat a delicious and inexpensive lunch or snack on the go. The pizzas—*Margherita,* marinara, onion, and potato—are all served by the slice and priced by weight; they look like nothing special seen from across the glass cases, but the mob fighting for them returns again and again for their stunningly rich flavor. The sandwiches, usually on focaccia, are also excellent; I've enjoyed the tuna, the roasted eggplant, and several others. This place is always crowded, and you have to either get your food to go or lean against a railing along the wall—not the most comfortable way to enjoy lunch, but very quick and easy, and right in the center of town between the Duomo and Piazza Signoria.

## I Fratellini ✳

**Via dei Cimatori 38r, 055/239-6096**
**Open daily 8 AM to 7 PM (sometimes closed Sunday); closed August**
**Map E5, Bus A**
**No credit cards**

Along with Forno Sartoni, Fratellini is a lifesaver for anyone who's hungry and in a hurry in the center of town. For years this little stall on Via dei Cimatori has been doling out small, perfectly proportioned sandwiches of pecorino and arugula, goat cheese and wild boar salami, mozzarella and tomato, and anchovies and butter—all accompanied by gulp-sized glasses of good wine or soda. Try the sun-dried tomato sandwich with goat cheese, or the truffle oil with pecorino and arugula. All the sandwiches are served on delicious warm rosette rolls. You eat standing on the street leaning against the wall or else crouching on the sidewalk, so if you're tired from walking around all day, this isn't your best option.

## I' Gottino

**Via Gioberti 174r, 055/244-797**
**Open Monday through Friday 9 AM to 10:30 PM; Saturday 9 AM to 2 PM**
**Map J5, Buses A, 8, 12, 33**
**No credit cards**

This bright sandwich shop near Piazza Beccaria attracts a young professional crowd. It's a little far from the Center but worth mentioning because it's so friendly and appealing as a place for a quick snack. The choice of sandwiches, which come on delicious *ciabatta*, includes salami and pecorino, tomato and mozzarella, or a custom combination. Well-chosen wines by the glass are an added bonus.

## Mediterranean Homesick Blues

You love penne, you're crazy about pizza, but when those primal instincts kick in and you crave ground beef on a bun, you have a few decent choices aside from the Golden Arches—often pubs where you can also pick up a pint of cold beer.

### Danny Rock
*Via Pandolfini 13r, 055/234-0307; open daily 7:15 PM to 1 AM, closed New Year's Day; Map F5, Buses A, 14; credit cards accepted.*
This swinging American-style eatery is actually quite popular with Florentines, as well as American college students abroad. They serve pizzas and pastas, but most diners seem to come for the enormous burgers, served with cheese and all the usual condiments on a sesame whole wheat bun.

### Angie's Pub
*Via dei Neri 35r, 055/283-764; open daily noon to 2 AM; Map F6, Bus B; credit cards accepted.*
A zero in terms of atmosphere, Angie's serve a good burger either plain, with cheese, or with frilly Italian-style toppings. Unfortunately, no french fries. There's a menu of familiar Italian *panini* as well.

## Mariano

**Via del Parione 19r, 055/214-067**
**Open Monday through Friday 8 AM to 3:30 PM and 5 PM to 7:30 PM;**
**Saturday 8 AM to 3:30 PM; closed two weeks in August**
**Map D5, Bus B**
**No credit cards**

You could wander around the center of Florence for a year without ever passing this place, which hides on a narrow street between the Trinità and Carraia bridges. The only sign on the outside says simply "Alimentari," but if you wander by close to lunchtime, you can't help but notice the buzz emanating from within. Florentines flock to this little place for their sandwiches, fresh and made to order, all for under €3. For some reason it's not that easy to find tasty, freshly made sandwiches in Florence, and this is one of the few places where you can actually sit, or at least lean, and relax while you eat one. Choose from tuna, sausage, prosciutto, *lardo*, cheese, roast beef, and a long list of other simple fillings. The *bresaola* with arugula and cream cheese (Italians call it "Philadelphia") is a surprisingly delicious combo. You can wash it down with a cold drink or an inexpensive glass of wine. Mariano reopens in the evenings as a place to grab a wine or an *aperitivo,* and opens early each morning in case someone in the neighborhood needs a coffee.

## Nerbone ✻

**Mercato Centrale, first floor, 055/219-949**
**Open Monday through Saturday 7 AM to 2 PM; closed part of August**
**Map E3, Bus 1**
**No credit cards**

Nerbone is more than a sandwich vendor, it's a contact sport. Your first challenge is to make eye contact with the man behind the cash register. If you succeed, you will be allowed to hand over €2.40 in exchange for a receipt and go on to obstacle number two, the sandwich mob. You make your way over to the bullying, hungry crowd as they watch the man behind the counter make his famous sandwiches. What you want is called a *bollito* (boiled beef), *bagnato* (dunked in the meaty juices), with *tutte le salse* (both the spicy red and refreshing green sauce). But first you have to shuffle, insinuate, muscle, and connive your way to the front of the line. Or you can come early, before the noon lunch crowd arrives.

Nerbone also serves delicious pastas, fresh salads, and meats such as a side of roast chicken, but the real reason to come is for the sandwich, which is Florence's answer to the hamburger. They also serve sliced *lampredotto* (intestine), but I usually stick with the *bollito.* At times it can be quite fatty, but it's always good and goes especially well with an ice-cold Coke.

## Pugi

Piazza San Marco 10, 055/280-981

Open Monday through Saturday 8 AM to 8 PM (Saturday 8 AM to 2 PM in
summer); closed part of August

Map F2, Buses C, 6, 11 (many others also pass through this piazza)

No credit cards

Any Florentine will tell you that Pugi makes the best *schiacciata* (see page
23) and *schiacciata* pizza in town, and in case you still had any doubt,
check out the mad rush of people flanking this place from well before
lunchtime until they close. This clean, inviting bakery makes perfect *schiacciata* with oil and salt in a wood-fired oven; you can get it unadulterated
or in pizza form covered with various toppings: thin-sliced zucchini,
tomato and basil, truffles. Some beautiful breads and a few fruit pastries
and sweet rolls are also available, but the people practically breaking
down the door come for the pizza. Pugi is right on the main bus transfer
spot, as well as in the middle of different university faculties. The original
location is on the outskirts of town, east of the Center past Campo di
Marte, and undoubtedly a calmer eating experience (Viale de Amicis 49r,
055/669-666).

## Stenio

Via Sant'Antonino 49r, 055/216-889

Open Monday through Saturday 7:30 AM to 1:30 PM and 3 PM to 7:30 PM;
closed Monday morning in winter and Saturday afternoon in summer;
closed August

Map E3, Bus A

No credit cards

For years this space, right across from the Central Market, was a well-
stocked *salumeria.* Now the same owners have refashioned it as a better-
than-average sandwich shop. Sandwiches are made fresh to order and
served on oblong *pugliese*-style rolls. You can choose from a long list of
combinations, including Tuscan *salame* and pecorino cheese, smoked
salmon with cream cheese, and *bresaola* with Parmigiano. Sandwiches are
under €5. The shop has a counter and a few stools on which to perch.

## Enoteca Baldovino

**Via San Giuseppe 18r, 055/234-7220**
**Open daily noon to 4 PM and 6 PM to midnight**
**Map G5, Buses 14, 23**
**Credit cards accepted**

Across the street from the popular Trattoria Baldovino, this enoteca of the same name offers an abundance of wines by the glass and bottle, as well as some unusual light meals. Choose from a long list of *crostoni* (open-face sandwiches) topped with every imaginable combination of cheese and vegetable, or a big salad with an abundance of ingredients. The menu also includes many different kinds of carpaccio, from meat to swordfish to vegetables, and a changing roster of daily pasta specials. The casual, subtly lit dining room plus bar up front has hardwood floors, and the walls, enlivened by contemporary paintings by a local artist, are painted the pleasing ochre that adorns so many Florentine restaurants. This is a hugely popular lunch spot, filled with the pleasant Babel of international tourists weary after exploring the church of Santa Croce. Service can be slow when the place is at capacity.

## Balducci

**Via dei Neri 2r, 055/216-887**
**Open Monday through Saturday 12:30 PM to 3:30 PM and 5 PM to 10:30 PM**
**Map F6, Buses B, 23**
**Credit cards accepted**

I often ignore Balducci's daily menu of hot specials—such as an excellent lasagne made with spinach or wild boar—in favor of a plate consisting of a little bit of this and a little bit of that. I like to make a mixed platter of their various cold salads—fava bean with Parmesan, little shrimp with celery, tomato, and mozzarella (though sometimes they use too much salt in the salads)—as well as one or two *crostini* and maybe a hot vegetable side dish. This is a family-run place with rough-hewn wooden chairs and tables and a perfect casual Florentine wine bar vibe. The service is friendly and laid-back. Order a glass of Rosso di Montalcino to go with your meal and enjoy the people-watching out on Via dei Benci.

---

## Cantinetta dei Verrazzano ✳

**Via dei Tavolini 18–20r, 055/268-590**
**Open Monday through Saturday 8 AM to 9 PM (lunch served 12:30 PM to 2:30 PM); closed two weeks in August; closed Christmas Day and New Year's Day**
**Map E4, Bus A**
**Credit cards accepted**

The Cantinetta is a kind of mini gourmet food hall. The bakery at the front sells outstanding breads, cookies, and cakes such as *torta della nonna* and a chocolate-semolina concoction. Beyond the baked goods you'll find a marble-topped bar serving top-quality Piansa coffee. Stop here in the morning for a cappuccino and pastry; you won't even have to pay extra to sit at the small number of tables. At lunch, squeeze into the train-car-sized room next-door for fantastic focaccia sandwiches straight from the wood-fired oven, tasting plates of Cinta Senese *salumi* (see page 22), cheeses paired with spicy *mostarda,* and other treats. Finish it off with a slice of *torta della nonna.*

The place has plenty of charm, with marble-topped tables and ornate wooden cabinets showing off bottles of Verrazzano wine (also for sale here). In all, this is a great place to have lunch before visiting the Duomo or Palazzo Vecchio. If the wait for one of the few tables looks long, you can always order a focaccia sandwich and a drink and eat while sitting on the long wooden bench or leaning against the bar. (By the way, the family who runs the Verrazzano vineyards in Chianti descends from Giovanni da Verrazzano, who in the years following Columbus explored the North American coastline around present-day Manhattan.)

---

## Capocaccia
**Lungarno Corsini 12–14r, 055/210-751**
**Open Tuesday through Sunday noon to 2 AM; closed August**
**Map D5, Bus B**
**Credit cards accepted**

At night it's almost impossible to wedge in here past the phalanx of fashionable young Florentines who come for an *aperitivo* (see page 135) and light snack. But in the daytime, Capocaccia is more peaceful than most eateries in the Center, despite its prime location along the Arno. The truly light lunch consists of an attractive cold buffet of salads, sliced meats, cheeses, and grilled vegetables for about €7 including drink. The interior is stylish, with blue walls, blue-and-white tile trim, and funky light fixtures that look like *funghi.*

## Coquinarius

**Via dell'Oche 15r, 055/230-2153**
**Open daily 9 AM to midnight; closed Sundays in summer; closed August**
**Map E4, Bus A**
**Credit cards accepted**

Coquinarius is a great combination of wine bar, restaurant, and stop for a light bite at odd hours. It also has the distinction of being about ten paces away from the Duomo, on a small side street. The evocative space, with its high ceilings and brick walls, is made comfortable and pleasant with modern track lighting, distressed furniture, and French and Italian posters from the 1920s and 1930s on the walls. A handful of white and red wines are available by the glass at reasonable prices, and there is a much longer list of bottles. The menu is distinguished by its popular *insalatone*, including the Greek salad with cucumber, tomato, and feta cheese; and the Californian, which includes shrimp, celery, and avocado. The kitchen also turns out simple but excellent pastas and other hot primi, including a great potato gnocchi with Gorgonzola sauce. Prices are reasonable and service is friendly, though it can be slow at peak times. Best of all, the kitchen is open every day (even Sunday) until 11 PM; you'd be surprised how rare and incredibly helpful this is in central Florence.

## Bar D'Azeglio

**Via della Mattonaia 55r, 055/247-9263**
**Open Monday through Saturday 6:30 AM to 8 PM; closed August**
**Map I3, Buses 31, 32, 6**
**No credit cards**

Casual would be an understatement for this bar with wood-paneled walls and pink tablecloths. But far from the tourist crowds, in the northeast corner of the city, Bar D'Azeglio serves excellent, reliable hot lunches at dirt-cheap prices. Secure a table, and then line up at the counter where you can choose from a changing daily roster of four pasta dishes and an assortment of secondi and salads. Afterward you can have a coffee at the bar. If you happen to be out this way, near the parklike Piazza D'Azeglio, this is one of the cheapest and best hot lunches around, always filled between 1 and 2 PM with businessmen and students from the nearby art history library.

## Oliandolo

**Via Ricasoli 38r, 055/211-296**
**Open Monday through Saturday 10:30 AM to 10 PM; closed most of August**
    **and Christmas Day**
**Map F3, Bus C**
**Credit cards accepted**

A crush of people clamor for the few wooden tables in this unpretentious lunch spot right between the Duomo and the Accademia. The small menu usually features a changing selection of roast meats (smallish portions), such as roast beef with mashed potatoes or a cold plate of *vitello tonnato* (thin-sliced veal with tuna sauce—a specialty of Emilia-Romagna). You can also get an *insalatone,* the "big salad" that is making more frequent appearances around town, and even some interesting vegetarian entrées, like a frittata with spinach, mozzarella, and grana. Oliandolo serves appetizing *panini* to go, as well as a small selection of good wines by the glass, the perfect complement to a small lunch between sights.

## Tavola Calda da Rocco

**Inside Mercato Sant'Ambrogio**
**Open Monday through Saturday noon to 1:30 PM; closed part of August**
**Map H5, Buses A, 14**
**No credit cards**

A *tavola calda* generally refers to an inexpensive place where the food is premade and kept hot and ready to serve (*tavola calda* literally means "hot table"). Florence doesn't have that many, which is okay because they're not generally very exciting. The exceptional *tavola calda* in town is Da Rocco, inside the Sant'Ambrogio market—a great stop for a cheap and unpretentious lunch. Possibly the best thing about Da Rocco is Rocco himself, a graying, slightly paunchy man with a great sense of humor who will tease you, flirt with you, and sometimes tell you what to eat. The food here is usually very good; I've eaten excellent *panzanella* and prosciutto with *melone* in the summer months, and in the winter I've hunkered down with Rocco's porcini risotto and stuffed eggplant. *Panna cotta,* crème caramel, and other classic desserts are served, and prices are rock-bottom.

## Rose's

**Via del Parione 26r, 055/287-090**
**Open Monday through Saturday 8 AM to 1:30 AM; Sunday 12:30 PM**
   **to 3 PM and 7:30 PM to 1:30 AM**
**Map D5, Buses A, B**
**Credit cards accepted**

At night Rose's is a stylish place to get an *aperitivo* or take a date for sushi (see page 129) or a late-night drink. During the day, however, calm reigns here as the kitchen offers light pita sandwiches and large salads instead of *maki* and *nigiri.* The atmosphere is crisp and tranquil, and the place is filled with actual workers on their lunch hour. Patrons perch on dark blue stools and banquettes and order up salads fortified with roasted vegetables, crab and shrimp, or various cheeses. Rose's is a very good choice for resting between sights and eating something besides heavy pasta.

## Il Santo Bevitore

**Via Santo Spirito 64–66r, 055/211-264**
**Open Monday through Saturday noon to 2:30 PM and 7:30 PM to 11:30 PM**
**Map C5, Buses D, 6**
**Credit cards accepted**

Though abounding in inexpensive quality restaurants, the Santo Spirito neighborhood lacked a place where you could sit down for a good glass of wine and small bite. Now it has one: Santo Bevitore, which skipped over the usual settling-in period and became immediately popular. The spacious vaulted room with red tile floors was already a restaurant, but the new owners have tastefully refashioned it with white-washed walls, modern custom-built shelves to hold bottles of wine, and a large wooden bar lining the wall. The atmosphere is casual and collegial; locals gather and chat at the dark wooden tables, and at dinner the room is softened by candlelight.

On the limited menu you can choose from tasting plates like a trio of paper-thin slices of excellent prosciutto, *finocchiona,* and *pancetta;* and an arrangement of mixed cheeses. The kitchen also makes salads, including spinach with pine nuts and pears and a *nizzarda* (Niçoise salad). There are ususally four or five hot primi to choose from, as well as one or two secondi. The primi might be a risotto with zucchini, *pappa al pomodoro,* or something equally straightforward. The wine list, devised by my favorite wine shop, Millesimi (see page 145), includes about ten wines by the glass—a mix of inexpensive Tuscans, whites from the north, and even some French wines. The elegant selection by the bottle focuses on Tuscany and Piedmont. The cooking here is satisfying without being stellar, but with fair prices, good wines, and a rustic-chic atmosphere, it's perfectly suited for a light meal—the kind of neighborhood place you can drop into day or night.

## Tuscan Takeout

Take-out food, often packaged in Styrofoam and approaching maximum sogginess by the time you get it home, is antithetical to the slow-food aesthetic of Florentine eating. Pizza delivery exists here, but the quality is embarrassing and I would recommend it only in cases of desperation. Most *alimentari* and *salumerie* offer a selection of cold food from which you can put together a terrific light meal of marinated artichokes, eggplant, cheeses, and cold cuts. If you're looking for quick cooked food, the answer is in the *rosticceria.* Most *rosticcerie* are so-called because they feature meats roasted on a turning spit, though most also sell vegetables and baked pastas like lasagne. The food is generally good but can also be quite salty and greasy. Once in a while, though, when you don't feel like cooking or eating out, a *rosticceria* chicken with roasted potatoes and marinated eggplant can be just the thing.

### Da Noi
*Via Fiesolana 46r, 055/242-917; open Monday through Saturday 8 AM to 2:30 PM and 4:30 PM to 7:30 PM, closed Wednesday afternoon; Map G4, Bus C; credit cards accepted.*

People who have lived here for years still wax fondly about Da Noi, a small restaurant that served simple home-cooked Tuscan food. The restaurant is long gone, but owners Bruno Tramontana and Sabine Busch still run a take-out and catering service in the same space. You can come here before dinner to pick up a pasta or entrée to go, but their main business is catering at people's homes for parties of five or more. They will make everything from savory tarts and *crostini* as appetizers, on through to special cakes and pastries for dessert.

## La Ghiotta
*Via Pietrapiana 7r, 055/241-237; open Tuesday to Sunday 11:30 AM to 2:30 PM and 6:30 PM to 10 PM, closed August; Map H4, Buses A, C; no credit cards.*
Hungry Florentines head to Ghiotta, close to the Sant'Ambrogio market, for the savory roast chicken and pork, fresh peas, spinach and other vegetables, and tempting thick-layered lasagne. It is unceasingly crowded here during prime lunch hours on weekdays.

## La Mangiatoia
*Piazza San Felice 8–10r (Via Romana), 055/224-060; open Tuesday through Sunday noon to 3 PM and 7 PM to 10 PM; Map D7, Buses D, 11, 36, 37; credit cards accepted.*
This clean and modern little *rosticceria*-restaurant serves excellent roast chicken, flattened under a brick and charred over an open flame. The potatoes can be great or disappointing depending on how long they've been sitting around, but the eggplant, peas, and spinach are all good. They also serve a rich lasagne with a hint of cinnamon, and a good homemade tiramisù. Hidden in back is a dining room for those who want to sit and eat an inexpensive pizza, a dish of pasta, or a plate of one of the roast meats. Overall this is a convenient full-service eatery and take-away for those who live in the area or are looking for a snack near Palazzo Pitti or Boboli Gardens.

# 6
# INTERNATIONAL FOOD

No one comes to Florence to eat *kung pao* chicken or baklava, but for the beleaguered expat, the adventurous local, or even the homesick traveler, these forays into international cuisine can be extremely welcome. Florence lags well behind Milan and Rome (don't even bring Paris or London into it) with respect to ethnic and international restaurants. First, it is simply much smaller and less cosmopolitan than those cities, with fewer immigrants; second, the Florentines tend to be extremely conservative in their eating habits, wary even of other regional Italian cuisines, let alone Thai red curry. Also, Florence is a highly tourist-conscious town and tourists want to eat the real thing: *ribollita, spaghetti con funghi porcini,* a thick, grilled *bistecca alla fiorentina.* For those who can recite a Florentine trattoria's offerings by heart and have perhaps eaten one *bistecca* too many, however, the new invasion of trendy Japanese, inexpensive Greek, and exotically spiced Indian cuisine is long overdue.

Chinese people make up the largest quotient of immigrants to Tuscany; the town of Prato in particular attracts a huge number of Chinese workers to its enormous textile factories. Everywhere in Florence—and the rest of Italy—you'll notice bright red lanterns illuminating the entrances to restaurants with names like Pearl of China or Bella Beijing. Unfortunately the quality of these restaurants is generally mediocre. Florence has also seen a fair amount of immigration from India and North and West Africa, and it is now possible to choose from among several Indian restaurants, as well as Egyptian and Turkish rotisseries. Spanish tapas are also making inroads, but the most striking phenomenon of late is the influx of chic Japanese restaurants offering high-priced, high-quality sushi to the curious crowds.

For other international offerings, see Amon (page 108), Asia Masala (page 158), and ViviMarket (page 165).

## La Festa dell'Unità

Every August, those few Florentines who have not hightailed it to the beach head to the Fortezza da Basso, an enormous open-air stone pentagon that was once Florence's military stronghold, for the Festa dell'Unità. The annual carnival/food fair/dancing-and-music party has political roots: it has long been sponsored by Italy's Communist party as a celebration of different cultures and the workingman and -woman. In postmillennial Italy the Communist Party has lost much of its former oomph, and the Festa is now sponsored by the softer Center-Leftist grouping called L'Uliva and by the leftist newspaper *L' Unità*. Aside from the political underpinnings, this is a free carnival where you can wander around in the warm summer night and peruse Indian scarves, Communist literature, and sample all kinds of international cooking. The atmosphere is a cross between a Mexico City street fair and the parking lot at a Grateful Dead show. Many Italian and non-Italian restaurants and bars set up booths here, including the restaurant India of Fiesole, a Cuban restaurant, a Moroccan one, a smokin' Argentinian steak barbecue, and several gelaterias and beer gardens. Late at night the place gets more crowded as people come to dance and hang out. Mainly it's a great chance to sample some different foods, drink beer, and listen to bad live music—what more can you ask for on a hot summer night?

## Dioniso

**Via San Gallo 16r, 055/217-882**
**Open Monday through Saturday 11 AM to midnight**
**Map F2, Buses 6, 11**
**Credit cards accepted**
**€**

The family who runs Dioniso has created a lively updated version of a Greek taverna in this student-filled area near the Central Market. You can choose among a sampling of smaller *stuzzichini* (à la carte pita sandwiches), as well as little bites of olives, or salads of chickpeas or egg-plant. You might opt for the *piatti unici,* which include moussaka, or an assortment of whole plates of grilled pork or beef with a side of Greek salad and *tzatziki,* made with creamy yogurt, fresh cucumber, and lots of garlic. I don't usually love Greek desserts but couldn't leave without try-ing the little syrup-soaked phyllo sweets wrapped in tiny fibers like a bird's nest; I very much enjoyed this and the other homemade treats, including halva and baklava.

In the short time since it opened, Dioniso has become immensely popular. The atmosphere is bright and slightly modern, with white walls, blue trim, and blown up black-and-white posters of Greek celebrities: Melina Mercouri, Anthony Quinn (actually Mexican), and Maria Callas gaze out imperiously at diners. The food is also a fresh and welcoming change from heavy Tuscan cooking. My one complaint is that the main dishes are too small; I was left hungry even after grazing from the plates of my indulgent companions. Prices here are certainly reasonable, and this is an excellent stop for a light lunch after visiting San Lorenzo or the Palazzo Medici.

## Eito

**Via dei Neri 72r, 055/210-940**
**Open Monday through Saturday 12 PM to 2 PM and 7:30 PM to 11 PM;**
   **Sunday 7:30 PM to 11 PM**
**Map F5, Bus B**
**Credit cards accepted**
**€€**

The red walls, red-cushioned chairs, smooth black tables, and stylish wait staff dressed in black all contribute to the sensation of being inside a lacquered Japanese box, an appropriate environment in which to dine on sushi and other Japanese preparations. Owner Laurent Chauvet (half Ital-ian, half French) lived for many years in Japan and the United States, learning the ins and outs of raw fish. As he explains, "In order to be fresh enough for sushi, the fish must be alive that morning." He buys his seafood from a number of different purveyors in Tuscany, depending on what's available each day.

Many diners order one of the prix fixe menus. The Edo menu consists of almost all sushi: tuna, salmon, and mackerel sashimi, *nigiri,* and *maki* (rolls), along with miso soup and little antipasti. The Osaka menu comprises delicious tempura of shrimp and vegetables, a plate of sashimi, and skewers of yakitori. The menus cost about €30 each, but include a huge amount of food. You can also order à la carte, either sushi or cooked fish and entrées. The service is discreet but attentive. For dessert, soy ice cream tastes a bit like Cool Whip, but cheesecake and other non-Japanese sweets are also offered.

---

## La Habitacion Liquida
**Borgo Ognissanti 87r, 055/280-922**
**Open Monday through Saturday 12:30 PM to 3 PM and 7:30 PM to 10 PM**
**(the bar is open until midnight); closed one week in August**
**Map B4, Buses B, D**
**Credit cards accepted**
**€**

Here is a brightly painted and high-spirited place to stop for a light Spanish lunch or full meal. Start with a plate of mixed tapas, including small portions of *serrano* ham, manchego cheese, stuffed tomatoes, and savory cheese turnovers. The brick-red gazpacho is delicious and refreshing, with little croutons and quality olive oil sprinkled on top. The tortillas come in several incarnations, as do the paella, with a choice of chicken or seafood. The paella is a little lackluster, but the sangria and charming atmosphere make up for any small shortcomings in the food.

---

## India
**Via Gramsci 43a, Fiesole, 055/599-900**
**Open Wednesday through Monday 7:30 PM to 10:30 PM**
**Bus 7**
**No credit cards**
**€€**

The owners of India have created not just a restaurant but a complete atmosphere that engages all the senses. The sprawling rooms, painted bright orange with green, red, and yellow accents, are dimly lit by lanterns and other soft lights, and the ceiling is covered with patterned fabric. Servers hustle about in colorful Indian dress while sitar and other mellow Indian music wafts in the background along with the smell of cumin and cardamom. The whole effect is mesmerizing and romantic, as if you were eating inside a luxurious scented tent.

The menu is traditional northern Indian. To start you can choose from standard *papadam* and samosas, both meat and vegetarian. The tandoor oven turns out excellent dishes of mainly chicken, and the enticing curries are spicy with deliciously complex flavors. The restaurant also serves rice *biryani* dishes and several vegetarian options. For dessert they make an assortment of sweets using mango, cream, and rice, or you can have a soothing *chai*.

You can catch the No. 7 bus in the Center at the station or closer to the Duomo and it will take you all the way up to the main square of Fiesole, from which you need walk about one block up the main street (Gramsci) to the restaurant. The bus runs until midnight, so you can take it there and home, though you should factor in a bit of waiting time as it only comes about every twenty minutes at night. Or, the restaurant will be glad to call you a cab, which should cost about €20 to the city center.

---

## Momoyama ✳

**Borgo San Frediano 10r, 055/291-840**
**Open daily 8 PM to 11:30 PM; closed two weeks in August**
**Map C5, Buses 6, D, 11**
**Credit cards accepted**
€€

Momoyama, like its groovy sushi counterparts around town, features a striking minimalist, modern Japanese-inspired interior. Much bigger than it initially looks, the restaurant sprawls out into a series of elegantly designed, simply furnished rooms in whites and light woods, with colorful contemporary paintings on the walls. There is a large upstairs room, as well as a tranquil back patio covered by big white canvas umbrellas and lit by flickering votives.

The menu is divided into sushi and Japanese food and what the chef calls "inventive cuisine," which I think is intended for the sheepish dining companion who came along for the meal but is terrified by raw fish. The beautifully presented platters of sushi include various *nigiri* and both classic and creative *maki* (rolls) all lovingly made by sushi chef Eric Stedman. You can stick with excellent California rolls (with real crab), spicy tuna, and simple tuna rolls or branch out to special creations such as scallop rolls with spicy sauce and avocado, or delicious shrimp tempura rolls. Abundant platters of tempura, some interesting Japanese salads, and miso and *soba* noodle soup are also served. The wine list is heavy on whites, though Tuscan reds and Japanese beer are available, too. Service is attentive and smart, and the whole place has a snappy, professional feel that can be hard to find in Florence. Prices are high, but the gleamingly fresh fish and ample portions make this place a sushi-lover's nirvana.

---

## Nin Hao

**Borgo Ognissanti 159r, 055/210-770**
**Open daily 11 AM to 2 PM and 6 PM to midnight; closed Monday dinner;**
    **closed two weeks in August**
**Map B3, Bus A, D**
**Credit cards accepted**
€

Most Chinese restaurants in Florence are fairly mediocre, using frozen ingredients to make very cheap meals. Nin Hao (which means "ciao") is exceptional in its inviting atmosphere, friendly staff, and nongreasy, better-than-average Chinese cooking. This place is open late and is almost always packed, mostly with locals but also with the occasional homesick American or Asian traveler who wanders in. The owners have fashioned a sort of exotic lounge setting with lacquered walls, potted plants, and music wafting in the background. Start your meal with the superb steamed dumplings (called *ravioli al vapore*) or fried spring rolls (*involtini di primavera*). I've tried many of the choices on the menu but usually return to my standby dishes: a respectable *kung pao* chicken and the spicy shredded pork with mushrooms (*maiale piccante con funghi*), accompanied with steamed white rice. Wash it all down with a cold Tsing Tao. I am always amazed at how inexpensive the bill is once it arrives; two can easily eat here for under €25.

## Rose's

Via del Parione 26r, 055/287-090
Open Monday through Saturday 8 AM to 1:30 AM, Sunday 7:30 PM
  to 1:30 AM
Map D5, Buses A, B
Credit cards accepted
€€

This stylish place, tucked away on a side street that runs between the Trinità and Carraia bridges, acts as both cocktail lounge and sushi restaurant, serving good raw fish at very high prices. (A light lunch is also offered, see page 119.) The fish is extremely fresh, and one person would do well to order the Super Sushi mixed platter of nine (tiny) tuna rolls and nine (bigger) *nigiri* pieces of raw salmon, tuna, yellowtail, and shrimp. There are also *soba, udon,* yakitori, and big plates of tempting shrimp or vegetable tempura that are strangely expensive (for raw fish I am willing to pay extra; when it comes to fried vegetables, I'm not). The minimalist decor consists of dark blue velvety banquettes, light wood tables and stools, modern art adorning the walls, and cool jazz playing in the background. The Kirin and Asahi beers were a welcome sight, but also wildly overpriced. The chef is a little miserly with the wasabi and ginger, but otherwise I left here feeling slightly more hip than usual and with my sushi craving satisfied, for the time being.

*Casa del Vino is a popular spot for a glass of wine or a snack.*

# 7

# WINE BARS
# AND WINE SHOPS

No region of Italy has made greater strides in winemaking in the last twenty years than Tuscany. On the production side, both small and large vintners have turned the traditional preference for quantity over quality on its head, making wines of class and distinction, particularly in the Chianti Classico zone and in Bolgheri. The marketing campaign has been equally impressive; savvy promoters have overhauled the image of Chianti wine, created a sales and marketing bonanza with the Supertuscan, and made the name Tuscany synonymous with quality Italian wine, eclipsing even Piedmont in terms of appreciation among foreigners.

Florence, with its casual wine bars and well-stocked shops, is the perfect place to begin or further a Tuscan wine education.

## WINE BARS

According to Leonardo Romanelli, head of Slow Food Florence, the most exciting change happening in the normally conservative Florentine food scene is the advent of creative, sophisticated wine bars. Places like Beccofino and Enotria purposely call themselves wine bars instead of *enoteche* to differentiate themselves from the more traditional gulp-and-go outposts. Now you have a choice in Florence. More traditional *enoteche* are havens where you can stop in for a moment, often before dinner, chat with old friends, and quaff a glass of good, often inexpensive, wine while standing at a casual bar. Or, you can opt for one of the even greater number of trendy wine bars, which tend to have a cool international atmosphere, an impressive wine list full of interesting labels, a rotating selection of top wines by the glass (often quite pricey), and, in the case of those that serve food, a chef that doesn't consider innovation a dirty word. Many wine bars offer delicious snacks—mainly Italian cheeses and *salumi*—while others serve a full menu of primi and secondi, always with a bit more experimentation than what's allowed in the more tradition-bound trattorias; there's also less pressure to order a multicourse meal.

---

## Enoteca Baldovino

**Via San Giuseppe 18r (Piazza Santa Croce), 055/234-7220**
**Open daily 11:30 PM to 2:30 PM and 7 PM to 11:30 PM**
**Map G5, Bus C**
**Credit cards accepted**
**€**

Across the street from the slightly more upscale Trattoria Baldovino (see page 60), this small enoteca's light menu is oriented somewhat around the vast wine list. You can have a whole meal in the relaxed back room or outside, or stop by for a glass of wine at the bar in front.

---

## Beccofino

**Piazza degli Scarlatti 1r (Lungarno Guicciardini), 055/290-076**
**Open Monday through Saturday 7:30 PM to midnight; Sunday 12:30 PM**
**to 2:30 PM and 7:30 PM to midnight**
**Map C5, Buses 6, D**
**Credit cards accepted**
**€€**

Everyone looks good in the warm wash of lighting at this impeccably designed restaurant and wine bar. Close to the entrance is a graceful horseshoe-shaped bar and several seats and tables where people without reservations can come in and sample from the changing list of wines by the glass, including about half a dozen reds, whites, and dessert wines, mostly from top or emerging producers. Among the reds you might try an inexpensive Primitivo from Puglia or a reliable glass of Morellino, Merlot, or Chianti *riserva.* If you don't like to sip on an empty stomach, you can order something light like *crostini* with such original toppings as mascarpone and sausage or escarole with pecorino. Or enjoy something heavier like a plate of hearty pasta. (For full review, see page 45.)

## Boccadama ❊

**Piazza Santa Croce 25–26r, 055/243-640**
**Open daily 8:30 AM to midnight; closed Monday afternoon**
**Map G5, Bus C**
**Credit cards accepted**
**€€**

Though mainly a restaurant, Boccadama is a great place to meet up with friends for a glass of wine and a plate of French or Italian cheeses, and perhaps some *bruschetta* or *salumi*. The outstanding location on the south side of car-free Piazza Santa Croce, the casual yet smooth atmosphere, and the smartly chosen wines make it well worth a stop. Servers are often multilingual and can be quite knowledgeable about wine (and if they don't know something, they have no problem calling in the owner). This is also a fine place to have a full meal (see page 63); there is a nonsmoking room in back and outdoor seating in summer months.

## Casa del Vino

**Via dell'Ariento 16r, 055/215-609**
**Open Monday through Friday 8:30 AM to 3 PM and 5 PM to 7:45 PM;**
   **Saturday 8:30 AM to 3 PM; closed most of August**
**Map E3, Buses 1, 6**
**Credit cards accepted**
**€**

Like Zanobini around the corner (see below), here is a narrow, good old-fashioned place outside the Central Market where you can duck in, sample a glass of wine, munch on *crostini* or other snacks, and duck back out blinking into the sunshine, all without sitting down or spending more than about €5. Different wines are featured on different days, but you can count on seeing respected labels from Tuscany, Piedmont, and Friuli. Among the reds you might find a Morellino di Scansano or an Umbrian Merlot, and the whites are equally well chosen.

# Enotria

Via delle Porte Nuove 50, 055/354-350

Open Monday through Saturday noon to 3:30 PM and 7:30 PM to midnight; closed Monday evening; closed most of August

Map A1, Buses 2, 17, 35

Credit cards accepted

€€

It's surprising to find this refined little wine shop, wine bar, and restaurant so far off the beaten tourist path, beyond the Porta al Prato, but it's worth the walk or ride for someone really serious about wine and food. The menu is divided into antipasti, primi, secondi, and dolci, and below each dish is a recommended wine by the glass. In other words, it's a menu clearly designed by a sommelier. The antipasti include a flavorful and delicate salad of smoked duck breast, whereas the primi are a little more standard, with several pastas and a soup. The ravioli and the *garganelli al pomodoro* are good without being too exciting, but the accompanying wines, including a Barbera from Piedmont and a Vernaccia di San Gimignano, are excellent. For the secondi, you can order a steak or rabbit dish, but you may want to opt for the tasting plates—either of exceptional Cinta Senese *salumi* (*coppa,* prosciutto, *soppressata*) or an equally impressive plate of Italian cheeses, from pecorino to pungent Taleggio, served with unusual little tomato, onion, and fig confits. The gregarious owner likes to talk wine and, if the restaurant isn't too crowded, is happy to chat with customers and answer questions.

You can also come in just for an inexpensive glass to drink at the bar, a bottle of fine Chianti or Chardonnay to take home, or something from the deli case, which features Cinta Senese cured meats and selected cheeses. The atmosphere is elegant but not too fussy, with lots of wood, white tablecloths, and wine bottles adorning the walls. The food, like everything in Florence, seems to have experienced some euroflation, but the wines by the glass are generally better better priced than in the center of town. I was surprised to learn there are smoking and non-smoking sections here, very rare for Florence, until I realized that it was not for health reasons but because smoke is said to interfere with the taste of wine.

## Aperitivo alla Fiorentino

Dario Cecchini, Tuscany's most famous—and headline grabbing—
butcher, recently held a mock funeral for Via Tornabuoni to mourn the
death of the street and the historic businesses that were being crowded out to make room for yet more designer shops. The crowd grum-
bled that Florence is becoming one giant upscale outdoor mall while
they swilled an *aperitivo* (predinner cocktail) called a Negroni, a mix
of red vermouth, Campari bitter, and gin. Most of the well-dressed
crowd's contempt had been roused by the loss of Giacosa, a historic
and elegant nineteenth-century bar-café where the Negroni was invented by a heavy-drinking Italian noble. Giacosa still exists as a small
leopard-striped accessory attached to the Roberto Cavalli fashion
boutique that took over its space. (Strangely, a lot of Florentines seem
to like this new incarnation, and in summer the establishment even
puts tables out on the street.) But if you'd rather not make your way
past rock star leather pantsuits to Giacosa, choose one of the other
fine places in town to linger, sip an early-evening *aperitivo,* or nurse a
late-night cocktail.

The *aperitivo* hour—or hours, usually from about 7 to 9 PM—is
a particularly Florentine pastime. It's a chance for locals and in-the-
know visitors to get dressed up before dinner (which happens late
here), sit outside if it's warm, and drink brightly colored concoctions
while socializing in style. The classic *aperitivi* are the Negroni and
the Americano (red vermouth, Campari bitter, and soda water), or a
Prosecco or other *spumante* (sparkling wine). Recently some trendy
Florentine bars have started serving slushy, fruity drinks like Margaritas
and Daiquiris—great on a hot summer night but not exactly authentic
to the region. The most popular *aperitivo* haunts put out impressive
displays of food to go along with the alcohol; some stick to *crostini*
but others go whole hog, with pasta salads, polenta, paella, even
sushi. Some people have been known to scrounge together a full meal
from the offerings, which goes a long way toward justifying the bank-
breaking price tag on most Florentine cocktails.

## Il Riffrulo

*Via di San Niccolò 53–57, 055/234-2621; open daily 8 AM to 1 AM, closed two weeks in August; Map G7, Buses D, 23.*

With atmospheric identity in crisis between an English pub and a French bistro, Riffulo has plenty going for it, including French doors in the front that open in summer months for an indoor-outdoor feel and a big back room with blazing fire in winter. Servers bring you a platter of snacks when you order an *aperitivo* here, or you can munch on shared plates at the bar, where drinks are a bit cheaper. Rifrullo has to stay on its toes to compete for its clientele with bars Zoe and Negroni around the corner.

## Dolce Vita

*Piazza del Carmine, 055/284-595; open daily 11 AM to 2 AM; Map B5, Bus D.*

Dolce Vita, right next to the Chiesa del Carmine and the Brancacci Chapel, was *the* in place in the early 1990s, went through a slight doldrums period, and now has been relaunched with new owners and a design makeover. The crowd here is stylish, mainly thirty-something Florentines who come to chat, have an *aperitivo*, and check out what one another are wearing. Since its rebirth the bar serves some interesting little snacks to go along with the booze, like marinated chicken on skewers and fish carpaccio. The owners also opened a little wine bar where you can choose wines by the glass to sip inside or out on the large and happening patio. You can order a light meal at lunchtime, though the too-hip slanted tables might not make for the most comfortable dining experience.

## Gilli

*Piazza della Repubblica 36–39r, 055/213-896; open Wednesday through Monday 7:30 AM to 10 PM, closed one week in August; Map E4, Bus A.*

If you want to sidle up to an art nouveau bar serviced by a liveried *barista* and have your aperitivo in old-world style, here's the place.

The drinking starts early—you'll sometimes see older Florentines sipping bright red Campari and soda before lunch rather than dinner—and the buffet spread is always impressive, brimming with a colorful assortment of olives, cheeses, and little sandwiches. This is probably the most classic bar in town to have an *aperitivo*.

### Caffè La Torre
*Lungarno Cellini 65r, 055/680-643; open daily 10:30 AM to 3 AM; Map H7, Buses D, 23.*
This is a trendy locale for young Florentines and expats to gather, both inside and on the hopping shaded front patio. Drinks are expensive but the clientele doesn't seem to mind as they flirt and fill up their plates with quite good free food; this is one of the most abundant *aperitivo* buffets in town. La Torre is so-called because it sits in the shadow of the tall Porta San Niccolò, a tower at the foot of the ramps leading up to Piazzale Michelangelo. It's right along the river, slightly east of the Center in the Oltrarno.

### Capocaccia
*Lungarno Corsini 12–14r, 055/210-751; open Tuesday through Sunday noon to 2 AM, closed part of August; Map D5, Bus B.*
Capocaccia is a bar of superlatives: most fashionable clientele, best buffet of free food, and unfortunately worst attitude, among both staff and the Florentines who frequent the place. It also has an excellent location right along the river, a really cool interior with bright blue and red walls, and sushi for a small supplement above the price of a cocktail on Tuesdays. If you come early (between 7 and 8 PM) you'll avoid some of the crowd and are much more likely to get a table, or at least be able to elbow your way to the bar. Capocaccia is also packed on most Sunday afternoons, a time when nobody is working and everyone is up for a long, slow drink. If all this sounds like too much trouble for a hip cocktail, definitely go elsewhere, but if you want to see a real Florentine scene, it's worth a visit.

# Fuori Porta

**Via Monte alle Croci 10r, 055/234-2483**

**Open Monday through Saturday 12:30 PM to 3 PM and 7 PM to 12:30 PM;**
**closed two weeks in August and Christmas Day**

**Map G7, Buses D, 12, 13, 23**

**Credit cards accepted**

€

This extremely charming casual enoteca is run efficiently by three partners; it's a great choice if you want to sample wines by the glass, buy a
bottle, or sit and have a light meal. The list of wines by the glass changes
every two weeks or so and usually is a pleasing mix, with wines representing Piedmont and other areas as well as Chianti, Nobile, and IGT
labels from closer to home. (The wines by the glass are dwarfed by the
number offered by the bottle, where this place really shines as an enoteca;
many people come here just to buy wine.)

Fuori Porta is also very popular for its light meals, both at lunch and dinner. The menu is essentially ten pages of *crostoni*—very tasty open-face sandwiches of melted cheese and other good things on toasted Tuscan bread—though it also has a short rotating list of pastas and meats. You should call ahead and reserve at night, unless you just want to hang out while standing at the counter. In summer the wine bar has outdoor seating on their choice patio, which looks down onto one of the medieval gates of the city (hence the name, which means "outside the gate").

## GustaVino

**Via della Condotta 37r, 055/239-9806**
**Open Monday through Saturday 11 AM to 3 PM and 6 PM to 11 PM;**
  **closed one week in August**
**Map F5, Bus A**
**Credit cards accepted**
€€

This is the latest of the newfangled wine bars, made of polished glass and stainless steel, to conquer Florence. In the early evening you can belly up to the sleek bar for a glass of wine from their ample list and a taste of unusual savory appetizers. (For full review, see page 53.)

## Pitti Gola e Cantina

**Piazza Pitti 16, 055/212-704**
**Open Tuesday through Sunday 9 AM to 9:30 PM; closed most of August**
**Map D6, Bus D**
**Credit cards accepted**
€

Take a seat at the inviting marble-topped bar or at one of the few small tables scattered inside or—when it's warm—outside, where you can look straight across at the enormous Renaissance bulk of the Palazzo Pitti. The walls are covered with floor-to-ceiling shelves of bottles, beginning with Supertuscans on one end, progressing along to Brunello and Vino Nobile, rounding the corner to Chianti Classico, and finally reaching wines from other regions, whites, and dessert wines. A light plate of assorted Tuscan *salumi* and cheeses goes well with a glass of wine. Downstairs in a side hallway Pitti Gola stocks a well-chosen selection of cookbooks in Italian, English, and German, including titles on wine and food published by *Gambero Rosso* and Slow Food.

---

## Le Volpi e L'Uva  ✳

**Piazza dei Rossi 1r, off Via Romana, 055/239-8132**
**Open Monday through Saturday 10:30 AM to 8:30 PM; closed most of August**
**Map E6, Bus D**
**Credit cards accepted**
€

Although it's in prime tourist territory, just off the foot of the Ponte Vecchio, unassuming Volpi e L'Uva (the "foxes and the grapes," named after a fairy tale) has resisted the temptation to get fancy. The tiny interior has only a dozen or so seats at the marble-topped bar and some room for standing, and in summer you can sit outside in the car-free piazza.

Giancarlo Cantini and his small crew of dedicated sommeliers and wine enthusiasts seek out only small, unknown producers from all over Italy in search of the holy grail of *un buon rapporto prezzo/qualità* (a good ratio of price to quality). They've done an exceptional job. Categorically ignoring big-name wines that have been overly hyped, they find new producers at various wine fairs, when traveling around simply for pleasure, or when friends or associates bring them wines to try. When a wine they serve becomes too famous and raises its price, they discontinue it, such is their dedication to bargain *bicchieri.* According to Cantini, the most fertile regions in Italy right now for finding bargain small producers are Umbria, where they are making good Sangiovese and Merlots; Abruzzo and the Marches, where the Montepulciano grape does well; and places in Sicily.

The frequently changing chalkboard list of wines by the glass has about a dozen whites and reds to choose from, probably the most varied and interesting—not to mention well-priced—list in the city. On a given evening they might feature unusual wines from Alto Adige, including several reds from this area more associated with whites. I've tried many great wines here, including a fruity Tuscan Viognier and a Chablis from

Burgundy. They don't list the wine estate names on the chalkboard, but if you look behind you on the shelves, you can usually spot what you're drinking that night. Unlike other wine bars where they have laid down tablecloths, lit a candle, and become overpriced restaurants, you can't get a full meal here, just little mixed plates of delectable *salumi* and cheeses that go extremely well with the wine. Le Volpi e L'Uva was begun with the desire to evoke the atmosphere of a Venetian *bacaro*, a place to stop off before dinner and taste an interesting glass of wine with a little snack before dinner. They do sell bottles here and at good prices, but otherwise they've stuck to this premise—they even close at 8 PM, before the typical Florentine dinnertime.

---

## Zanobini

**Via Sant'Antonino 47r, 055/239-6850**
**Open Monday through Saturday 8:30 AM to 2 PM and 4 PM to 8 PM**
**Map E3, Buses 4, 12**
**No credit cards**
€

The good food vibes emanating from the Central Market spread out to the crowded surrounding streets, including the one-block stretch where you'll find both a *friggitoria* selling fried goodies and this old-school wine bar run by brothers Simone and Mario Zanobini. Like the ubiquitous stand-up coffee bars, this is meant to be the kind of place where businesspeople can stop in between meetings, or on the way home for dinner, for a glass of Chianti or Nobile for under €3—nothing fancy or time-consuming. They sell their own label of inexpensive wine, and also stock several tall shelves with mostly Tuscan reds, so if you particularly like what you're tasting, you can buy a bottle.

Many wine shops in the center of Florence cater to tourists and offer the same few bottles of Chianti and Brunello at big markups. But fortunately Florence does have a number of fine specialist shops owned by passionate oenophiles that carry a larger stock of harder-to-find wines, have a helpful and knowledgeable staff, and feature wines from all over Italy. The following list of small and large places, some in the Center and some farther out, should please anyone looking for an elusive Supertuscan, special Chianti *riserva,* or something more exotic from Sicily or Puglia. Winemakers all over Italy, from the heel and toe to the Alps, are thriving right now; there's never been a better time to drink up.

---

## Alessi

**Via dell'Oche 27–29r, 055/239-6987**
**Open Monday through Saturday 9 AM to 1 PM and 4 PM to 8 PM;**
   **closed August**
**Map E4, Buses 14, 23**
**Credit cards accepted**

On its ground floor, Alessi is divided into a candy and gourmet sweet-shop on one side and a wine-tasting bar on the other. None of this seems particularly exciting until you descend the staircase into the wine cellar below. Giorgio Alessi's wine selection is simply mind-boggling. You'll find bottle after bottle arranged by region; one room filled entirely with Tuscan wines is the size of most *enoteche,* and another equally big space is filled only with wines from Piedmont. This is also one of the few central *enoteche* to store the wines horizontally, in specially designed brick racks that resist heat and cold. Aside from the vast selection of contemporary wines, Alessi has assembled a sort of wine museum, kept in a dark, locked area, which includes bottles from 1900 on. When I asked if a Chianti Classico from 1968 would actually be any good, he equivocated, but I was impressed by the selection nonetheless.

Upstairs you'll find spirits and dessert wines, including a choice of quality *vin santo.* Because of its reputation and central location, Alessi is very popular with tourists and has a multilingual staff.

## Bonatti

**Via Gioberti, 66–68r, 055/660-050**

**Open Monday through Saturday 9 AM to 1 PM and 4 PM to 8 PM; closed Monday mornings in winter; closed Saturday afternoon in summer**

**Map F1, Buses A, 8, 12, 31**

**Credit cards accepted**

Bonatti was recently declared the best enoteca in Florence by the Italian food and wine magazine *Gambero Rosso*. If you make it to this area of town east from the Center, you'll be rewarded by a modern and spacious shop where the three young partners are more than happy to spend time explaining their wares or simply talking wine—in English. Bonatti's two large rooms full of shelves are well organized and easy to browse. In addition to primarily Italian wines, they carry a decent selection of wines from Chile, Australia, South Africa, and France. They also sell crystal wineglasses, high-tech bottle openers, and other accoutrements. The focus, however, is always on the wine itself: everything from Supertuscans to grappas from Tuscany and the Veneto.

Via Gioberti is a culinary goldmine. If you do make it out this way, take a minute to sample some of the other goodies on this street. **I' Gottino** (174r, see page 110) makes delicious light sandwiches on *ciabatta,* and **Caffè Serafini** (168r) serves wonderful cookies, cakes, éclairs, and cappuccinos.

## Bussotti

**Via San Gallo 161r, 055/483-091**

**Open Monday through Saturday 8:30 AM to 1 PM and 4 PM to 7:30 PM; closed most of August**

**Map J5, Buses 6, 11, 17**

**Credit cards accepted**

The Bussotti family has run this tidy, comfortable wine shop a little ways north of the Center since 1935. They stock mainly high-end bottles from Tuscany and Piedmont, including a generous selection of Supertuscans and Brunellos. The wide choice of good Chiantis includes Querciabella, Brolio, Villa Vistarenni, and Castello di Ama. Among the bottles of

Brunello, you'll find Col d'Orcia, Castelgiocondo, and some smaller producers. The front room holds a broad stock of grappa, *vin santo,* and even French Sauternes. The clear grappas in their elegantly designed bottles from Sassicaia and Ruffino make excellent gifts. While you are out on this unusually peaceful stretch of Via San Gallo, take a minute to explore the other food offerings on the same block, including a cute bakery and a good butcher shop.

---

## Gambi

**Borgo S.S. Apostoli 21–23r, 055/292-646**
**Open Monday through Saturday 10 AM to 7 PM; closed Saturday mornings;**
**closed August**
**Map E5, Bus B**
**Credit cards accepted**

The Gambi family has run this thriving wine shop since 1957. *La Mamma* is still in attendance, but daughter Elena, with a sommelier degree and several languages under her belt, has taken over much of the responsibility. Downstairs you'll find gourmet gift items like *limoncello, biscotti di Antonio Mattei* (see page 188), and balsamic vinegar from Modena, but the main action is upstairs in the wine room. The Supertuscans, including much-requested bottles of Tignanello and Le Pergole Torte, are kept in a glass case at the top of the stairs. Gambi stocks the major Chianti producers and also some interesting smaller estates, such as Terreno of Greve in Chianti, both a *riserva* and Chianti Classico from Il Tarroco, and a Sangiovese-Cabernet mix from Podere San Luigi. They carry a wide selection of wines from Piedmont and other Italian regions, and an impressive stock of white wines—often an afterthought in wine shops. Among the whites you'll find a Verncaccia di San Gimignano from Pernizzi, with cool modern label design, as well as Batar, a white made by Querciabella, better known for its Chiantis.

Gambi has another location outside the Porta Romana at Via Senese 21r, 055/222-525.

## Millesimi ✳

**Borgo Tegolaio 33r, 055/265-4675**
**Open Monday through Friday 3 PM to 8 PM; Saturday 10 AM to 8 PM**
**Map C6, Bus D**
**Credit cards accepted**

Housed in a sixteenth-century palazzo, Millesimi has the feel of a contemporary art gallery more than a wine shop. Come here not for a cheap everyday wine, but when you want to seek out a special bottle or try something interesting and new. The wines are divided into little islands of Supertuscans, Chianti Classicos, wines from Piedmont, and so on. The store's owner, Marie Parrocel Pirelli, is a transplanted Frenchwoman from Marseilles, so in addition to stocking most Italian regions there is also an unusual selection of Pinots and whites from Burgundy. Best of all, the manager Gianni (who is learning English) is happy to spend the time to talk you through the various offerings; his suggestions are always spot-on, whatever your price range. The inventory is selective instead of exhaustive. There is a great choice of wines from Puglia, Campania, and Sicily—often hard to find in Florence. I like to come here, chat with Gianni, and experiment, be it with a Sangiovese-Merlot mix from an up-and-coming Tuscan producer or an earthy Primitivo from Puglia. They stock reds and whites from Cusumano and Planeta in Sicily, and many excellent Reislings and Sauvignons from Trentino–Alto Adige. Millesimi is also the Tuscan distributor for *Wine Spectator* magazine, which it flaunts at the front of the shop.

## Enoteca Ognissanti

**Borgo Ognissanti 133r, 055/287-505**
**Open Monday through Friday 10 AM to 1 PM and 4 PM to 8 PM;**
**Saturday 10 AM to 1 PM; closed ten days in August**
**Map B3, Bus D**
**Credit cards accepted**

This is a small but well-stocked wine shop whose owner, Jonathan Ferace, is half English and half Italian; if he is not in, often there are other English-speaking staff on hand. The shop offers a nice selection of Morellino di Scansano wines and La Corte from Puglia, which is a Zinfandel aged in barrique. They have plenty of bottles of Brunello and Nobile (Bindella, Poliziano, Biondi-Santi), as well as wines from Gaja, a well-known producer from Piedmont. From the promised land of Bolgheri they have Grattamacco, Ornellaia, and others. They keep a small selection on hand from Sicily, including a Cabernet, Merlot, and Nero d'Avola blend from Mandarossa. In addition to Tuscan whites such as Fontodi's Meriggio, they stock Greco di Tufo and offerings from Friuli, the Veneto, and Alto Adige. The wines are well displayed on sturdy wooden shelves. Look for occasional free tastings on Saturday evenings.

## Vino Olio

**Via dei Serragli 29r, 055/239-8708**
**Open Monday through Friday 9:30 AM to 1 PM and 4 PM to 8 PM;**
    **Saturday 4 PM to 8 PM; closed most of August**
**Map C6, Buses 11, 36, 37**
**Credit cards accepted**

At first glance this small, dimly lit enoteca in the Oltrarno doesn't inspire much confidence. Although it may not have a huge selection, the wine and especially the olive oils are well chosen. The shop carries all the big local names like Antinori and Frescobaldi, but more importantly, a wide selection of lesser-known and lower-priced wines, such as a Chianti Classico from Spaltenna (a good deal at €10), a plethora of low-priced Tuscan and northern white wines, as well as some very unusual Sicilian reds. Bottles of *spumante* and white wine are kept in a refrigerated case, which comes in handy if you're rushing to a dinner party in the neighborhood. Clients from as far as the United States order the *olii novelli* (new harvest oils) every November, and this is the place to come to find the delicate Laudemio oil from Frescobaldi/Antinori, as well as other fine estate oils like those from Col d'Orcia and Capezzana. In addition the shop carries *biscottini* from Antonio Mattei, a number of fine bottles of grappa, and a small selection of artisanal *limoncello* from Sorrento and the island of Procida.

*Aged pecorino cheese rounds for sale.*

*One of the busy produce stands at the Sant'Ambrogio market.*

# 8

# MARKETS AND SHOPS

One of the great pleasures of living in Florence is shopping for food. Whether you forage among the vast displays of produce in the Central Market or make your way from butcher to baker to *salumeria* in your own neighborhood, you'll know you're not in Kansas anymore. I take visiting friends on a tour of the Central Market as if it were the Uffizi, proudly showing off my adopted city's unbelievable displays of cheese, prosciutto, and sides of Chianina beef. Huge wedges of Parmigiano-Reggiano, whole ducks and pigeons, specialties like tripe— all of this is available in Florence's markets at surprisingly low prices. I've grown so accustomed to butchers who grind the beef fresh while I wait, fishmongers who patiently fillet the sole for me to fry later, and cheese experts who point out which Gorgonzola will go best with my dinner that I am not sure how I would ever live without all these perks. Small, independent, usually family-run businesses thrive here because the owners take pride in their wares. The prices are sometimes higher in smaller shops than in the supermarkets, but so is the quality. If you want to buy apples individually wrapped in plastic, head to Esselunga supermarket; if you want to buy them straight from the farmer who may have picked them that day, you'd better head to Santo Spirito or Sant'Ambrogio.

I've heard rumors that market chains Esselunga and Standa are partly owned by Italian President Silvio Berlusconi, and to this day I'm not sure if these reports are true or merely arise from a commingling of his right-wing Americanized politics and the culture that the supermarkets represent. Florence does have supermarkets, but the big ones are all on the outskirts and the few in the Center are discreet and inoffensive. It is inevitable that Italians would want to use supermarkets for the same reason Americans began to fifty years ago: they are cheaper, quicker, and more convenient. But without the small food stores and specialty shops, much of the aesthetic and culture in Florence as we know it would essentially come to an end, and the only shops left will be those selling either boxer shorts depicting David's genitalia or three-hundred-dollar Gucci shoes. So when you spend half your day hunting and gathering at your local butcher, baker, and produce seller who know you by name and ask how that chicken came out, remember that your act is partly a political one.

■ ■ ■

The word *siesta* (or *pausa*, as they call it here) rolls off your tongue like a lullaby, bringing to mind a world of Latin light and fun and long, sweet naps in the shade. Unfortunately siesta has a darker side, which is that year-round, winter or summer, stores close down in the afternoon between about 1 and 5 PM. Many also close Monday mornings and Wednesday afternoons—though less so with food stores—in addition to all day Sunday because, well, they can. This means shopping for food, either in the morning or the evening, takes more ahead-of-time planning than most foreigners are used to. It's certainly challenging and often annoying, but if the shopkeepers can keep the frantic workaholic world at bay for a little while longer, I'm with them.

## Words to Shop By

Whereas many of us are accustomed to browsing and shopping in silent anonymity, here a customary exchange of greetings between buyer and seller is an integral part of the commercial endeavor. At first it may seem almost comical how strictly Florentines stick to their stock civilities, but after a while you might grow to appreciate this token of friendly banter. Every time you enter a store, you should greet the owner with a hearty *buon giorno* or *buona sera,* depending on the time of day. *Salve* (pronounced sall-vay), which literally means "good health" but essentially has come to stand in as "greetings," is also a respectable if slightly casual hello any time of day. When you buy your loot and go, you'll probably engage in a rally of *grazie* and *arriverderci.* You should never use the informal *ciao* in these situations unless the person serving you is the same age as you and gives hints of being a friendly, casual sort. But if and when they start ciao-ing you, feel free to say it back, especially as a final shout on the way out the door.

Other important shopping vocabulary:

*Alimentari* = General store selling food items

*Forno* = Bakery

*Latteria* = "Milk shop," typically a small market with a refrigerator case containing milk and packaged cheeses; usually also carries some dried goods (pasta, cookies, coffee)

*Macelleria* = Butcher shop

*Mesticheria* = General store selling kitchen and household supplies

*Pescheria* = Fishmonger

*Pizzicheria* = Store selling *salumi,* cheeses, and assorted gourmet and dry goods

*Polleria* = Butcher specializing in chicken

*Salumeria* = *Pizzicheria* specializing in cold cuts

*Opposite: The Baroni gourmet cheese and* salumi *stall at the Central Market.*

## Mercato Centrale ✳

**Piazza del Mercato Centrale**
**Open Monday through Saturday 9 AM to 2 PM**
**Map E2, Buses 12, 4**

This hulking nineteenth-century structure was built as Florence's central market, and it, along with Sant'Ambrogio (see page 157), continues to serve as one of the best and least expensive places in the city to buy a huge variety of fresh meats, fish, cheeses, and produce. On the ground floor you'll find the meat, poultry, fish, *salumi,* and cheese—it's almost too much to take in, and not for the squeamish, as you'll occasionally run into a bloody sheep's head, and certainly plenty of tripe and other offal. The selection of cheeses from all over Italy can be dizzying. Downstairs is also home to the sublime quick lunch and sandwich spot **Nerbone** (see page 112) and a couple of other outlets for coffee and sandwiches, though the market's sometimes damp and chilly interior isn't always the most appetizing place to linger.

The fish stalls cluster to one side of the first floor, and together offer by far the best choice of seafood in the city. The fruit and vegetable vendors are concentrated upstairs, also one of the best places in the city to find specialty herbs like dill and cilantro, as well as dried fruits and nuts. The competition among stands selling essentially the same wares keeps prices down; if one apple seller is asking €3 a kilogram, his customers can just walk across the hall. In terms of singling out individual sellers, **Macellerie Soderi, Ieri,** and **Del Soldato** all have excellent reputations for gourmet meat. **Baroni** (055/289-576), located to the left when you enter from Via dell'Ariento, has the widest selection of Italian and French cheeses I've seen in Florence, as well as a host of *salumi* and an array of appetizing jars of condiments to go with cheeses and salami. The cheese- and meat-producing cooperative **Il Forteto** sells a range of excellent pecorini cheeses, as well as honey and selected *salumi* from a stand on the Piazza Mercato end of the first floor. Even if you just follow your nose and your senses, you're bound to do well here: if a stand has other

*Fresh seafood at the Central Market.*

buyers, the meat (or cheese, or produce) looks and smells fresh, and you like the look of the operation, go with it.

Even if you aren't looking to buy veal shoulder or pecorino cheese, it's still a worthwhile experience to come in and have a look around, and while you're at it, explore the surrounding area. If you can navigate past the *shmatta* hawkers of the adjacent San Lorenzo open market, Via Panicale, Via dell'Ariento, and Via Sant'Antonino in particular abound with excellent little wine bars, shops, and casual restaurants.

## Season's Eatings

In Florence's markets and restaurants, eating seasonally isn't a trend, it's just a fact of life. If you really try, you could probably track down strawberries shipped from South America in winter or fava beans in fall, but why would you want to when they look sort of pitiful next to the abundant local seasonal fruits and vegetables? There are some exceptions to this rule: Italians love imported pineapples all year long, and there's nothing wrong with the occasional mango. In general, however, it's best to eat what's abundant at the time.

### Spring
Spring is the time to make the most of fava beans, artichokes, and asparagus. Most good pastry shops boast their *schiacciata alla fiorentina* (a cake, not like regular *schiacciata*) before and after Carnival time in February and March, and around Easter you'll see special treats like *frittelle*, fritters with rice or custard inside, at the *pasticcerie*.

### Summer
With the hot weather comes all the best fruits: cherries, grapes, watermelon, peaches, and berries. It's also the time for peppers, eggplant, zucchini flowers, and, of course, tomatoes—either the big fleshy red ones to be sliced into salad or mashed to sauce, or the little *ciliegini*, so delicious you can eat them like candy. Toward midsummer you can sometimes find early figs as well as tart little plums.

## Fall

Figs make a cameo appearance from early to mid-September, so stock up, while continuing to enjoy good tomatoes, peppers, and other summer produce that lingers into the fall. In September the market vendors compete to sell their fresh porcini, and later, in November, prized white truffles from Umbria will pop up on menus at some of Florence's poshest restaurants. November is the time for *vino novello* (see page 37), and by early December sharp new Tuscan olive oils start to appear on the shelves.

## Winter

The apples and pears of winter are decent enough, but I've gone through several kilos a week of the delicious seedless *clementini,* tangerines that ward off winter colds. When the *clementini* begin to wilt toward January, try the *mandarini* instead. Winter is the time for carrots, spinach, all types of onions and bitter greens, and *cavolo nero* (see page 16) and other cabbages. It's also hunting season, so you will see more *cinghiale* (wild boar) and *lepre* (hare) on menus around town, as well as abundant local chestnuts. Christmas brings the dense, nut-filled *panforte,* as well as panettone, those big top-hat-shaped puffy breads filled with raisins and candies so adored by Italians but regarded skeptically by the rest of the world. I prefer festive *cenci,* fried dough shaped like wide ribbons and dusted with powdered sugar.

# Santo Spirito

Perhaps everyone is partial to his or her own neighborhood piazza, but I honestly think that Piazza Santo Spirito is one of the best public spaces in Florence. The elongated rectangle is fronted on one side by Brunelleschi's butter-colored Renaissance church and on the other with a series of graceful sixteenth-century palazzi. The central space is occupied by a gurgling fountain, benches for sitting and reading, and best of all, trees—a godsend in greenery-deprived Florence.

Food lovers also have reason to head here. Next door to the unusual dry-goods store **Morganti** (see page 162), a mostly young crowd gathers at **Cabiria** (Piazza Santo Spirito 4r, 055/215-732) for an *aperitivo* on the patio in summer, or packs into the somewhat cramped interior for a warm drink in winter. A few doors down, the agile *bariste* at **Caffè Ricchi** (Piazza Santo Spirito 10r, 055/282-173) make some of the best coffee in town. While **Borgo Antico** (see page 64) pleases diners with pizza and *riso* on its ample patio, **Osteria Santo Spirito** across the way (Piazza Santo Spirito 16r, 055/382-383), which belongs to the same owners, serves similar fare in a warm and colorful dining room.

Farmers used to drive their little trucks up in front of the church and sell directly to consumers only on Wednesdays, but their appearance has become more and more frequent, and you will now find one or two out there selling their eggplant, basil, leeks, lettuce, and apples almost every weekday and on Saturdays. And if you don't see the farmers, you'll find a good retail stand selling fresh fruit and vegetables almost every day in front of the tobacco shop. One Sunday a month the piazza hosts an organic market, where artisans come and sell everything from batik scarves to good local olive oil and pecorino cheese. Every summer the piazza is the site of an open-air bar with lots of tables and chairs, and a stage where live musicians sometimes play. It seems like the whole city comes to the piazza on hot summer nights to revel in the truly festive, and sometimes chaotic, atmosphere.

# Mercato Sant'Ambrogio ✻
**Via dei Macci, Piazza Lorenzo Ghiberti**
**Open Monday through Saturday to 7:30 AM to 1:30 PM**
**Map H5, Buses A, 14**

Because it's smaller than the Central Market, Sant'Ambrogio feels a little less hectic and overwhelming. It's also a more pleasant place to spend time, with a large section outdoors. Although still within the old medieval circuit of walls, this neighborhood is a little farther from the Center, so you'll hear considerably more Italian spoken.

Outside, on the Via dei Macci side (the front, if you're coming from the Center), you'll find a stunning, colorful quilt of seasonal fruits and vegetables. The farmers out to sell what they just picked that morning—often only two or three things, like leeks and chicory—cluster on the far right end. Inside is a smorgasbord of cheeses, meats, dry goods, and an excellent fishmonger. On either side of the building there is a daily flea market where you can pick up cheap socks and towels, as well as flowers and plants.

Right when you walk in from the Via dei Macci side, you'll see the excellent meats of **Macelleria Luca Menoni;** and on the north end of the hall, a stand called **Sant'Ambrogio Formaggi** that sells excellent goat cheese (*caprino*), Gorgonzola, and a Parmesan-like aged cheese called Gran Sardo. Toward the northwest edge of the hall you'll find fish merchant **Fabio Gallerini** (these places aren't signed, but just look out for the selection of fresh fish) selling shellfish and a changing array of fillets and whole fish, such as fresh cod (*merluzzo*), sea bass (*spigola* or *branzino*), and sole (*sogliola*), though the fish selection will always be more abundant at the Central Market.

## Antica Gastronomia

**Via degli Artisti 58r, at Via Masaccio, 055/505-8769**
**Open Monday through Saturday 8 AM to 2 PM and 5 PM to 8 PM; closed**
     **Wednesday afternoon in winter; closed Saturday afternoon in summer;**
     **closed August and Christmas Day**
**Map I1, Bus 11**
**Credit cards accepted**

The chaotic jumble of food in this busy neighborhood shop is focused around the hot take-out items. The *rigatoni al ragù* (pasta with meat sauce), lasagne, mashed potatoes, roast chickens, and pepper side dishes all look terrific. You can also buy imported and domestic cheeses: Cheddar and Muenster side by side with real provolone cheese from Ragusa (in Sicily) and little goat cheese balls spiked with raisins. Plus you'll find Do Mori chocolates, DiCecco pasta, and *carnaroli* and *arborio* rice. Only the selection of wines is uninspired. Perhaps most important, Antica Gastronomia—unfortunately way out on the north side of town—acts as a kind of clearinghouse for the local chapter of Slow Food; it sells a range of the Slow Food books (some in English), and it is the only place in Florence where you can sign up in person to become a member.

## Asia Masala

**Piazza Santa Maria Novella 21–22r, 055/281-800**
**Open Tuesday through Sunday 10 AM to 1 PM and 4 PM to 7 PM;**
     **Monday 4 PM to 7 PM; closed Christmas Day**
**Map D3, Buses 36, 37**
**Credit cards accepted**

Asia Masala sells everything you need to cook Indian food at home, including cardamom pods, cumin, and turmeric; various types of basmati rice; green and orange lentils; and mango chutney in jars. You'll find ginger and plantains in bins toward the front of the shop, plus a few yams and yucca that have perhaps seen better days. They also sell hard-to-find products from Thailand, China, Sri Lanka, and the Philippines.

## Azzarri

**Borgo Sant'Jacopo 27r, 055/238-1714**
**Open Tuesday through Saturday 9 AM to 1:30 PM and 3:30 PM to 7:45 PM;**
    **Monday 3:30 PM to 7:45 PM; closed for part of August**
**Map D6, Bus D**
**Credit cards accepted**

Adriano Azzarri now runs this elegant little gourmet foods and butcher shop, originally founded by his grandfather, near the Ponte Vecchio. They sell *salumi* specially produced for them according to the *nonno*'s old recipes. Many of the specialty cheeses and meats here are vacuum-packed, and intended to be given as gifts, not taken straight home and eaten. You'll pay more for the shop's high-quality goods, which also include fine local wines, stuffed peppers in jars, and premium fresh veal and beef. Azzarri is very proud of his bilingual website, www.azzarri-firenze.it, where you can also order foods and have them shipped.

## Bizzarri

**Via della Condotta 32r, 055/211-580**
**Open Monday through Friday 9:30 AM to 1 PM and 4 PM to 7:30 PM;**
    **closed August**
**Map F5, Bus A**
**No credit cards**

Bizzarri seems like an appropriate name for this odd little shop, a kind of antique apothecary that sells spices and extracts for cooking (as well as boric acid and chemicals for photo development), but in fact it's named after the owner, Alessandro Bizzarri. The place is decked out like a stage set, with creaky looking test tubes and Pyrex jars. When you ask for vanilla extract, they bring out a big glass container and suck it up with a straw before decanting it into an individual glass container. This shop isn't just ornamental, a backdrop for those who would rather be living in the nineteenth century—it's actually an extremely useful source for spices like cumin, cardamom, whole nutmeg, and saffron, and a host of herbs and extracts that you'll have great difficulty finding anywhere else in town.

## Sending It All Back Home

Several places around town will vacuum pack and ship anything from a kilogram of Parmesan cheese to a leg of prosciutto—U.S. Customs permitting, of course.

**Conti** (055/239-8501), a good-looking gourmet goods stand on the ground floor of the Central Market, will vacuum pack and ship porcini, estate-bottled oils, balsamic vinegars, and wine to anywhere in the world.

**Baroni** (055/289-576; www.baronialimentari.it), located in the Central Market, will ship cheeses and other goods.

**Vino Olio** (Via dei Serragli 29r, 055/239-8708) ships olive oils to clients in the States and elsewhere.

**Azzarri** (see page 159) will pack and ship abroad all kinds of *salumi*, cheeses, and gourmet goods.

# Convivium

**Viale Europa 4–6, Gavinana, 055/681-1757**
**Open Monday through Friday 9 AM to 7:30 PM, Saturday 9 AM to 1 PM;**
    **closed August**
**Buses D, 23, 33**
**Credit cards accepted**

Housed in a perfectly kept two-story Spanish-style house on the outskirts of town, Convivium is a gleaming tribute to Italian gastronomy. In its two rooms you'll find two huge glass cases, one filled with an extraordinary selection of cheeses, the other with house-made delicacies of all types. The cheeses are divided between French and Italian; the latter come mainly from the mountains in the north, including several fontinas and Asiagos. A veritable mountain of pecorino is on display, aged and semi-aged, some from Pienza. You can choose from fresh ricotta, several Gorgonzolas, and lovely Brie. Above the cheese case are shelves lined with *salumi*, including fennel-scented *finocchiona,* salami varieties from Abruzzo and even Hungary, *speck*, and prosciutto from Parma.

In the next room an equally attractive case displays platter after abundant platter of prepared foods: squid *in inzimino* (a kind of tomato sauce); roast pork loin; steamed crayfish; delicacies like prosciutto mousse in aspic; and little round spicy peppers stuffed with anchovies. Choose from among an assortment of sweets, including the local favorite *torta della nonna.* The small wine selection is exclusively Tuscan: Avignonese, Biondi-Santi, and Guado al Tasso Bolgheri Superiore are among the standouts. Finally, Convivium has one of the better selections I've seen of savory and sweet jellies and condiments, including confitures and fruit *mostarde* to be eaten with aged cheeses. It also does a big catering business for weddings and events of all kinds. The prices here are steep, and the location is inconvenient, but it is one of the finest and most sophisticated *gastronomie* in the city. You can get here either by taking two buses from the Center or by bike or car.

The owners of Convivium have recently opened a new, much more convenient location in the Oltrarno (Via Santo Spirito 4, 055/265-8198; open Monday through Saturday 11 AM to 7 PM; Map D5; credit cards accepted). Here they offer a light lunch, wine tastings, and even olive oil tastings.

## Da Fernando

**Via Don Minzoni 38r, Piazza della Libertà, 055/587-540**
**Open Monday through Saturday 7 AM to 8 PM; closed Christmas Day and**
    **New Year's Day**
**Buses 1, 7, 11**
**Credit cards accepted**

I was originally attracted to this store by the fresh, wonderful-looking apples, ginger, potatoes that look like they just came from the ground, and assorted vegetables displayed out in front. Inside, Da Fernando is more of an all-around gourmet specialty shop than just a produce shop. I was mesmerized by the selection of goods: whole walnuts, dried figs, big rounds of French and Italian blue cheeses, organic and whole wheat pastas and rice from small producers; jar upon colorful jar of little round peppers stuffed with anchovies, spicy pickled fruits (*mostarde*), all tastefully arranged in a small space. In the adjacent room is a modest selection of wines, including interesting and well-priced Zinfindels from the south, Ruffino Chianti *riserva* at a good price, and a shelf of Solaia, Tignanello, Brancaia, and other special bottles.

## Morganti

**Piazza Santo Spirito 3r, 055/289230**
**Open Monday through Saturday 8:30 AM to 1 PM and 4:30 PM to 8 PM in**
    **winter; daily 8:30 AM to 7:30 PM in summer; closed part of August**
**Map C6, Bus D**
**Credit cards accepted**

This odd little store on Piazza Santo Spirito is worth knowing about for their excellent grains, rices, and beans, which they sell in bulk from huge sacks. Some of the wares are traditional, like *toscanelli* (white beans), *farro,* and *arborio* rice, and some more difficult to find in Florence, such as black beans and wild and basmati rice. It also carries an eclectic assortment of organic goods for people and pets, in addition to straw mats and baskets of all sizes.

## Pegna

**Via dello Studio 8, 055/282-701**

**Open Monday through Saturday 9 AM to 1 PM and 4 PM to 8 PM in winter;**
**daily 9 AM to 1 PM and 3:30 PM to 5:30 PM in summer**

**Map F4, Buses 14, 23**

**Credit cards accepted**

You could easily walk right by Pegna, adjacent to the Duomo, without realizing what awaits inside. The front section resembles a posh drugstore, with ordinary household items like toilet paper and toothpaste for sale. But beyond that, the good stuff begins. First you come to the spice counter where you can pick up shelled pistachios, fennel seeds, and other baking and cooking ingredients. Next is the chocolate and sweets section, filled with Lindt and Perugina, as well as lots of gifty items, followed by the liquors, with Champagne, cognac, organic local wine, and the like. Turn the corner and you'll find an array of gourmet dried pastas, estate-bottled oils, and aged balsamic vinegars, along with specialty goods like stuffed peppers in jars. In a small imports section expats will thrill to Marmite, Tabasco, Mexican-style salsa, and French foie gras terrines. A tiny deli offers some ready-made pestos and sauces, as well as imported Cheddar and Stilton cheeses, and beautiful but very expensive Norwegian smoked salmon.

## Procacci

**Via Tornabuoni 64r, 055/211-656**

**Open Monday through Saturday 10:30 AM to 8:30 PM; closed August**
**and Christmas Day**

**Map D4, Buses A, 6, 11, 37**

**Credit cards accepted**

For a long time I ignored this little shop, squeezed as it is between the Puccis and Guccis on Via Tornabuoni. I usually try to avoid entering anything on this street, lest they put me under fashion arrest. Luckily I soon got wise to this little gastronomic gem. Procacci, now owned by the wine-making Antinori family, has specialized in truffles since 1885, but it also serves finger sandwiches with smoked salmon and arugula, Brie cheese

and walnuts, and salami and butter in addition to the classic one with truffles. It carries a selection of gourmet goods, including its own line of truffle and mushroom spreads, cherry tomatoes in oil, and scallions in sweet-and-sour sauce. It also stocks elegant chocolates by local maker Amadei and a selection of French and Italian cheeses, and serves wines by the glass, including several from Antinori, naturally.

## Tassini

Borgo S.S. Apostoli 24r, 055/282-696

Open Monday through Saturday 8:30 AM to 2:30 PM and 4:30 PM to
    7:30 PM; closed Wednesday in winter and Saturday afternoon in
    summer; closed most of August, Christmas Day, and New Year's Day

Map D5, Bus B

Credit cards accepted

Despite its touristy trappings (the color brochure is in Italian, English, and Japanese), this little *alimentari* on a side street near the Ponte Vecchio is worth a stop to pick up certain gourmet food items or wine. It sells a fine assortment of Italian wines from Tuscany, Piedmont, and other areas, including names like Gaja, Barbi, and Castello di Ama; and stocks several impressive shelves with jams, *mostarde,* honey, and expensive concoctions made with white and black truffles. You'll also find a small sampling of estate-bottled olive oils, dry pasta in funny shapes and colors, and biscotti from Antonio Mattei of Prato (see page 188). A pristine glass case shows off an excellent choice of picnic stylings: cured fish, fresh and aged cheeses, grilled vegetables in oil, and *salumi.* The shop also sells some cooked foods after noon.

## ViviMarket ✳

Via del Giglio 20–22r, 055/294-911

Open Monday through Saturday 9 AM to 2 PM and 3 PM to 7:30 PM

Map D3, Buses 6, 36, 37

Credit cards accepted

This mainstay for mostly Asian but also other international foods recently moved to bigger and brighter digs on Via del Giglio. At this point it's like a little international supermarket, and perhaps the best thing to happen to expats living in Florence since the introduction of Laundromats. Here you can buy the staples of several Asian cuisines, including basmati rice, garam masala, and a huge assortment of spices such as cumin, cardamom, coriander, mustard seeds, and fenugreek for making Indian food; rice paper, hoisin sauce, and many things I have never heard of for Chinese and Japanese cooking; and even hard-to-find fresh ingredients like galangal, limes, and lemongrass for cooking Thai food. Homesick Americans can fill up their carts with Jif peanut butter and Duncan Hines cake mix, and Brits abroad will take solace in Marmite and Coleman's mustard. (To top it off, there are unusual exported American candies like Nerds and Gobstoppers next to the cash register.) ViviMarket also sells woks, fry-strainers, and a small selection of ceramic dishes. If you live in Florence and want to cook non-Italian food at home, this place is a lifesaver.

## Fresh Pasta

## La Bolognese

**Via dei Serragli 24r, 055/282-318**
**Open Monday through Saturday 7 AM to 1 PM and 5 PM to 7:30 PM;**
**closed the week of August 15**
**Map C5, Buses 11, 36, 37**
**No credit cards**

In Bologna's city center you can hardly walk a block without seeing a delectable vision of fresh tagliatelle or tortellini laid out in shop windows, but in Florence that sight is less common. La Bolognese is a tiny, no-frills shop on a busy street in the Oltrarno that sells only fresh pasta, including potato-stuffed ravioli, an assortment of tortellini, and even some little potato gnocchi. Take some home, heat up a little tomato puree, and you've got an easy, delicious meal.

## Pasta Fresca di Giancarlo Bianchi

**Via dell'Albero 1r, 055/282-246**
**Open Monday through Saturday 9 AM to 1 PM and 4:30 PM to 7:30 PM; closed**
**Wednesday afternoon; closed August**
**Map C3, Bus D**
**No credit cards**

This is another excellent shop that sells fresh pasta, not far from the train station. Here, you can watch through glass as dough is rolled and stuffed in an adjacent room. Especially good are the potato-stuffed *tortelli*, the tortellini, and ravioli. The staff also makes the thick, wormlike *pici*—a Tuscan specialty.

## La Bottega delle Chiacchiere
**Via San Miniato 2r, 055/234-2864**
**Open Monday through Saturday 8 AM to 1 PM and 5 PM to 8 PM; closed**
**Wednesday afternoon**
**Map G7, Buses D, 23**
**Credit cards accepted**

La Bottega delle Chiacchiere has a bright, clean, and organized look that I particularly like. It sells *salumi,* smoked duck breast carpaccio, imported smoked salmon, smoked provolone cheese (see a pattern here?), and other more usual offerings in a long glass case. A little *cantinetta* in back stocks a small assortment of inexpensive local wines, and the shelves are lined with Mulino Bianco cookies and other snacks.

## Pane & Co.
**Piazza San Firenze 5r (Via della Condotta), 055/213-063**
**Open Monday through Saturday 8 AM to 7:30 PM; closed part of August,**
**Christmas Day and New Year's Day**
**Map F5, Bus A**
**Credit cards accepted**

Carlo Agostini has a burgeoning food and wine empire on Via della Condotta, right off the Piazza Signoria. Pane & Co. calls itself an *enogastronomia,* which is fitting, as it's about three-quarters *alimentari* and one-quarter enoteca. The *alimentari* is a nice-looking space selling pecorino and other Tuscan cheeses, *prosciutto di Parma,* and special Cinta Senese *salumi.* A small room in back acts as the enoteca, stocked with mainly high-end bottles of Brunello, Nobile, and Supertuscans, including the biggest names in all of those categories. Agostini and partners also own the nearby wine bar GustaVino (see page 139) and conduct wine tastings at both locations.

## Pizzicheria Paolo e Marta

**Via dei Serragli 32r, 055/214-127**

**Open Monday through Saturday 7:30 AM to 1:30 PM and 4 PM to 8 PM; closed**
   **Wednesday and Saturday afternoons; closed Christmas Day**
   **and New Year's Day**

**Map C6, Buses D, 11, 36, 37**

**Credit cards accepted**

This little cheese and *salumi* shop is much like a lot of other high quality *pizzicherie* in town, but the proprietors are more friendly and helpful than most and all the offerings are top-notch. In particular they carry a larger-than-usual selection of cheeses, mainly Italian varieties such as aged Taleggio, Asiago, and, of course, the usual pecorinos, Gorgonzolas, and Parmigianos. You can also find Greek feta cheese, French Roquefort, and some less common Italian cheeses. The *salumi* are excellent as well: sweet and Tuscan prosciutto, *bresaola,* Tuscan and Milanese salami, and more. If you are giving a dinner party, you can come here to assemble an antipasto of cheeses and *salumi,* as well as other savory bites like fresh green and garlic-cured olives, marinated artichoke hearts and eggplant, and sardines and anchovies. They also sell dried pasta, tuna in glass jars, and assorted gourmet sauces and condiments. The prices are not particularly low, but they reflect the quality of the goods sold.

## Produce

The best places to buy produce are without doubt the two big markets, Centrale and Sant'Ambrogio, but both close at midday and might not always be convenient.

---

## Braccini

**Borgo Ognissanti 121r, 055/213-078**
**Open Monday through Saturday 8 AM to 7:30 PM; closed Wednesday afternoon**
**Map B4, Bus D**
**No credit cards**

Half of this pleasant, well-stocked shop is a *gastronomia* selling excellent cheeses and *salumi,* while the other half focuses on fruits and vegetables, including fresh radicchio—both round and elongated—and all the usual greens and fruits of Florence. It has a slight health-food bent, so you can also pick up some sugar-free chocolate if you are so inclined.

---

## Colivicchi

**Via Sant'Agostino 24r, 055/210-001**
**Open Monday through Friday 7:30 AM to 1:30 PM and 4 PM to 8 PM;**
**Saturday 7:30 AM to 1 PM; closed three weeks in August**
**Map C6, Bus D**
**No credit cards**

You might want to rehearse your order before entering this tightly packed, no-frills produce shop. The battalion of men (young, old, toothless, nicotine stained) who run the place will cut you no slack. If you're not ready, get out of the way because there's always someone else right behind you. Quick, do you want the red onions or the yellow? The spinach or the *cavolo nero*? And what's the Italian word for plum? Of course it's all worth the hassle; this is one of the cheapest places to buy good fresh produce outside the big markets. And if you come in the afternoon instead of the morning things tend of be more calm. A poster on the door shows all kinds of vegetables and their names in Italian, if this helps, but pointing always works well. Colivicchi also sells big inexpensive bottles of its own brand of extra virgin olive oil (fantastic), vinegar, and white wines.

## Look but Don't Touch

As tempting as it is to squeeze the tomatoes, shake the melons, and inspect the winter greens, try to hold back, as you might get your hand slapped by an indignant Italian vendor. In fact, you'll often see signs that say "Do Not Touch" written in English at some markets to guard against such clumsy handling of fragile wares. For better or worse, Italians don't get to pick out their fruit, and they believe it is unhygienic to let whomever lay hands on. Of course this also means that while choosing your apples or lettuce, the vendor gets the chance to unload some less-than-perfect merchandise in the process. One word of advice: It is not considered rude, and is in fact almost expected, that you will watch carefully as they pick out your fruit and vegetables, and you are well within your rights to say "that one please" and "not that [brown, bruised] one, please." Florentine matrons demand the best produce, and so should you.

*Summer fruit at the Sant'Ambrogio market.*

## L'Ortolano Ciasky

**Via dell'Orto 3r, 055/220-7041**
**Open Monday through Saturday 7:30 AM to 1 PM and 5 PM to 8 PM;**
   **Sunday 7:30 AM to 1 PM; closed most of August**
**Map A5, Bus D**
**No credit cards**

*Orto* is an old word for vegetable garden, and there's a good chance this street was full of produce vendors way back when, which bodes well for this unassuming shop next to an equally appealing butcher. The young guys working here will help you to beautiful artichokes, cauliflower, oranges and tangerines, and all the usual offerings. The displays of fruit and vegetables outside the shop look enticing, though I have to wonder about the exhaust they might be soaking up—perhaps better to stick to the interior.

---

## Vettori

**Borgo Sant'Jacopo 63r, corner of Via Maggio, 055/212-797**
**Open Monday through Saturday 7 AM to 1:30 PM and 4:30 PM to 9 PM;**
   **closed Wednesday afternoon; closed most of August**
**Map D6, Bus D**
**No credit cards**

Vettori occupies a rather touristy corner near the Santa Trinità bridge; they nonetheless sell fruit and vegetables of excellent quality, including a range of lettuces, arugula, hard-to-find fresh mushrooms, cherries and apricots in season, and more.

## Fish, Meat, and Poultry

The best place to buy fish is at the Central Market (see page 152). One whole side of the first floor is dedicated to fish; some fishmongers have been here forever, while others are relative newcomers, but all offer basically similar fare in terms of freshness, price, and quality. On any given day you can choose among shrimp of every size, mussels, clams, and oysters imported from France. You can ask for fresh sardines by the kilogram, and have the monger cut sole into fine fillets while you wait. You might see shiny little mackerel and red mullet, eels, thick cuts of shark and swordfish, and fine turbot and sea bass.

The Central and Sant'Ambrogio (see page 157) markets are also a good bet for meat, but several butchers in different neighborhoods have been selling local chicken, pigeon, milk- and grass-fed veal, and Chianina beef

### Butcher Boys

Two of the best local butchers are not actually in Florence. **Falorni** of the tranquil town of Greve in Chianti, is known for its fine Tuscan prosciutto and salami, their offerings from the Cinta Senese pig, local *cinghiale,* and Chianina beef. Their *salumi* sometimes shows up in the city's better *pizzicherie* and *alimentari.* **Dario Cecchini** in Panzano, about ten minutes further from Greve, has made his name as possibly the world's first celebrity butcher; his stuff is that good, his personality is that large. His name also turns up on Florentine menus, or you can make the pilgrimage to his shop in order to buy his famed Chianina beef, *crema di lardo,* handmade *soppressata,* and other marvels of the flesh. (For more on Falorni and Cecchini, see pages 235 and 236.)

**Antica Macelleria Falorni**
*Piazza Matteotti 69, Greve, 055/853-029*

**Antica Macelleria Cecchini**
*Via XX Luglio 11, Panzano, 055/852-020*

for generations. If you're unsure of what to do with a given cut of meat, you can always ask them for advice, and without missing a beat they'll give you the recipe their *nonne* always make.

## Macelleria Lanini

**Via dell'Orto 1r, corner of Via del Leone, 055/229-8677**
**Open Saturday and Monday through Wednesday 7:30 AM to 1 PM;**
    **Thursday and Friday 7:30 AM to 1 PM and 5 PM to 7 PM; closed August**
**Map B5, Bus D**
**Credit cards accepted**

The butchers in this clean, bright shop in the San Frediano neighborhood will cut you off a nice slab of *fiorentina* T-bone to grill at home. They also sell an assortment of veal, chicken, rabbit, and even pigeon—all at very reasonable prices.

## Macelleria Zagli

**Via Valori 6r, off Piazza Savonarola, 055/587-571**
**Open Monday through Wednesday 7:30 AM to 1 PM and 5 PM to 7:30 PM;**
    **Thursday through Saturday 7:30 AM to 1 PM; closed August**
**Map H1, Buses 11,13, 33**
**Credit cards accepted**

Zagli is a veritable meat boutique, proudly displaying huge slabs of Chianina beef on the bone, ready to be turned into *bistecca alla fiorentina;* fresh locally raised chickens; and whole turkey. It's known for semi-prepared (raw but fixed and seasoned) meats, such as delicious-looking *speck* (smoked prosciutto) rolled around veal, and stuffed chicken. The shop also carries a small selection of pecorino cheese from Pienza, organic and whole wheat pastas, and a few bottles of wine, the best of which is probably the Selvapiana Chianti Rufina.

## Pescheria Silvestri

**Via dei Macci 117r, 055/241-022**

**Open Monday through Saturday 7:30 AM to 1 PM and 4:30 PM to 7:30 PM;**
**closed August**

**Map H4, Bus 14**

**No credit cards**

This bare-bones fish shop outside the Sant'Ambrogio market is popular with locals, including some restaurateurs. If Sant'Ambrogio is already closed for the day, come here for scampi and other seafood.

## Pescheria Tirrena

**Via dei Cerchi 20r, 055/216-602**

**Open Monday through Wednesday and Saturday 8 AM to 2 PM;**
**Thursday and Friday 8 AM to 2 PM and 5 PM to 7:30 PM**

**Map E5, Bus A**

**No credit cards**

Baccalà *(salt cod) for sale.*

Sauro Bartoli gets his fresh fish every day from "wherever there's an ocean," as he tells it with some cheek, though they are often caught in the Mediterranean Sea. The selection changes all the time, but you might see beautifully chunky monkfish (*coda di rospo*), as well as whole turbot (*rombo*), and sparkling scampi.

## KITCHENWARE AND GIFTS

### Bartolini ✳

**Via dei Servi 30r, 055/211-895**
**Open Monday through Saturday 9 AM to 1 PM and 3:30 PM to 7:30 PM;**
    **closed Monday morning in winter and Saturday afternoon in summer;**
    **closed most of August**
**Map F3, Bus C**
**Credit cards accepted**

Bartolini is my favorite place to buy kitchen goods. On one end of the (huge) store are nicely displayed shelves of fancy wares like Wedgwood and Richard Ginori china, gleaming espresso machines, Riedel crystal wineglasses, copper pots, and a whole line of goods by Alessi. On the other end are the practical cooking items like inexpensive stainless steel pots with heavy bottoms, Wüsthof knives, and every conceivable gadget for making Italian food: pasta machines and cutters, pie rollers, olive oil taps, and more sizes, shapes, and styles of stove-top coffeemakers than I've ever seen. Check out the *chitarra,* an extraordinary little device that looks like a musical instrument but is actually meant for cutting fresh pasta into long squared-off strands. Upstairs you'll find food scales, butcher blocks, and some other big items. At any given time, at least one English-speaking staff member should be able to help you.

## Cascine Market

**Viale Lincoln, Parco delle Cascine**

**Open Tuesdays 8 AM to 2 PM; Sundays before Easter and Christmas Day**
**8 AM to 2 PM**

**Buses 1, 9, 12, 13, 17**

Most of what's sold at Florence's main flea market is fairly junky: polyester teenybopper clothing and shoes that will break down after one wearing. But you can find good deals here on simple cooking items like stainless steel pots, strainers, and other little implements. Occasionally you might find some attractive dishes at a good price, or nice place mats or tablecloths, but first you have to decide if it's worth braving the crowds. Final caveat: Don't be tempted by sausages sold from the mobile caravans—they're not as good as they look.

## Coin Casa

**Via dei Calzaioli 56r, (basement of Coin department store), 055/280-531**

**Open Monday through Saturday 9:30 AM to 8 PM; Sunday 11 AM to 8 PM**

**Map E4, Bus A**

**Credit cards accepted**

I'm not crazy about the clothing upstairs, but downstairs, the national chain Coin sells some excellent goods both for the kitchen and dining room. Stock up on colorful woven place mats, well-made cotton tablecloths, both traditional and Japanese-influenced ceramics, and accessories like candles and cloth napkins. You can also buy all sorts of kitchen utensils, pots, pans, mitts, and most basic necessities, all well displayed. The styles tend to be casual, and prices reasonable.

## Mesticheria Mazzanti

**Borgo La Croce 101r, 055/248-0663**
**Open Monday through Saturday 8 AM to 1 PM and 3:30 PM to 7:30 PM;**
**closed August**
**Map H5, Bus A**
**No credit cards**

Mesticheria Mazzanti is a bustling all-purpose hardware and home store, but they have a big selection of very inexpensive kitchen goods like glasses, mugs, silverware, cheap pots, and wooden implements of all kinds—very useful for setting up a temporary kitchen. It's often crowded, so take a ticket and wait to be helped. You can enter the store either on Borgo La Croce or from Piazza Ghiberti (where the Sant'Ambrogio market is).

## Richard Ginori

**Via Rondinelli 17r, 055/210-041**
**Open Monday through Friday 10 AM to 7 PM; Saturday 9 AM to 1 PM;**
**closed Saturday and Monday in winter**
**Map D4, Buses 6, 11, 36, 37**
**Credit cards accepted**

Richard Ginori makes some of the most beautiful bone china and hand-painted porcelain in the world, and it all began in eighteenth-century Florence. This fancy showroom displays china, porcelain, stunning silver trays and serving pieces, and some vases and larger pieces that have "wedding gift" written all over them. The prices are lower here than in the United States and elsewhere, but remember to factor in the price of shipping your purchases home. Come dressed to impress if you want any attention from the dead-eyed saleswomen.

The Richard Ginori kitchen and bath headquarters also has a showroom farther out of town in Sesto Fiorentino (Viale Giulio Cesare 21, 055/420-491; fax: 055/420-4934); call for an appointment.

## Sbigoli

**Via Sant'Egidio 4r, 055/247-9713**

**Open Monday through Saturday 9:30 AM to 1 PM and 3 PM to 7:30 PM;**
**occasionally closed Saturday afternoon**

**Map G4, Bus 23**

**Credit cards accepted**

I've come here often to buy wedding presents for friends when I want something that exudes true Italian-ness. Sbigoli sells lovely pieces, both hand-painted ceramics typical of Deruta, in Umbria, and the studio's own largely floral designs. You can choose from mugs and teacups, large and small serving bowls and platters, and decorative as well as everyday plates. The owners speak English, accept credit cards, and are adept at packing and shipping.

## Le Telerie Toscane

**Sdrucciolo dei Pitti 15r, 055/216-177**

**Open Monday through Saturday 10 AM to 1:30 PM and 2:30 PM to 7 PM;**
**closed Saturday in summer**

**Map D6, Bus D**

**Credit cards accepted**

Florence was once known for its luxurious fabrics, and neighboring Prato is still an industrial center of cloth production. This Tuscany-wide chain of fine table and bed linen shops specializes in traditional, rather regal patterns in muted colors and decadent fabrics. Prices are in line with the manor-house feel of the place.

## Veneziano

**Via dei Fossi 53r, 055/287-925**
**Open Monday through Saturday 9 AM to 2 PM and 5 PM to 8 PM;**
    **Monday through Friday in summer**
**Map C4, Buses A, 11**
**Credit cards accepted**

Veneziano specializes in the kind of chic, modern kitchenware for which Italy has become known. The shop has a particularly well-chosen selection of designer Murano glass dishes and bowls, as well as cut-glass wine stems, and architectural pieces from brands such as Driade and IVV. If you want to send something home, Veneziano uses an expensive shipping service, so you may be better off carrying your purchases with you or going across the river to Mail Boxes Etc. (or the post office) and shipping it yourself. The staff may seem chilly at first, but in time they warm up and speak fluent English.

## Vice Versa

**Via Ricasoli 53r, 055/239-8281**
**Open Sunday through Friday 9:30 AM to 7:30 PM; Sat. 9:30 AM to 1:30 PM;**
    **closed Mondays in winter and Saturdays in summer**
**Map F3, Bus C**
**Credit cards accepted**

This sleek little shop specializes in gift items, such as every imaginable kitchen and bathroom gadget from Alessi, Guzzini, and its own house brand, Vice Versa. You can pick up an espresso machine, a garlic press designed by Ross Lovegrove, or modish plastic place mats. There is a roomful of furniture downstairs, but the fun stuff—espresso cups, Parmesan cheese boats, smiley-face spatulas—is all upstairs. A bonus: The store will wrap up and ship your goods to anywhere in the world.

## Cookbooks

### Libreria Edison
**Piazza della Repubblica 27r, 055/213-110**
**Open daily 9 AM to 9 PM**
**Map E4, Bus A**
**Credit cards accepted**

With its four floors of books, a small café with tables and chairs for reading, and American-style open-all-hours schedule, Edison is a dream come true. It is often the only place to hang out on a rainy Sunday or to find air-conditioned solace on an August afternoon. It stocks a fair number of English-language cookbooks and food-related guidebooks on the ground floor near the cash registers, including huge stacks of *Gambero Rosso*'s wine guides and other favorites. The third floor houses a decent Italian-language cookbook and food history section.

### Feltrinelli International
**Via Cavour 12r, 055/292-196**
**Open Monday through Saturday 9 AM to 7:30 PM**
**Map F3, Buses 1, 11**
**Credit cards accepted**

All English speakers staying in Florence should be aware of Feltrinelli International since it has one of the best selections in the city of English-language books, mainly stocked on the second floor. On the first floor near the entrance, look for a stash of English-language guidebooks to the region and one whole shelf of cookbooks, including works by Marcella Hazan, Lorenza de' Medici, and Elizabeth David.

## Paperback Exchange

**Via Fiesolana 31r, 055/247-8154**
**Open Monday through Friday 9 AM to 7:30 PM; Saturday 10 AM to 1 PM**
    **and 3:30 PM to 7:30 PM**
**Map G4, Bus C**
**Credit cards accepted**

This small shop is filled entirely with English-language books; in fact many study-abroad programs buy their textbooks here. It's called the Paperback Exchange because you can turn in several of your own used books in exchange for one of their used books; however, this ends up being kind of a raw deal, and is more of a way to unload books that you don't want to schlepp back home with you on a return trip. In any case, most people come here to peruse and buy new books, and there are several shelves stocked with volumes on food and wine. The shop sells many popular coffee-table books on Tuscany and Florence, as well as wine guides by Oz Clarke and Hugh Johnson and cookbooks, including titles by Benedetta Vitali of Zibibbo (see page 92) and Jamie Oliver. It even sells books on sushi and *The Joy of Cooking,* for those tired of Italian fare.

## Pitti Gola e Cantina

**Piazza Pitti 16, 055/212-704**
**Open Tuesday through Sunday 9 AM to 9:30 PM; closed most of August**
**Map D6, Bus D**
**Credit cards accepted**

Pitti Gola is first and foremost a wine bar, but around to the side of the bar it stocks a small but interesting selection of books in English, German, and Italian, including Faith Willinger's cookbooks and current Italian wine guides.

*A raspberry tart on display at Dolci & Dolcezze.*

# 9
# Coffee, Pastries, and Chocolate

I used to bait friends at home by saying that you can get a better cappuccino in the train station in Florence than you can in any café in San Francisco. I said it partly to provoke, but I'll stand by that claim—the cappuccino in the station bar is truly good (though the atmosphere may be a tad hectic). It's hard to go wrong with coffee in Florence. Is it the water, the machines, the cleaning of the machines, or a certain Italian *non so cosa* that makes every shot of coffee here like a little liquid rush of bliss? I can't tell you what a great pleasure and relief it is to a coffee-hound like me to know that no matter where I am in Italy, how far north or south or in what small town or hamlet, I am almost never more than half a block from a good coffee.

But even in Italy, there's coffee and there's coffee. Some swear by Illy Caffè. I sometimes buy Lavazza Qualità d'Oro, which I like for the stove-top *caffettiera*. The biggest name in local coffee roasting is **Piansa**, famous for their mix of Arabica beans, but its main bar is far from the Center on the southeast side of town (Viale Europa 126–128r, 055/653-2117; open Monday through Friday 7 AM to 9 PM, Saturday and Sunday mornings). Luckily you can also buy Piansa coffee in the center of town at **Caffeteria Piansa** (Borgo Pinti 18r, 055/234-2362; open Monday through Saturday 8 AM to 8 PM) and **Cantinetta dei Verrazzano** (see page 115).

It's helpful to know the difference between *pasticceria, forno,* and *bar,* though they very often end up blended together (and so you get places with names like Caffè Bar Pasticceria da Lorenzo). A bar is a place to stop in and get a coffee or alcoholic drink at any time of day, usually while standing. Some bars have excellent homemade pastries, while others have a little bread-box-sized case of dry brioche from the day before. You can tell immediately, just by eyeballing, whether you've stepped into the former or the latter. Trust your senses.

A *pasticceria* sells primarily cakes and sweets; sometimes the goodies will be divided between breakfast sweets like brioches and the *bomboloni* and evening or party sweets like cakes, little custard tarts, and éclairs. In Italy, the price of a coffee and brioche is never high *as long as you are standing.* Also, outside the Center, if a place has a couple of chairs and tables set up, you can usually sit without worrying. All of the *pasticcerie* I have included are also bars, except Becagli, which calls itself a *forno* anyway.

A *forno* (which literally means "oven") is a bread bakery. The name harks back to the time when families would bring their own loaves to the communal wood-burning oven to be baked. It was too dangerous and expensive for every family to have such a hot oven in the house, so the community *forno* did the job. Now *forni* sell bread and related items such as *schiacciata*, bread sticks, and some sweets, too.

*Delicious yogurt tartlets at Patrizio Cosi.*

## Words to Eat By:

*Bignè* = Éclair

*Biscotti(ni), cantucci(ni)* = Hard Tuscan cookie, almost always made with almonds (the *–ni* suffix means they are extra-small)

*Bombolone* = Doughnut without the hole, often filled with custard

*Brioche* = Croissant

*Budino* = Dense pudding, often made with rice, formed into a little mound and eaten with one's fingers

*Cenci* = Fried dough covered with powdered sugar, served at Carnival time

*Ciambella* = Doughnut with the hole (or anything doughnut shaped)

*Cornetto* = Croissant (used less often in Florence than brioche)

*Crema* = Custard filling inside many pastries (the Italian word for "cream" is *panna*)

*Frittelle* = Sweet fritters

*Gianduia* = Mix of dark chocolate and hazelnut

*Marmellata* = Jam or jelly filling inside many pastries

*Mignon* = Cream puff

*Ricciarelli* = Almond cookies from Siena

*Schiacciata* = Tuscan focaccia

*Schiacciata alla fiorentina* = Yellow cake flavored with orange peel, served at Carnival time

*Torta della nonna* = Custard tart topped with almonds or pine nuts (the *tortina della nonna* is a smaller version of the same name that many Florentines take with their midmorning coffee; you'll sometimes see *tortina del nonno,* with chocolate custard instead of vanilla)

# Becagli

**Borgo Ognissanti 92r, 055/215-065**
**Open Thursday through Tuesday 6:30 AM to 2 PM and 5 PM to 8 PM;**
  **Wednesday 6:30 AM to 2 PM; closed most of August**
**Map B4, Buses A, D**

You know you're in the right place when you see the line of Florentines snaking out of here every day of the week, patiently waiting to squeeze inside and buy bread and *schiacciata* fresh from the oven or the perfect *torta della nonna* to bring home. The cookies filled with chocolate and hazelnut and little semolina tarts covered with ruby red strawberry sauce are tops here. This place is abundance itself, overflowing with cookies, fruit pies, and savory breads and *pizzette*—a rare equilibrium between forno and pasticceria. There's no bar, but an unconnected place next door serves coffee and cappuccino if you need a pick-me-up. If you're here on Monday, Tuesday, or Saturday between 9 AM and noon, you should go see Domenico Ghirlandaio's *Last Supper* in the refectory next to the Ognissanti church, right down the street.

# Buscioni

**Via Centostelle 1r, Campo di Marte, 055/602-765**
**Open Tuesday through Saturday 7:30 AM to 2 PM and 3 PM to 8 PM**
**Buses 11 17**

Occasionally you'll see handwritten signs on the windows of *pasticcerie* that say *Bomboloni Caldi, 16:30* (hot doughnuts at 4:30 PM). Compared to *schiacciata* or sandwiches with truffle oil, hot filled doughnuts are not exactly an exotic novelty to the average traveler, but Tuscans really take to them (they even opt for hot doughnuts as a beach snack instead of something cold like a Popsicle), and Florentines will all tell you that Buscioni makes the best *bomboloni caldi* in town. I wouldn't advocate a special trip to this out-of-the-way spot just to taste the doughnuts, but if you happen to find yourself near the Campo di Marte stadium around 4:30 PM, you could do worse than to stop by Buscioni and pick up a soft, warm bun straight from the oven, filled with custard, chocolate, or marmalade, and topped with the usual granulated sugar for good measure. The other baked goods here look quite good, too, but everyone seems to come for the *bomboloni*.

## Coffee Basics

I had a rude awakening on my first visit to Italy when, fresh from the cafés of my California youth, I strolled into an Italian bar, asked for a latte, and predictably was given a large glass of milk. If you need a coffee or two before you are capable of contemplating Caravaggio, it's a good idea to know your coffee vocabulary.

*Caffè* = Espresso (also called *caffè normale*)

*Caffè affogato* = Dessert dish of gelato "drowned" in a shot of espresso (some cafés and many restaurants offer this after a meal)

*Caffè americano* = Espresso with extra hot water added to resemble American coffee

*Caffè corretto* = Espresso with a shot of grappa

*Caffè decaffeinato* = Decaffeinated (usually made with the grain orzo)

*Caffè latte* = Hot milk with espresso, served in a glass

*Caffè lungo* = Same as *caffè americano*

*Caffè macchiato* = Espresso with a dollop of milk foam

*Caffè shakerato* = Sweet summertime drink of cold coffee and ice "shaken" and served in a cocktail glass

*Cappuccino* = Espresso with hot milk and foam

*Latte* = Glass of milk

*Latte macchiato* = Hot milk with a dollop of espresso

*Tè* = Tea

*Tè detèinato* = Decaffeinated tea

## Biscottini di Prato

The biscotti that are a favorite snack and dessert of Florence originate in the nearby town of Prato, about twenty minutes away by train. **Antonio Mattei** first opened his shop there in 1858, baking small, crescent-shaped almond cookies, and his company, now run by the Pandolfini family, is still the first name in biscotti (you'll sometimes see them called *cantucci* or *cantuccini*, but it's the same thing). Mattei also makes other cookies, including the *brutti ma buoni* (ugly but good) type made with almonds and *pan di ramerino,* another local favorite combining raisins and rosemary in a sweet and savory bread that's great for breakfast. You can find Mattei cookies for sale at most good wine and gourmet food shops in town, including **Vino Olio, Gambi,** and **Alessi** (see chapter 7). The best way to avoid breaking a tooth when indulging in these twice-baked sweets is to immerse them in a small glass of *vin santo,* which many Florentines do after a meal for dessert.

### Antonio Mattei
*Via Ricasoli 20–22, Prato, 0574/257-56; open Tuesday through Friday 8 AM to 7:30 PM, Saturday 8 AM to 1 PM and 3 PM to 7:30 PM, Sunday 8 AM to 1 PM; credit cards accepted.*

---

## Castaldini
**Viale dei Mille 47r, Campo di Marte, 055/579-684**
**Open Wednesday through Monday 7:30 AM to 1:30 PM and 4:30 PM
to 8:30 PM; closed most of August**
**Buses 11, 17**

Enzo Castaldini and his wife have been filling the community's need for cakes and cookies since 1956. If you do make it out this way, northeast of the center, you might want to try the specialty of the house called *torta fernanda,* two layers of vanilla cake lightly soaked in liqueur, split in two and filled with whipped cream, and topped with powdered sugar and a little bit of cocoa powder. The refrigerated case holds frozen cakes, profiteroles, and other goodies. During Carnival season, at the end of January and beginning of February, they also sell a fair number of *schiacciata alla fiorentina,* actually not a *schiacciata* at all, but a delicate yellow cake flavored with orange zest, topped with powdered sugar and the lily emblem of Florence etched in cocoa powder. They also sell an array of little chocolate candies, including chocolate-covered cherries and sugared oranges, as well as house-made butter cookies. Plus, it's a pleasant place to get a coffee.

## Chiaroscuro

**Via del Corso 36r, 055/214-247**
**Open Monday through Friday 8 AM to 8:30 PM, Saturday and Sunday**
    **8 AM to 9:30 PM; closed Sunday in summer**
**Map E4, Bus A**

An oasis of calm right in the heart of town, Chiaroscuro is the perfect place to take shelter from the busy Corso shopping street. You can either stand at the bar or sit in the Frenchified back room filled with cane bistro chairs and a few little tables, and sip a *nocciolina*—a delicious concoction of coffee with cream and hazelnut served in little glass cups. I have a life-long grudge against flavored coffee, but I make an exception for the *nocciolina* or *bicchierina,* an equally divine mix of coffee, chocolate, and cream. They also sell roasted coffee from all over the world, and at lunchtime you can order something light like a Niçoise salad or one of the heaping pastas and salads from the glass case in front. In the evening they serve *aperitivi* and snacks.

## Caffè Cibreo

**Via del Verrocchio 5r, 055/234-5853**
**Open Tuesday through Saturday 8 AM to 1 AM; closed August, Christmas Day,**
    **and New Year's Day**
**Map H5, Bus 14**

Part of the Cibreo food complex (see page 42) outside the Mercato Sant' Ambrogio, little Caffè Cibreo is decorated in the same dark woods and Parisian greens as the restaurant and trattoria. They don't make many pastries, usually just a brioche or two plus a special plum cake or unusual tart, but it's always a good stop for a cappuccino, and a way to capture a taste of Cibreo without the wait of the trattoria or the price of the restaurant. They serve a light lunch in the daytime, and at night people sit around the tiny round tables waiting to be seated in the other dining rooms, sometimes eating meals from the restaurant kitchen here.

## Patrizio Cosi ✳

**Borgo Albizi 11r, 055/248-0367**
**Open Monday through Saturday 7 AM to 8 PM; closed August**
**Map G4, Bus A**

Cosi (pronounced "cozy") is the first word out of anyone's mouth when you mention pastries in Florence. As in, "Do you know what time the *bomboloni* come out of the oven at Cosi?" or, "Have you tried the chocolate brioche at Cosi?"

You walk in the door and immediately see row upon row of glistening tarts, cookies, and treats in the glass case. I particularly love the tiny little éclairs and tarts that are exactly the size of one bite; they're so small you don't even feel guilty eating them. If you want to feel guilty, check out the tall refrigerated display cases on the other side, containing the full-sized chocolate cakes, tremendous raspberry tarts, and *torte della nonna.* I once made the mistake of ordering a *brioche con cioccolato* for breakfast, and almost needed to go home for a second shower to get the melted dark chocolate off my face. Next time, I had a much tidier *brioche con crema.* The interior of Cosi has been redone, with a light wood bar and tiled floor. At the marble-topped bar in back you can taste one of the best cappuccinos (or coffees) in town; you'll also find a few tables and chairs where you can sit for a moment to recharge.

## Dolci & Dolcezze ✳

**Piazza Beccaria 8r, 055/234-5458**
**Open Tuesday through Saturday 8:30 AM to 8 PM; Sunday 9 AM to 1 PM**
**and 4:30 PM to 7:30 PM**
**Map I5, Buses A, 8, 12**

Dolci & Dolcezze, to the east side of town in Piazza Beccaria, is special. It even looks different, like a sweetshop out of a nineteenth-century fairy tale, with lime green walls, marble counters, lace trim, and gilded moldings. You could come just for an amazing cup of Piansa coffee and a flaky, buttery croissant, but then you'd be missing out on a specialty that has made the shop a pilgrimage site for chocophiles—the place to try Giulio Corti's famous chocolate torte, either in party-sized rounds or little personal cakes dusted with cocoa powder. It's so rich that just a couple of bites will do you in. The little tarts filled with lemon curd or topped with raspberries or miniature wild strawberries and powdered sugar are also incredible.

*The* bariste *at Patrizio Cosi.*

## Donnini

**Piazza della Repubblica 15r, 055/213-694**
**Open Wednesday through Monday 6 AM to 11:30 PM; closed part of August**
**Map E4, Bus A**

Donnini is literally dwarfed by the other cafés in this grand nineteenth-century piazza, so I was glad when a Florentine friend directed me there to try the *caffè macchiato*, which he finds to be the best in the city, and a special pastry called a *scendiletto* (a *scendiletto* is literally a bedside rug—basically a soft landing for when you wake up, much like this pastry). This decadent confection of pastry and custard, flattened into a little rectangle, comes out of the ovens at 9 AM; they sell out within the first two hours or so but are by far best when still warm, in the first half hour. The coffee is very good, served in elegant little glass cups by some of the most dextrous and attentive *bariste* in central Florence. At lunchtime Donnini fills with a crowd eager to partake of their inexpensive and delicious hot pastas, which emerge from the kitchen in big serving dishes. Try the lasagne or *farfalle* with asparagus.

## Gilli

**Piazza della Repubblica 36–39r, 055/213-896**
**Open Wednesday through Monday 7:30 AM to 10 PM; closed August**
**Map E4, Bus A**

Part of Piazza della Repubblica's troika of elegant, Viennese-style cafés, which also includes Paszkowski and Giubbe Rosse (once the hangout of Risorgimento-era rabble-rousers), Gilli is known both for its chocolates and its *aperitivi,* and like the others it's a good central stop for a coffee and brioche or *bombolone* (doughnut). The drinking starts early, so don't be surprised to see fur-clad women and old men in hats lined up against the impressive wood-and-mirror art nouveau bar at noon on a weekday, sipping a Prosecco and partaking of the impressive spread of snacks. A glass case next to the cash register displays a beautiful array of chocolates, both light and dark.

## Gualtieri

**Via Senese 18r, Porta Romana, 055/221-771**

**Open Tuesday through Sunday 7 AM to 1:15 PM and 4 PM to 8 PM;**
**closed August**

**Buses 27, 36**

If you find yourself out by the Porta Romana, Gualtieri is a small, bustling place to come for a French-style éclair, a sweet rice fritter (*frittella*) made around Easter, or just a very good cappuccino and brioche. The specialty of the house is a *torta tirolese,* a round semolina tart made with fresh pears, but everything is high quality here. The shop makes its own chocolate candies, and even sell chocolate bars with the house label. In the summer months you can stop here for a homemade gelato.

## Hemingway

**Piazza Piattellina 9r, 055/284-781**

**Open Tuesday through Saturday 4:30 PM to 1 AM; Sunday 11 AM to 8 PM**
**(brunch from 11:30 AM to 2:30 PM); closed August**

**Map B5, Bus D**

Hemingway is primarily a nighttime hotspot, but it also specializes in excellent locally made chocolates. In fact, it's a great place to go at night after dinner if you don't feel like smoking and drinking. Cocktails are served, but hot drinks are the focus, from hot chocolates to coffee drinks to a long list of teas. The menu offers a choice of puddings and cakes, as well as a platter of assorted candies from Slitti, a top chocolatier from Monsummano Terme (see page 201), and chocolates made by Paul De Bondt of Pisa, another leader in the field. Even a regular coffee comes with a little spoon made of fine chocolate and cocoa. Stop in for a late-afternoon coffee or hot chocolate after you visit the Brancacci chapel in the church of Santa Maria delle Carmine, just down the block. On Sunday doors open early for a big brunch (see page 55).

# Sweets for the Homesick

Here's a twist: An American bakery churning out chocolate chip cookies, peanut butter cookies, and pumpkin pies in the heart of Florence, owned by a Florentine, and patronized mostly by homesick American college students. On Saturdays people line up at **Mr. Jimmy's** for hot dogs and bagels, toasted and topped with cream cheese and smoked salmon. The chocolate chip cookies are about on par with what you would get at a café in the States—not great, but passable. Mr. Jimmy's also supplies the café at Edison bookstore (see page 179) and several restaurants around town with their brownies and other desserts, and sells specialty cakes for holidays like Halloween and Valentine's Day. Once in a long while, an apple pie can be a welcome change after all those *torte della nonna*.

Masha Innocenti is an Italian American whose whole family long ago moved back to Italy, where she began to teach cooking and in 1993 opened **La Boutique dei Dolci,** which despite its Franco-Italian name turns out American-style sweets. It specializes in cheesecake, but also makes apple and blueberry pies as well as custom-made decorated cakes for birthdays and weddings. The shop has supplied multitiered wedding cakes to happy couples, cakes that look like bright green soccer fields for little kids' birthdays, and even plied Anthony Hopkins and the rest of the cast of *Hannibal* with American cakes during filming. It is out of the way, in northwest Florence near Piazza Leopoldo, so most people access it by car.

### Mr. Jimmy's
*Via di San Niccolò 47, 055/248-0999; open daily 11 AM to 8 PM; Map G7, Bus D.*

### La Boutique dei Dolci
*Via Fabroni 18r, Piazza Leopoldo, 055/499-503; open Tuesday through Saturday 9:30 AM to 1 PM and 4 PM to 7:30 PM; Buses 8, 20, 28.*

## Caffè Italiano
**Via della Condotta 56r, 055/291-082**
**Open Monday through Saturday 8 AM to 8 PM; closed August**
**Map E5, Bus A**

This elegant belle epoque–style café with dark wood paneling, crystal chandeliers, and wrought iron chairs is another welcome refuge in the center of town: an excellent place to duck in for a morning hot chocolate while you browse the various international newspapers hanging on hooks. There is also a cozy upstairs room, where you can order coffee and pastries, or a light lunch of soup or pasta, which only runs about €6.

## Migone
**Via dei Calzaiuoli 85–87r, 055/214-004**
**Open Tuesday through Saturday 9 AM to 7:30 PM; closed Christmas Day**
**Map E4, Bus A**

Next to the expensive leather goods and high fashion *botteghe* on Via dei Calzaiuoli, Migone is a gift boutique of sweets. You can stock up on locally made biscotti, all manner of candy kitsch such as chocolates shaped like the Duomo and the Baptistry, colorful Sicilian marzipan fruits, or different flavors of *torrone* (almond nougat).

## Minni
**Via Antonio Giacomini 16, Piazza Savonarola, 055/578-836**
**Open Monday through Saturday 7:15 AM to 8 PM; Sunday 7 AM to 1:30 PM;**
**   closed August**
**Buses 11, 17**

On the north side of town, wedged between Piazza Libertà and Piazza Savonarola, Minni is a great stop for a coffee and a sweet or for cookies and cakes to bring home or to a dinner party. Inside, the first thing you'll notice is the unmistakable smell of fresh-baked sweets; next you'll see a baker emerge from the kitchen in back with a fresh tray of sweet fritters hot from the oil; and finally you'll stop to take in the endless variety of incredibly appealing tarts, cookies, and cakes of all kinds. Brioches in Florence tend to

*A few of the sublime cakes at Dolci & Dolcezze.*

be of a pretty consistent decent quality, but Minni makes some of the freshest, highest-quality ones around, with raisins, filled with custard, and so on. In the refrigerated case, you'll find different sizes of *tartufi* and mounds of gelato covered in chocolate that look like little chocolate *bombe.*

## Alessandro Nannini

**Via Borgo San Lorenzo 7r, 055/212-680**
**Open daily 7:30 AM to 8 PM**
**Map E3, Buses 6, 11**

From outside, Nannini looks just like any other crowded and touristy coffee bar, but on closer inspection you'll find it's the Florentine outpost for tasting authentic specialty cookies of Siena, made by the longstanding bakery. Many of the excellent biscotti are made with soft, sweet almond paste, including the *ricciarelli* (roughly translated as "curlicues") and the *brutti ma buoni* (ugly but good). It's a pleasant stop for a cappuccino, especially if you want to sit down, as it's much more spacious than most cafés.

---

## L'Olandese Volante

**Via San Gallo 44r, 055/473-240**
**Open Monday through Saturday 10 AM to 1:15 PM and 3:45 PM to 7:45 PM;**
**closed August**
**Map F1, Buses 6, 11**

The main display case at L'Olandese Volante (The Flying Dutchman) features row after neat row of imported artisanal Dutch chocolates, milk and dark, filled with cognac, almond paste, and other delectables. It sells a small selection of Goudas and other Dutch cheeses, as well as some dry goods and such for homesick Dutch people, but the fine little chocolates are the main attraction.

---

## Paszkowski

**Piazza della Repubblica 31–35r, 055/210-236**
**Open Tuesday through Sunday 7:30 AM to 1 AM**
**Map E4, Bus A**

Paszkowski has been serving Florence's best dressed since 1846. It may be a bit snooty, but it's all part of the buttoned-up ambience, and is worth putting up with once you discover the little tarts: yogurt tarts with berries, custard tarts with chocolate, orange-flavored and lime-flavored custard with little pieces of fruit on top, all lined up like a beauty pageant under glass. People come on weekends and fill up elegant boxes to bring to a party or a family lunch. On top of the counter you'll see thick bars of *nocciolato* (chocolate hazelnut) prettily wrapped in cellophane with the house label. The little chocolate cookies, meringue kisses, and babas floating in a big bowl of rum are all equally tempting. Paszkowski has a large indoor room for eating, as well as plenty of space outside, but I wouldn't recommend either if you're on a budget.

## Petrarca

**Piazzale di Porta Romana 6r, 055/221-092**
**Open Sunday through Friday 6 AM to 8:30 PM; closed August and**
**Christmas Day**
**Buses 11, 12, 13, 36, 37**

If you are staying in the Porta Romana area, south of the Center, or happen to find yourself over this way—maybe after a visit to the Boboli Gardens—stop in at Petrarca. This multifaceted bar fills several important functions: you can get an excellent cappuccino and pastry, a quick lunch of either pasta or one of the prepared foods in the glass case, an afternoon éclair, or buy an entire cheesecake, apple tart, or *torta della nonna* for a party, all made in-house and all terrific. (For the record, cheesecake in Italy means something slightly different than in America: it's more like a sweet quiche). Best of all, it's open all day on Sunday (though not Saturday). Don't be put off by the fancy uniforms or occasionally chilly attitude; the people are actually very friendly.

## Rivoire

**Piazza della Signoria 5r, 055/214-412**
**Open Tuesday through Saturday 8 AM to 12:30 AM in summer,**
**8 AM to 9 PM in winter; closed Christmas Day**
**Map E5, Bus B**

If you choose just one tourist indulgence, instead of going for a ride in one of those horse and buggies, find a table outside Rivoire. From this prime spot right on Piazza Signoria in view of the Palazzo Vecchio and the Uffizi, you can order a hot chocolate with whipped cream (*cioccolata calda con panna*). The hot chocolate for which this venerable café is famous bears no resemblance to what normally goes by that name; it's more like a hot dark chocolate custard, thick and extremely rich, which explains the need for whipped cream to balance it out. They also sell their own mark of gourmet packaged chocolates (many filled with liqueur) and make an excellent *torta della nonna* to enjoy while people-watching and gazing at the copy of *David* in front of the Palazzo Vecchio.

## Robiglio

**Via dei Servi 112r, 055/214-501**
**Open Monday through Saturday 7:30 AM to 7:30 PM; Saturday 7:30 AM**
**to 2 PM in summer; closed August and New Year's Day**
**Map F3, Bus C**

**Via dei Tosinghi 11r, 055/215-013**
**Open Monday through Saturday 8 AM to 8 PM; closed August and**
**New Year's Day**
**Map E4, Bus A**

The original location of Robiglio on Via dei Servi is an incredibly popular place for locals to stop for a coffee and delicious pastry. The *bariste* are constantly singing and there's a lot of loud and lively chatter in the very packed space around the bar. Among the specialties are *tortine della nonna* and *nonno* (with chocolate), lemon-custard tartlets, and fresh croissants. The savories (very small *panini* and slices of rustic vegetable tarts) are also good, and crowds stand around eating them at lunch. The shop sells row after row of small chocolate candies, as well

### Late-Night Nutella

The **Forno Stefano Galli** has several locations in Florence dishing out *schiacciata* pizzas by the slice, Tuscan breads, sweet brioche, and a Nutella sandwich that is exactly what it sounds like—luscious chocolate-hazelnut spread on a sweet roll. The best part of the equation is that the most convenient Galli, on Via Faenza near both the train station and the Central Market, is open seven days a week until four in the morning, catering to late-night revelers and anyone else in need of a snack.

**Forno Stefano Galli**
*Via Faenza 39r, 055/215-314; open daily 7 AM to 4 AM; Map D3.*

as a variety of European packaged brands. Here's a tip for pastry success: The top shelf holds whatever just came out of the oven.

If you're shopping in the city center you might stop in at the location on Via dei Tosinghi, between Via dei Calzaiuoli and Piazza della Repubblica. The always festive window displays show off the delectable-looking cakes and tortes inside. Robiglio also serves an excellent cappuccino and *macchiato*, as well as an assortment of treats.

## Ruggini

**Via dei Neri 76r, 055/214-521**
**Open Monday through Friday 7:30 PM to 8 PM, Saturday and**
   **Sunday 7:30 AM to 1:30 PM; closed most of August**
**Map F5, Bus B**

Though you might enter this sedate little bar on a street behind the Palazzo Vecchio just to grab a cappuccino, you can't help but be distracted by the golden-hued cookies piled high in the window on your way in. This pastry shop, with its long, narrow standing room decorated with large mirrors, seems to attract an older well-dressed crowd. The *bomboloni al cioccolato* (chocolate doughnuts) are especially good here. You can also buy an assortment of cookies, *gianduia* cake, or Sacher torte to take away.

## Scudieri

**Piazza San Giovanni 19r (Piazza del Duomo), 055/210-733**
**Open daily 7:30 AM to 9 PM; closed August**
**Map E4, Buses 1, 6, 11**

Scudieri occupies prime real estate right behind the Baptistry, and certainly doesn't lack for foot traffic. With its mirrored bar and colorful display cases full of tempting sweets, it's a convenient spot for a fresh, delicious brioche (high turnover is a good indicator of pastry freshness), or more adventurous treats, as well as any kind of coffee or tea. Other treats include impressive blocks of chocolate and various flavors of *torrone* (almond nougat) from Sicily.

# Chocolate Valley

One of the latest trends in Tuscan gastronomy is high-quality artisanal chocolates. The critical mass of some of the biggest names in Italian chocolate, including **Catinari** in the small town of Agliana, near Pisa; **Paul De Bondt** of Pisa; **Slitti** (pronounced *zlee-tee*) from the spa town of Monsummano Terme; and **Amadei** in Pontedera, near Pisa, has led food and wine magazine *Gambero Rosso* to dub the northeast corner of Tuscany "Chocolate Valley." In 2001 Slow Food helped sponsor the first Tuscan chocolate fair, called *Cioccolosità*, in Monsummano Terme, where local makers went head-to-head with some of the more established names from Piedmont and Liguria. You can find chocolates from Slitti and Paul De Bondt at **Hemingway** (see page 193), and Amadei can be found at **Chiaroscuro** (see page 189), **Procacci** (see page 163), and **Gambi** (see page 144).

### Catinari
*Via Provinciale 378, Agliana, 0574/718-506; open Tuesday through Saturday 8 AM to 1 PM and 3:30 PM to 7:30 PM.*

### Slitti
*Via Francesca Sud 240, Monsummano Terme, 0572/640-240; open Monday through Saturday 8 AM to 1 PM and 3 PM to 8 PM.*

### De Bondt
*Via Turati 22, Pisa, 050/501-896; open Tuesday through Saturday 9:30 AM to 1:30 PM and 3 PM to 8 PM.*

### Amadei
*Via San Gervasio 29, Pontedera, by appointment only, 0587/484-849.*

## Torrefazione Fiorenza

**Via Santa Monaca 2r, 055/287-546**
**Open Sunday through Friday 8 AM to 1 PM and 4:30 PM to 7:30 PM;**
**Saturday 8 AM to 1 PM; closed August**
**Map C6, Buses D, 11, 36**

This little shop between Piazza Santo Spirito and Piazza del Carmine has been in business since 1957, and the two older men who run it look as if they might have been here just as long. The main reason to come is for a selection of fresh-ground coffee, the smell of which infuses the place. Behind the counter is a small *spezzeria,* a collection of old-fashioned apothecary jars filled with bulk herbs and spices such as nutmeg, oregano, and local *nepitella* (an herb in the mint family), as well as other specialty items like unsweetened cocoa, pistachios, vanilla beans, and gelatin for making *panna cotta.*

## Vestri ✳

**Borgo degli Albizi 11r, 055/234-0374**
**Open Monday through Saturday 10 AM to 7:30 PM; closed August**
**Map G4, Bus A**

A recent addition to the Florentine food scene, Vestri appeared out of the blue as a full-fledged artisanal chocolate shop in the heart of town. The company, based in Arezzo, specializes in chocolate candies and handmade ice creams in chocolate, chocolate mint, and a few other outstanding flavors. The candies come filled with *gianduia,* walnut, coffee, puffed rice, and other flavors; the ganache come in Kahlúa, Earl Grey tea, pepper, and some other unusual flavors. Chocolates are beautifully displayed in this alluring shop, which happens to be right next to Patrizio Cosi pastries.

*Olive groves in the countryside near Pienza.*

*Eating gelato outside Vestri.*

# 10
# GELATERIAS

Italian gelato differs from American ice cream in that it is made with more milk and less butterfat so the texture is softer and creamier and the flavor often more intense. Most of the fruit flavors are made with no milk at all.

The gelato in Florence is of such a consistently high quality that it is actually difficult to determine who makes the best gelato in town. Many swear by Vivoli, the old stalwart, while others deride it as touristy, over-priced, and past its prime. I've had friends lobby for Neri, while loved ones pledge allegiance to Carabé and Carraia. If you are truly obsessed, it's worth the bus ride out to Badiani, where the *Buontalenti* (rich cream) flavor will make your head swim with delight. Otherwise, you can hardly go wrong at any of the places listed below, favorites of Florentines and expats both in and outside the city center.

If you are craving gelato in the winter, be aware that most shops have shorter hours.

## Gelateria L'Alpina

**Viale Strozzi 12r, 055/496-677**
**Open Wednesday through Monday 7 AM to 9 PM in winter; 7 AM to midnight
in summer; closed mid-August, Christmas Day, and New Year's Day**
**Map D1, Buses 7, 10, 13, 25**

Like Cavini (see page 209), Alpina is a neighborhood hangout as well as gelato joint and bar. It's a walk from the Center, just by the Fortezza da Basso. The *Buontalenti* flavor is a bit disappointing (too much rum), but the chocolate, *nocciola* (hazelnut), and *croccante al rhum* are rich and creamy.

## Badiani ✳

**Viale dei Mille 20r, Campo di Marte, 055/578-682**
**Open Wednesday through Monday 7 AM to midnight**
**Buses 11, 17**

Badiani is the queen bee of Florentine gelaterias. You'll want to make a trip out to this inconvenient spot near the Campo di Marte for one reason: *Buontalenti.* Named after a late sixteenth-century engineer and architect (he designed several Medici villas and the famous grotto in the Boboli Gardens), this is Badiani's signature flavor, and you'll notice that almost every customer orders it as part of their mélange of scoops. *Buontalenti* has the hue of buttermilk, and no discernable flavor like vanilla or liqueur; instead it tastes like some kind of heart-stopping quadruple cream straight from the cow. It's decadent, delicious, and goes extremely well with their other flavors, hazelnut, coffee, and pistachio among them. Unlike most gelaterias, Badiani is also a pleasant bar where you can get a coffee and brioche and hang out with a book or newspaper. There's often a big rush after soccer matches at the nearby stadium.

## Carabé ✳

**Via Ricasoli 60r, 055/289-476**
**Open daily 9 AM to 1 AM**
**Map F3, Bus C**

Carabé's Sicilian owners make excellent fruit- and nut-flavored gelatos. The almond, walnut, and pistachio gelatos are all standouts, and the perfectly tart-sweet lemon flavor is the most refreshing thing you could eat on a hot summer day. They also make a deliciously creamy and slightly tart yogurt flavor, as well as fig—straight from the Central Market—when in season. People will tell you to try the granitas here, either coffee, almond, or lemon, but I found them disappointing. These Sicilian slurpeelike ice creations for some reason only taste right in Sicily; once north of the Straits of Messina, even natives lose either the recipe or the capacity for making them well. But never mind the granitas, the gelato is really, really good.

## La Carraia
**Piazza Nizario Sauro 25r, 055/280-695**
**Open daily 10 AM to 11 PM; occasionally closed during winter months**
**Map C5, Buses 11, 36, 37**

La Carraia has somehow escaped the notice of most Florentine food critics and food-obsessed people in general, but there it is, clear as day, and right in the Center, too, on the Oltrarno side of the Carraia bridge. Simply put, this is some of the best gelato in the city: fluffy, creamy, decadent, no-nonsense flavors like coffee, *fior di latte* (cow's milk mozzarella), and chocolate are all excellent. It even sells a Nutella yogurt for those who aren't sure if they're on a diet or a binge (actually this is a great flavor, the yogurt giving a slightly sour kick to the otherwise sweet taste). You might go elsewhere, however, for your fruit flavors; here they are cream-based and not as appealing as the water-based flavors at Neri and Carabé.

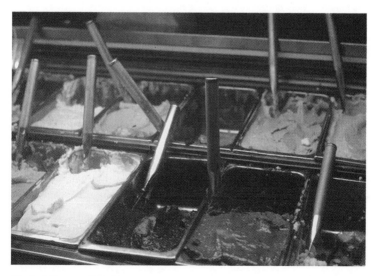

*The fruit flavors at Vivoli.*

*Friendly server at Carrozza.*

## Carrozza

**Piazza del Pesce 3–5, 055/239-6810**
**Open Thursday through Tuesday 11 AM to 1 AM**
**Map E5, Bus B**

Before I moved to Florence, people who had lived there kept telling me to make sure to got to "the gelateria near the Ponte Vecchio." And even once I arrived, friends would often discuss how the "one near the Ponte Vecchio" has some of the best gelato in town. The only problem being that there are about three gelaterias on each side of the Ponte. Soon I followed my nose—and the line of people—and figured out they were all talking about Carrozza, definitely the best gelato in this immediate vicinity. The shop makes an excellent chocolate flavor, and the pistacchio, *nocciola* (hazelnut), and yogurt are all a treat. The fruit flavors are deep and colorful, including a refreshing lemon and a dark and tempting *mirtillo* (blueberry).

## Cavini

**Piazza delle Cure 19-23r, Le Cure, 055/587-489**
**Open Tuesday through Sunday 7 AM TO 1 AM**
**Buses 1, 7**

Like a lot of the best gelato in town, this one is out of the Center in a more residential neighborhood. The draw here is an exceptionally wide variety of flavors, as well as the generally high quality of the ice cream. As a bonus, once you have your cone or cup in hand, you can relax outside in one of the chairs lined up on the piazza. Cavini's chocolate is rich and creamy, and there are variations on the theme: chocolate with orange, Mexican chocolate, and two kinds of chocolate chip, among others. It also has two varieties of pistachio (the Sicilian one is better), many fruit flavors, and an entire case of *semifreddi,* the half-frozen mousse counterpart to regular gelato. The *Buontalenti* flavor had a hint of saffron or some other mystery flavor that I liked, though it's not quite as good as at Badiani. Locals come by to pick up a frozen cake or *cassata* (Sicilian ricotta cake) to take home. Cavini also serves as a neighborhood hangout, staying open late to serve coffee, hard alcohol, and many, many cones of gelato.

## Neri

**Via dei Neri 20-22r, 055/210-034**
**Open daily noon to midnight**
**Map F5, Bus B**

Gelateria Neri has taken over where Vivoli, just around the corner, lets off: it's a little less touristy and a little less expensive than the older gelato grande dame. If you want to really indulge, try a cup or cone of their excellent coffee flavor, paired with chocolate or *nocciola* (hazelnut) and topped with a "correction" of whipped cream. The fruit flavors are equally appealing, especially in summer. The tiny shop is arranged so that you can lean against a kind of wall support but can't actually sit, which works out fine for the short time it takes to devour the excellent gelato.

# Perchè No?
**Via dei Tavolini 19r, 055/239-8969**
**Open daily 11 AM to midnight; closed Christmas Day and New Year's Day**
**Map E5, Bus A**

*Perchè no,* indeed. If you're walking around the center of town, in between visits to the Duomo, the Palazzo Vecchio, the Uffizi, and Orsanmichele, why not stop in for a nice gelato at this respectable outpost? The interior was remodeled to no noticeable effect, except the ice cream counter now looks a little like a disco ball. The flavors here are good (probably the best of the central gelaterias right off Via dei Calzaiuoli) without being particularly outstanding. I like the mousses, as well as the excellent lemon gelato.

# Veneta
**Piazza Beccaria 7r, 055/234-3370**
**Open Wednesday through Monday 10 AM to midnight; 10 AM to 8 PM**
**    in winter; 5 PM to midnight in August**
**Map I5, Buses A, 8, 12, 31, 32**

It's difficult to decide which flavors to choose at Veneta because everything looks good. One time I tried a delicious mix of *mirtillo* (blueberry) with a fantastically creamy *Buontalenti.* The *nocciola* (hazelnut) flavor is superb, as is the chocolate, and they are great when paired. I also like the little treats on offer, including homemade ice-cream sandwiches, frosting-dipped cones, and the like. Special cakes to take away are lined up in the frozen case. Coffees are served from a little bar, but most people come here for the gelato.

# Vestri
**Borgo degli Albizi 11r, 055/234-0374**
**Open Monday through Saturday 10 AM to 7:30 PM; closed August**
**Map G4, Bus A**

A recent addition to the Florentine food scene, Vestri is completely devoted to chocolate: chocolate candies, hot chocolate, and all kinds of creative variations on chocolate gelato, such as chocolate-orange, chocolate-cinnamon, chocolate-mint, and, of course, pure unadulterated chocolate. The chocolate-mint here is rare in that it is the color of chocolate and not a fake mint green.

## Vivoli
**Via Isola delle Stinche 7r, 055/292-334**
**Open Tuesday through Saturday 7:30 AM to 1 AM, Sunday 9:30 AM to 1 AM;**
    **closed for two weeks in August**
**Map F5, Buses A, 23**

This gelateria near Santa Croce has a long reputation as the best gelato place in Florence, and at this point I'd have to say it has rested a bit on its laurels and other gelaterias are threatening the crown. Vivoli still makes some of the best ice cream in town, but puts some people off with its tiny portions and high prices. One reason to come is for the terrific *riso* (rice) flavor; another is for the array of fresh fruit gelatos—always a mix of mundane and unusual, like pear, kiwifruit, or blood orange—all vibrantly colored, pure, and delicious. It also makes great chocolate and yogurt flavors.

*Pamela Sheldon Johns of Culinary Arts conducts a tasting of aged balsamic vinegars.*

# 11
# COOKING CLASSES

In a city that's as food-saturated as Florence, it's natural that the abundance would extend to cooking instruction, from one-day classes for beginners to semester-long courses complete with chefs' toques and test kitchens. In essence, two different kinds of programs in and around Florence cater to the needs of food lovers seeking a Tuscan culinary education. The first type of program is geared toward residents or long-term visitors to the city. These schools offer both short- and long-term study, and professional (or at least semiprofessional) courses aimed at people truly interested in working within the restaurant industry. Then there is the large (and ever-growing) number of programs aimed at short-term vacationers, where in some cases the cooking course *is* the vacation. It's not hard to see the appeal: what could be nicer than spending a week at a restored Tuscan villa, learning to cook traditional recipes with local ingredients?

Because some programs ask for payment in American dollars, prices are given as such. At the time of publication, the exchange rate of euros to dollars was more or less one to one.

## IN FLORENCE

### Apicius
**Via Guelfa 85, 055/287-143; fax: 055/239-8920**
**www.apicius.it**
**Map D2, Buses 4, 12**

This cooking school has refurbished its facilities on Via Guelfa to an extremely impressive professional level. In the cooking classes, students stand at their own stainless steel work station until the end of the semester, at which point they try out what they've learned in a fully stocked facsimile of a restaurant kitchen. The wine courses are held in a small classroom equipped with marble-topped desks containing little troughs for discarded wine.

Apicius, named for an ancient Roman cookbook author, offers so many different programs that it can be hard to sort them all out. Courses are divided into professional and amateur programs. The professional programs in the wine, cooking, and the hospitality trades each last two semesters, at the end of which you receive a certificate of graduation (the school is private and not accredited by the state, but is a member of the International Association of Culinary Professionals). You can also choose to take just one semester. Each semester is a full load of Italian language plus four subject courses and an internship at a restaurant or enoteca in Florence. Each semester (approximately fifteen weeks) costs US$4,500, which includes two knives and a jacket. The courses are all taught in English by Italian experts in the field, and attract a mix of Americans and others from all over the world. Many are recent college graduates, while others are older professionals interested in changing careers.

The amateur programs are less intensive, and can be taken either for a month, a week, a summer, or a whole semester. Subjects range from wine appreciation to regional cooking. You can also combine different subjects. Group amateur classes are sometimes taught in Italian, so make sure to check in advance. Or sign up for one-on-one lessons in another one of their sparkling test kitchens. The school will help students find housing in Florence (not an easy thing) at fairly reasonable prices.

---

### Cooking in Florence
**Via dei Pilastri 52, 055/242-128 in Florence; 212/753-0811 in New York**
**www.bugialli.com**
**Map H4, Bus C**

Giuliano Bugialli is known for his numerous books on Tuscan and Italian regional cooking (*The Fine Art of Italian Cooking, Foods of Italy*), but even before he began writing cookbooks he founded this cooking school to teach his craft to others. He now divides his time between New York and Florence, teaching, cooking, consulting, writing, and appearing on television cooking shows.

In 1996 Bugialli opened the new location for his school in a restored farmhouse outside Florence in the Chianti region. Students still stay in a hotel in Florence, but are bused to the farmhouse for all classes. The school offers what it calls classic courses and traveling courses. The classic courses, which last one week, include Florence in the Spring, Italian Tradition, and Florence in the Fall. An example of the traveling courses is Umbria, Assisi, and Black Truffles. The cost of the classes are US$3,600, including a double room, lessons, and some dinners at night.

## Cordon Bleu

**Via di Mezzo 55r, telephone/fax: 055/234-5468**
**www.cordonbleu-it.com**
**Map G4, Buses 14, 23**

Cordon Bleu is run by Gabriella Mari and Cristina Blasi, two energetic Tuscan women with a passionate knowledge of wine and food. They offer two different types of courses. The first is a week-long intensive course taught in English, on either basic Italian cooking, regional Italian cooking, or new Italian cooking. The courses are taught in four lessons of three hours and cost €360 each. These are usually taught at intervals in April, June, July, and September, so you need to catch them at the right time in order to partake.

For the rest of the year the school is aimed at residents and long-term visitors, offering weekly courses of three hours that can be anywhere from one lesson to eight depending on the subject, anything from basic cooking (eight lessons) to summer vegetables (three lessons) to Christmas sweets (one lesson). The best thing about these classes, and what sets them apart from the majority of cooking ventures in Florence, is that they are taught in Italian (often lightening-fast Italian) and attract a large number of Florentines in addition to international attendees—especially if you take a night course, which runs from 8 to 11 PM. Some of the best classes here are Primi Piatti, Cucina Mediterranea, and any of the vegetable classes.

One drawback here is that, due to the kitchen design, only one or two students at a time usually participate hands-on, while the others sit, watch, and take notes. Another is that a lot of recipes are squeezed into each lesson, often giving things a hectic feel, but you do learn a lot of different techniques. A full semester course includes all the classes on offer. Prices are reasonable, usually about €50 per lesson. (New students should know that this school, Scuola Cucinaria di Cordon Bleu, is not related to the Cordon Bleu of Paris.)

## Divina Cucina—Judy Witts Francini

**Via Taddea 31, telephone/fax: 055/292-578**
**www.divinacucina.com**
**email: info@divinacucina.com**
**Map E2, Bus 12**

Judy Witts Francini earned her chops as a pastry chef for five-star hotels in San Francisco before ever setting foot in Italy. When she first arrived in the 1980s, she wasn't even sure she liked Italy or Italian food. But soon she was learning the fine points of Tuscan cuisine, working in various kitchens and apprenticing with butcher Dario Cecchini in Panzano. In 1988 she began teaching classes to small groups. She now offers lessons

*Judy Witts Francini and students in the Central Market.*

three days a week, generally from 10 AM to 4 or 5 PM, Tuesday through Thursday. Classes begin with a trip to the Central Market, literally across the street from her kitchen; include tastings of olive oils, balsamic vinegars, and local cheeses; and finish with the cooking and eating of a full Tuscan meal. Students can come for just one class or up to three, as they choose; the cost is US$250 per day. Francini has an outgoing, lively personality and a thorough knowledge of Tuscan cooking.

## Jeff Thickman
**055/730-9064**
**email: jig@dada.it**

Also known as Jeff Lo Chef, Jeff Thickman studied at the Cordon Bleu in Paris and has catered parties for the first families of Florence, as well as fashion and music royalty from around the world. He has worked as the private chef to Zubin Mehta, and at various times has cooked for Shimon Peres, Hillary Clinton, Sophia Loren, Luciano Pavarotti, Madonna, and Sting. Friendly, shy, and self-effacing, Thickman has gained his clientele solely by word of mouth, and was recently featured in *Gambero Rosso,* Italy's premier food and wine magazine.

Though he works mostly as a caterer and private chef, Thickman has outfitted his home kitchen as a teaching space for small group classes where he can tailor the program to whatever his students would like to learn, from stretching pasta by hand to making classic Neapolitan-style *sfogliatelle* (flaky, ricotta-stuffed pastry). Classes are organized by request and should have a minimum of four people and a maximum of twenty. Classes cost €120 per person.

## Faith Willinger

Via della Chiesa 7, telephone/fax: 055/233-7014
www.faithwillinger.com
Map C7, Buses D, 36, 37, 11

Faith Heller Willinger has lived in Florence for twenty-five years, authored a cookbook on Italian vegetables (*Red, White, & Greens*), and a guidebook to eating in northern Italy (*Eating in Italy*). Every Wednesday she leads a small group on a tour of the local market and proceeds to cook a full meal while explaining the niceties and peculiarities of living and eating *alla italiana* to her students. The classes, which last all day, start out with coffee and work their way through olive oil, balsamic vinegar, wines of the region, and whatever Italian specialties she is cooking that day. Willinger, a down-to-earth woman with a great sense of humor, is a member of the International Association of Culinary Professionals and extremely well-respected in both American and Italian food circles. Her Wednesday classes run US$450 per person and include bottles of olive oil, vinegar, and other little take-away gifts; you save $50 if you book directly through her website.

## Zibibbo—Benedetta Vitali

Via di Terzollina 3r, Careggi, 055/433-383; fax: 055/428-9070
www.zibibboline.com
email: zibibbofirenze@hotmail.com
Bus 14C (Capolinea, end of the line)

With a restaurant open for lunch and dinner (see page 91), a children's book, and a hit cookbook in the stores, perhaps Benedetta Vitali didn't feel busy enough, so she decided to start a small cooking school in her restaurant's kitchen. Courses are intended for people interested in working in a professional kitchen. For the one-week intensive lessons, Vitali and all the regular Zibibbo cooks take part in teaching the classes, which cover the basics of making *soffritto* (the base for savory Tuscan sauces) and stocks; frying vegetables, meats, and fish; cooking pasta and sauces; and making desserts from Zibibbo's recipe file. Courses go from 8 AM to 1 PM; the cost is €660, including wine tasting, apron, and hat, but not lodging.

The school also offers a more relaxed curriculum aimed at Florentine residents, held over four Saturdays, in which students learn about pasta, cooking basics, and fish, and at the end of each four-hour lesson make a complete meal. The cost for this is €385, also including apron and hat.

## OUTSIDE FLORENCE

### Badia a Coltibuono
**Loc. Badia a Coltibuono**
**Gaiole in Chianti, 0577/744-832**
**www.coltibuono.com**
**email: info@coltibuono.com**

Badia a Coltibuono is an eleventh-century monastery-turned–wine estate. Beautifully situated overlooking the Val di Orcia near Gaiole in Chianti, it is known for its excellent Chianti Classico. Here you can also enroll in popular classes that for years were taught by cookbook author Lorenza de' Medici and are now taught by chef Paolo Pancotti with additional help from John Meis, author of the coffee-table book *Taste of Tuscany*. These courses, which are offered many times throughout the year, last five days and cost around €3,300, including accommodations. The course might include a day trip to Florence's market and a visit to a nearby sheep farm, as well as extensive hands-on instruction in Tuscan cooking. The school also offers "mini classes" every Friday morning from 10 AM to 3 PM that include a visit to the cellars and a wine tasting. Definitely call or write ahead to reserve for both kinds of classes.

## Culinary Arts

**U.S.: 1324 State St., J-157, Santa Barbara, CA 93101, 805/963-7289**
**Italy: Via del Pelago 11, 53045 Sant'Albino di Montepulciano (SI),**
**  telephone/fax: 0578/798-370**
**www.foodartisans.com**
**email: pamela@foodartisans.com**

Pamela Sheldon Johns, author of a popular series of single-subject cookbooks, including *Parmigiano!* and *Balsamico!*, runs a cooking school in the country near Montepulciano. Students stay at Poggio Etrusco, Johns's restored fifteen-acre estate. Classes last one week and cost US$2,650, including lodging for two, food, wine, and ground transport. The workshops include visits to local farmers' and gourmet markets to highlight basic ingredients; wine tasting in nearby towns; local Italian guest chefs; pizza making; and a farewell dinner at Mondo X (see page 243).

## Tenuta di Capezzana

**Bacioni, Inc.**
**235 East 22nd Street, 9T, New York, NY 10010, 212/ 679-3660;**
**  fax: 646/ 473-0226**
**www.capezzana.it**
**www.bacioni2000.com**
**email: nikki@bacioni2000.com**

Tenuta di Capezzana is best known for its excellent Carmignano and Barco Reale wines. The venerable estate run by the Bonacossi family opens its doors to visitors about a half-dozen times per year for a five-day cooking program headed by Faith Willinger (see page 218). Each program has a theme, such as Summer Bounty or Fall Vegetables. The cost hovers around US$3,000 per person per week, including accommodations. Students might begin by working on pizza and focaccia and then move on to explore kitchen supplies, ingredients, local food artisans, and exceptional restaurants in Florence. Capezzana also offers one-day classes every Tuesday and Thursday featuring a lunch with Capezzana wines and a tour of the estate (these are taught by Patrizio Cirri, not

Willinger). You need a minimum of two people in order to sign up, and the cost is US$200 per person. The estate also has a pool, tennis courts, and hiking and jogging trails.

---

## Toscana Saporita

**Fattoria di Comporomano**
**Piano del Quercione, Massarosa Lucca 55054, 0584/92781 in Italy;**
  **212/219-8791 in New York**
**www.toscanasaporita.com**
**email: toscana@compuserve.com**

Anne Bianchi, author of several cookbooks, including *Italian Festival Food*, *Dolci Toscani*, and *From the Tables of Tuscan Women*, founded this cooking school with her Tuscan cousin Sandra Lotti. The instructors include Lotti and several Americans (many Italian Americans), all experienced chefs and food professionals.

Students come for one-week sessions to live and study in a fifteenth-century villa near Lucca. The classes are relatively small (twelve students maximum), and are taught in English. Emphasis is given to hands-on participation and traditional Tuscan seasonal cooking. The price per person is US$2,450, including accommodations in a double room, all food and wine, sightseeing tours, and pickup and drop off at the Pisa airport or train station. The cost is slightly higher for an advanced cooking course and a wine lover's course. The grounds also have a swimming pool, garden, and nearby hiking trails.

## Apicius
**See page 213.**

## AIS: Associazione Italiana Sommeliers
**Via Giosue Carducci 18, 055/257-1643**
**www.sommelier.it**
**Map H4, Bus C**

If you live in Florence, feel comfortable speaking and taking classes in Italian, and want to expand your knowledge of wine to a professional level, check out the courses offered by the Associazione Italiana Sommeliers (AIS), an official organization that graduates accredited sommeliers. The program includes three levels of classes; one must take an oral exam (including blind tastings) to become accredited as a sommelier, though you can also just take one level. Each level consists of three-hour classes once a week for twelve weeks. The cost is quite reasonable at about €600 per level, as this is aimed at Italians and not foreigners. The trick here is catching the level at the right time; each one is only offered in Florence once every year or so, though if you're mobile you might be able to catch the level you need in a nearby Tuscan city.

The first level course deals with an introduction to the role of the sommelier, the proper service of wine, how to organize a cellar, techniques of wine tasting, and the correct matching of glasses with types of wine. In the second level you delve into domestic and international oenology, wine geography, and a "complete immersion in the sensorial analysis and shared language of wine." The third level takes on ideas of pairing wine and food, and the memorization of the chart for evaluating the taste and smell criteria of both to complement one another.

# FISAR: Federazione Italiana Sommeliers

**Via Ghibellina 117r, 055/264-5201**
**(Patrizia Parretti at Affinity Travel)**
**or Francesca Curcio at 055/832-1477**
**www.fisar.com**
**email: firenze@fisar.com**

This association is very similar to AIS; in fact, it splintered off from it in 1972. They too offer three levels, with ten courses in each level focusing on everything from oenology to viticulture to the proper way to serve and taste wine. There is a strong focus on pairing food and wine, and not surprisingly, on Italian wines in particular. The beginning level always starts in late January so you can complete the whole series by the end of the year; in order to move on to the next level you must pass a final exam. The organization's courses are aimed at Italians and foreigners living in Italy who speak fluent Italian. At the end of the three levels you can take an exam to qualify as an officially designated sommelier. The course locations change from year to year.

FISAR has recently begun a less-intensive program aimed at English-speaking students called Florence Sommelier. The course consists of four lessons: techniques of wine tasting, how wine is made, Tuscan wines, and wine and food pairing. The program costs €150 and includes wine for all four lessons and food for the last lesson.

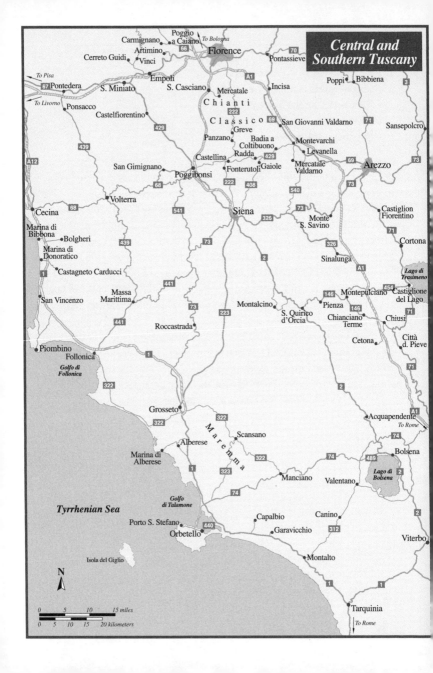

### Central and Southern Tuscany

*To Bologna*
*To Pisa*
*To Livorno*
*To Rome*
*To Rome*

Carmignano, Poggio a Caiano
Artimino
Vinci
Cerreto Guidi
Florence
Pontassieve
Poppi • Bibbiena

Pontedera
Empoli
S. Casciano
Mercatale
Incisa
Sansepolcro

S. Miniato
Ponsacco
C h i a n t i

Castelfiorentino
C l a s s i c o
San Giovanni Valdarno

Panzano
Greve
Badia a Coltibuono
Montevarchi
Levanella
Arezzo

San Gimignano
Castellina
Radda
Fonterutoli
Gaiole
Mercatale Valdarno

Volterra
Poggibonsi
Castiglion Fiorentino

Cecina
Siena
Monte S. Savino
Cortona

Marina di Bibbona • Bolgheri
Lago di Trasimeno

Marina di Donoratico
Sinalunga
Castiglione del Lago

Castagneto Carducci
Massa Marittima
Montalcino
S. Quirico d'Orcia
Montepulciano
Pienza
Chianciano Terme
Chiusi

San Vincenzo
Roccastrada
Città d. Pieve

Piombino
Follonica
Cetona

*Golfo di Follonica*
Grosseto
Acquapendente

M a r e m m a
Scansano
Bolsena

Alberese
Lago di Bolsena

Marina di Alberese
Manciano
Valentano

*Tyrrhenian Sea*
*Golfo di Talamone*
Capalbio
Canino

Porto S. Stefano
Garavicchio
Viterbo

Orbetello

Isola del Giglio
Montalto

Tarquinia

**N**

0    5    10    15 miles
0   5  10  15    20 kilometers

# 12
# CULINARY EXCURSIONS IN TUSCANY

If you want to taste the best that Tuscany has to offer, inevitably you will want to set out from Florence to explore the surrounding region. Some of the best restaurants in Tuscany can be found by the side of the road, in a small hilltop town, or seemingly in the middle of nowhere.

Tuscany covers a large swath of central Italy, bordered by the Apennines in the north, Umbria to the east, the region of Lazio straight south, and the Mediterranean Sea forming a border to the west. When you head toward Umbria, the cooking becomes more rustic, featuring wild game, heavy *ragù* sauces, and in season, prized white truffles. Along the coast you'll find excellent fish and seafood, plus some specialty items like *farinata,* a fried savory snack made from chickpea flour. The rolling hills of Chianti, just south of Florence, offer not only a wealth of wine but also a number of excellent country restaurants featuring simple, delicious Tuscan standards like braised wild boar and fresh *pici.*

In general I'd much rather travel by train than car in Italy; I prefer to read, relax, and leave the driving to some nice man in a conductor's cap and leave the autostrada to the maniacs who want to see what their Fiat Punto can really do when pushed to pass on a curve. Many of the destinations in this chapter can be reached by train or bus. However, I've come around to the reality that in order to see—and eat—the best of Tuscany, you need to have a car at least part of the time. With a car, you'll make short work of the curving country roads of Chianti, wandering from one winery to another. And you'll be able to reach that obscure enoteca or cheese shop that everyone's talking about without spending half your day looking mournfully into the distance for signs of the big blue SITA bus.

From Florence, you can hit the A1 Autostrada or a smaller, more scenic road and immediately you're in Greve, you're in Bolgheri, you're in Arezzo, trying out a little bit of what the rest of Tuscany has to offer.

## 1. WHITE TRUFFLES AND THE PIERO TRAIL IN EASTERN TUSCANY

Around Florence and Rome, you'll sometimes hear travelers talking about following the Piero Trail. Piero della Francesca was one of the finest painters of the fifteenth century, his work a kind of prelude to the coming sophistication of depth, color, and delicate features of Leonardo da Vinci. Part of Piero's allure is that so few of his works remain and you must travel to see them, as they are concentrated in a corner of eastern Tuscany and western Umbria. This book is about food, but there's nothing wrong with picking up a little culture before or after a meal—this is Italy, after all. One of my favorite restaurants, Da Ventura, happens to be in Sansepolcro, the birthplace of Piero and home to some of his finest works.

Visitors do not need a car to reach Arezzo or Sansepolcro, where Piero's greatest works are located; trains leave nearly hourly from Florence to Arezzo, and from there frequent buses traverse the hilly countryside toward the smaller walled town of Sansepolcro. There is also a small train line that runs from Perugia (in Umbria) to Sansepolcro, though it does not run very often.

---

### Da Ventura
**Via Niccolò Aggiunti 30, Sansepolcro, 0575/742-560**
**Open Tuesday through Saturday 12:30 PM to 2:15 PM and 7:30 PM to 10:30 PM;**
    **Sunday 12:30 PM to 2 PM; closed most of August and Christmas Day**
**Credit cards accepted**
**€€**

The first time I ate at Da Ventura, the experience left such an indelible impression on my gustatory memory that I was set on returning, which I did about four years later. Most meals would suffer under these conditions of fantasy and memory, but Da Ventura was, if anything, better on subsequent visits.

The atmosphere is simple and unassuming, with tablecloths and fine drinking glasses the only nods toward elegance; caricatures of Italian celebrities line the wood-paneled walls. The elderly owners who used to greet diners at the entrance are now retired and the restaurant is run by their children, who have changed a few menu items and keep the restaurant open on Saturdays, but otherwise have left things much the same.

One image that lingered in my memory from the first visit was of big platters of *porchetta* (herbed pork cooked on a spit) and pasta with truffles served family-style from a rolling cart, and sure enough the cart still makes an appearance tableside. My second visit was in November, white truffle season, and along with the rest of my group, I could not resist the tagliatelle topped only with clarified butter and the prized white truffle shaved directly onto it at table. (This isn't the only way to enjoy the prized fungus, however; an old man in sweatpants and a misshapen hat at a nearby table ate a simple meal of two fried eggs with truffles, followed by the same tagliatelle.)

If you arrive outside of truffle season, don't despair; all the offerings here are delicious. You might try the gnocchi with spinach and ricotta as a primo, and an outstandingly juicy and savory veal steak for two as a secondo. After the filling tagliatelle, I was satisfied with a lighter plate of veal carpaccio with arugula and Parmesan shavings. The wine list is full of well-priced bottles, including several choices of Nobile di Montepulciano and Umbrian wines. Da Ventura can accommodate big groups with its many long tables, though you should reserve in advance, as always.

■ ■ ■

**Sansepolcro** is a small, relaxed, and genteel town where you can happily pass a day. Aside from Da Ventura, its claim to fame is its **Museo Civico** (Via Niccolò Aggiunti 65, 0575/732-218; open daily 9:30 AM to 1:30 PM and 2:30 PM to 6:30 PM), home to two of the finest paintings by Piero della Francesca. The museum houses the *Madonna della Misericordia,* which shows members of the patrons' confraternity gathered under the Virgin's outspread cloak; and the *Resurrection,* painted in fresco for the nearby town hall in the 1450s and later detached and moved to the present site.

Located in the nearby town of **Arezzo,** Piero's masterwork, a fresco cycle depicting the *Legend of the True Cross,* was under restoration and out of public view for nearly a decade. (It was supposed to be finished for the five-hundredth anniversary of Piero's death in 1992, but the scaffolding stayed on until the late 1990s.) Fortunately, it is now back on glorious display in **the church of San Francesco.** You need to reserve a time slot to see the frescoes by calling the Centro Prenotazione (0575/240-01); you then pick up your tickets at Piazza San Francesco at the ticket office right next to the church. Viewers are allowed in only for fifteen-minute allotments. Pick up an audio guide (gratis) and let the gazing begin. When you're done, head across the street to refuel with a coffee or an *aperitivo* at the lovely Viennese-style **Caffè dei Costanti** (Piazza San Francesco 19).

Arezzo has had its brushes with fame: Piero's fresco cycle (a copy of it) was featured in the film *The English Patient,* and Roberto Benigni walked the streets of this, his hometown, in the movie *Life Is Beautiful.* The poet Petrarch and the sixteenth-century painter, architect, and historian Giorgio Vasari were born here, both still constant sources of pride to the local population. Arezzo is truly the epitome of an aesthetically pleasing and comfortably bourgeois Tuscan town. It is also a major antiques center, and every first Saturday and Sunday of the month an outdoor fair seems to take over half the city.

Those who are really dedicated in their quest for a comprehensive Piero binge will drive to the nearby tiny town of **Monterchi** just to see his strikingly unusual *Madonna del Parto.* The work is no longer in its original location; it is on display in a darkened, temperature-controlled room on Via Reglia. (Contradictory signs might have you going in circles, but don't worry, the town is so small you're bound to wind up here.) This painting is important as one of the only depictions of Mary as a pregnant woman, without the conventions of a Visitation scene. The fresco is worse for wear, but the beatific look on Mary's face transcends the passage of time.

## Follow That Food Fair

Throughout the year, but especially in the warmer months, you will begin to see brightly colored posters around Florence announcing *sagre* of various kinds, food fairs celebrating the local cuisines of Tuscany. You'll find the Sagra del Cinghiale (Festival of the Wild Boar), Sagra del Fungo Porcino (Festival of the Porcini Mushroom), and *sagre* for everything from fried pork chops to handmade pasta.

The one caveat is that these *sagre* are often in small towns on the outskirts of Florence that are reached with difficulty sans car. Once you arrive, the fairs are pretty much what you would imagine: casual, whole-hog celebrations of food with booths of different producers and purveyors offering their wares. Sometimes you pay a small entrance fee and other times you only pay for what you eat. In general, I find this systematic celebration of food a beautiful thing, another reminder of the prominence still given to local foods in Italian culture.

The exact dates and locations of the *sagre* change from year to year, so keep an eye out for the posters and take it from there. For more information contact the Tuscany tourism office at Via di Novoli 26, 055/438-2111, fax: 055/438-3084.

**Sagra della Frittella** (fritter)
Sambuca di Tavernelle Val
  di Pesa, near Florence
Mid-May

**Sagra del Tartufo** (truffle
mushroom)
Rignano sull'Arno, near
  Florence
Early July

**Sagra del Cinghiale**
Borgo San Lorenzo
Mid-July

**Sagra delle Pappardelle**
Montespetoli
End of August, beginning
  of September

**Sagra dei Tortelli** (potato-
stuffed ravioli)
Scarperia
End of August

**Sagra Funghi e Polenta**
Montramito, near Lucca
Mid-July

## 2. DA DELFNA AND THE
## MEDICI VILLAS

If you have a car, you might take a day and head to three Medici Villas, the town of Carmignano (home of great wines and a Pontormo masterpiece), and an excellent restaurant at the edge of an unreconstructed hill town, all within reach about forty minutes northwest of Florence.

Beginning in the mid-fifteenth century, the ruling Medici family established several country residences dotting the hills around Florence, though the heyday of Medici villa–building was in the late sixteenth century. Probably the most impressive to visit today is **Poggio a Caiano** (Piazza de' Medici 14, 055/877-012; open daily 9 AM to 4:30 PM, but the closing time changes frequently), well hidden behind a wall in the town of the same name (look out for a tiny placard reading *ingresso*). Once inside the courtyard, you're confronted with a grand manicured lawn and the Renaissance palace, fronted by a dramatic curved double stairway and Greek-style pediment (the first private home to incorporate one) with a terra-cotta frieze of mythological subjects. The inside is largely furnished, but not from Medici times. King Vittorio Emanuele II lived here for five years in the nineteenth century when Florence was briefly made the capital of Italy after unification. The most important thing to see is the grand Sala del Leone, covered with an impressive fresco cycle of Roman histories and mythological scenes painted by Andrea del Sarto, Franciabiagio, and Iacopo Pontormo between 1519 and 1521 and finished over half a century later (in a more mannerist style) by Alessandro Allori. Another room is graced with an almost comical ceiling fresco from the late seventeenth century showing Medici patriarch Cosimo the Elder being presented by an allegorical symbol of the city of Florence to the god Jove in heaven.

Next you can head to the sleepy, pretty little town of **Carmignano**, better known as an excellent appellation of wine, to see an important and stunning Pontormo altarpiece, *The Visitation*, in the church of San Michele. The painting (realized in the late 1520s) is of four women: Mary and Elizabeth, pregnant with Jesus and John the Baptist, respectively, and their older maidservants. Pontormo's vision of the visitation is an intimate and affectionate gathering, notable for the tranquil beauty of the

*A view of the Medici Villa from Artimino.*

faces (Mary and Elizabeth in profile, their maidservants directly facing the viewer), and the substantial figures draped in the vividly colored flowing garments for which the painter is well known. The women form a circle that seems to almost float in front of the obscure dark background of a narrow street in a quiet hill town.

Across from the small hill town of **Artimino,** the **Villa Medicea La Ferdinanda** (Viale Papa Giovanni XXIII 1, 055/875-1427) cuts a striking figure. This former hunting lodge designed by Bernardo Buontalenti in the last decade of the sixteenth century is now a privately owned villa that can be rented for private and corporate functions. Though it is not open to visitors, you can wander the grounds and admire the villa, with its plethora of jutting chimneys, or better yet stay in the former stables, now a swanky inn called **Paggeria Medicea** (055/875-141). The stable building houses an impressive restaurant, **Biagio Pignatta** (055/875-1406). The villa also produces a fine group of Carmignano wines under the Fattoria di Artimino label.

## Da Delfina

**Via della Chiesa 1, Artimino, 055/871-8119**

**Open Tuesday through Saturday 12:30 PM to 3 PM and 8:30 PM to 10 PM;**
**Sunday 12:30 PM to 3 PM; closed August**

**No credit cards**

€€€

At the edge of Artimino sits a stone farmhouse with a large patio overlooking a deep green valley across to the Medici Villa on the other side. This is Da Delfina, a quintessential Tuscan country restaurant: scenic, rustic, regional . . . the real thing. (It also provided inspiration for the name and menu at the acclaimed restaurant Delfina in San Francisco.)

To start the meal you are served a glass of local pink *spumante,* which complements starters like *crostini* of chicken liver and caramelized cherry tomatoes, a classic mixed *salumi* sampling, or a *sformato di ceci,* a deliciously light little soufflé of chickpeas. No matter what your feeling may be regarding *ribollita,* you must try the version here—a thick stew that is then

*Chef-owner Carlo Cioni of Da Delfina.*

grilled, bringing out the flavor of the beans and *cavolo nero*. The home-made *pappardelle* with rabbit *ragù* is also terrific. For secondi, try the *fritto misto* of chicken, meat, and veggies, each fried with a different batter; there is more than enough to share. A plate of young goat chops also comes with a side of irresistible fried vegetables, of which the zucchini and arti-chokes are especially good. If you order the succulent rabbit cooked with olives and pine nuts, no whistles or buzzers go off, but at the end of your meal you'll be given a special commemorative plate.

Da Delfina has now been written up in several guidebooks and maga-zines, but it is definitely not pandering to tourists. The menu is in Italian and credit cards are not taken. The town is hard to find at the end of a very windy road; this plus the extraordinary view make Delfina a better choice for lunch than dinner, when you would miss the view and have to navigate the hairy road in the dark.

■ ■ ■

Continuing on the villa tour, a quick stop is all that's needed at the Medici Villa in **Cerreto Guidi** (Via dei Ponti Medicei 7, 0571/55705; call for hours), also designed by Buontalenti. Not as grand or exciting as the other two villas, it is nonetheless the site of a grisly family murder: Isabella de' Medici, daughter of Duke Cosimo, was strangled by her husband here in 1576. Today the bare villa, reached via an enormous double ramp in front, leads to a small but elegant little trellised garden.

While in this area, you might want to stop in the nearby hill town of **Vinci** to see the small museum and birthplace of Leonardo, the town's most famous son. The **Museo Leonardiano** is located in Palazzina Uzielli (Piazza Conti Guidi; open daily 9:30 AM to 7 PM); for more information call 0571/568-012. None of Leonardo's few works remain in Vinci, nor are the Vinci sights essential visiting for those strapped for time. It does, however, remain a lovely village, beautifully situated along the ridge of a hill above the small Streda River.

## 3. A Food and Wine Tour of Chianti

The green and hilly area between Florence and Siena could hardly be more beautiful. This is what people are thinking of when they get that faraway look in their eyes and wax poetic about the Tuscan countryside: mile after mile of undulating hillside vineyards and olive groves occasionally interrupted by a sixteenth-century farmhouse, and navigable by the kind of winding country roads that make people go out and buy expensive cars. The map of this unspoiled terrain reads like a local wine list; every town evokes a vision of labels: Fonterutoli, Lamole, Olena, Querceto, and on and on. In an agricultural area with such good wine, you are bound to find equally impressive food, and Chianti does not disappoint, featuring any number of welcoming country restaurants and famous butchers selling the Chianina beef and signature *salumi* of this area.

Until a few years ago, the concept of oeno-tourism was unknown here, and seemed as odd to locals as someone asking to visit the cows on the farm. The wineries of Chianti have made dramatic leaps in allowing people to visit and taste the wares. Still, Chianti is no Napa, set up from top to bottom for tourists, and that's probably for the best. The drawback is that you will often arrive at a winery to find that the owners are having their lunch/are closed/are busy/don't do tastings/don't do tastings for small groups/don't do tastings on the first Saturday of the month/or simply don't like the look of you! This means that you are likely to spend a decent amount of time driving and enjoying the views without a lot of actual wine tasting and winery touring. To minimize wasted time, try to call in advance and make an appointment; otherwise, try to visit wineries on a weekday and in the morning, when many more of them are open. Some wineries will charge you for the tour and/or extensive tastings, but no matter where you are, it should not be too expensive. Happily, many Chianti wineries sell their wares directly to customers at a slight discount.

**Greve** is the heart of the Chianti region and its biggest city, though still a relatively small and tranquil place. The charmed, colonnaded triangle of Piazza Matteotti lies at its center, where you'll find four or five trattorias, a gelateria, one of Tuscany's best butcher shops, and a statue of local son Giovanni da Verrazzano, navigator and early explorer of North America's Atlantic coast.

If you're hungry for lunch, stop at **Nerbone a Greve** (Piazza Matteotti 22, 055/855-308; €), owned by the same foodie family that dishes out *bollito* sandwiches at Florence's Central Market and excellent Tuscan fare at Trattoria Vecchia Bettola (see page 75). You can order a *bollito* at the bar or sit down and enjoy a hearty pasta with peas and sausage, a Tuscan peasant bean soup, or even something lighter, like a chicken salad, all washed down with local wine.

Across the piazza, pilgrims from all over the world come to peruse the pork products at **Antica Macelleria Falorni** (Piazza Matteotti 69, 055/853-029, www.falorni.it), often credited with reintroducing Chianina beef back into the Tuscan food scene. Several menacing stuffed *cinghiali* keep watch over the vast expanse of musky salami, cured meats, fresh meats, and cheeses. Here you'll find every variation of salami, made from pork, boar, and the special pig called Cinta Senese (see page 22). They also stock vacuum-packed prosciutto and *bresaola,* and from behind an L-shaped butcher's counter sell fresh Chianina beef, milk-fed veal, and local chickens. The cheese is all pecorino, but this place seems to be in continual expansion; by my next visit I wouldn't be surprised to find a more varied cheese cave. The meats here are certainly top quality, especially if you are thinking of making a picnic while in Chianti.

If you want to see the full gamut of Chianti's viticultural output, plan a stop at **Le Cantine di Greve in Chianti** (Piazza delle Cantine, just after the footbridge into town, 055/854-6404; open daily 10 AM to 7 PM), which boasts the biggest selection of wines in Chianti, plus a nice assortment of extra virgin oils, *vin santo,* and other local goods.

On the third weekend of September, the towns of Greve and Panzano jointly hold a wine festival called **Vino al Vino,** with festivities taking place in both towns. For more information call the Greve tourism office, 055/854-51.

Driving south into town from Florence to Greve you'll pass the **Castello di Verrazzano** winery (Route 222, right side of road coming south, 055/853-211; closed December and January), where you can stop for a tasting of Chianti Classico wine, *vin santo,* olive oil, or honey at their roadside store, or, if you're there at the right time, explore the castle and wine cellars.

Less accessible but worth the detour is the **Castello di Querceto** winery (Via Dudda, on the road between Greve and Dudda, 055/859-21; open 9 AM to 5 PM), makers of highly respected Chianti Classico vintages. The castle and beatific grounds (complete with strolling peacocks) are set in isolated splendor on top of a hill, next to acres of sloping vines. Call in advance to set up a tasting, or better yet, stay in one of their *agriturismo* apartments for a night or two.

A short drive south from Greve you'll arrive in the small town of **Panzano**. Up a short hill in the center of town you'll find **Antica Macelleria Cecchini** (Via XX Luglio 11, 055/852-020, macelleriacecchini@tin.it; open Sunday through Tuesday, and Thursday, 9 AM to 2 PM; Saturday and Sunday 9 AM to 6 PM), presided over by Dario Cecchini, beaming like a bull in a red neck bandana behind his pristine meat case. "I'm going to Washington soon," he exclaimed on a recent visit, "and I am going to eat a whole cow!" At this he mugs for the visitors in the shop and gives a mischievous cackle. This is a man who loves meat. His shop is the sanctum sanctorum of the cow and the pig. Cecchini has a flair for the dramatic: he likes to quote Dante at length and rhapsodize about famous friends and acquaintances around the world. His cultivated image as celebrity butcher would ring hollow, however, if he didn't back it up with such extraordinary products. While classical music wafts through his shop, you can help yourself to tastes of his incredible *porchetta, finocchiona* salami, and Parmesan dipped in his signature sweet-and-spicy pepper jelly. No, that fluffy white mountain inside the case isn't mashed potatoes, it's lard—or as one German tourist indicated to me with a sly smile, schmaltz. And you can taste that as well, spiked with herbs and spread on little toasts. Of course you can also buy pork, lamb, and a huge selection of beef cuts, all overseen by Cecchini more or less from cradle to case. This is one butcher shop, and one butcher, unlike any other that you're likely to experience. On Sunday mornings the shop offers a "brunch" in a small adjoining room, but when pressed for details on the menu, he responded, "Look, we're a butcher shop, not a restaurant, we're serving meat."

Continuing on the main road south from Panzano, keep an eye out on the left-hand side for a small sign reading **Tenuta Fontodi** (Via San Leolino 87, 055/852-005, fontodi@dada.it; open daily 8 AM to 12:30 PM and 2 PM to 6 PM). Fontodi is one of the stars of the Chianti region; their Chianti

Classicos consistently receive high praise, and their expensive all-Sangiovese Flaccianello della Pieve is a constant among Supertuscans. You'll find a small tasting room where you can sample, gratis, some of their Chiantis, perhaps a white wine, as well as their excellent olive oil and *vin santo*. The Flaccianello doesn't make it into the tasting lineup too often, so you might have to buy a bottle in order to partake. Fontodi also offers lovely rooms in which to stay on the same estate, a great option among *agriturismi* in the area.

Beyond Panzano, eventually the road splits and you have a choice of heading east toward Radda or west to **Castellina**. Castellina is the more charming and slightly bigger of the two, a thoroughly medieval little village filled with wine shops and bars. It's a nice place simply to walk around and stop in at **Cantina Orlandi del Gallo Nero** (Piazza del Commune 13, 0577/741-110; open daily 10 AM to 1 PM and 4 PM to 7:30 PM). You'll find some of the big names of the Chianti and Montepulciano regions (Castello di Ama, Felsina), as well as many of the smaller producers from the hills right around Castellina. The selection is small but well chosen; I like to stop here to chat with Franco, the northern Italian who manages the place (he speaks fluent English and German) and taste the various wines of the day.

About ten minutes farther south of Castellina you'll come across the tiny town of **Fonterutoli,** where if you blink you'll miss the turn-off for the winery and restaurant of the same name. Like Fontodi, Fonterutoli (Via Ottone III di Sassonia 5, 0577/740-212, fonterutoli@fonterutoli.it; open daily 12:30 PM to 1:30 PM and 7:30 PM to 9:30 PM) is another star of the region, consistently winning the coveted Tre Bicchieri (Three Glasses) award from *Gambero Rosso* for their Supertuscan called Siepi, a mixture of Sangiovese and Merlot. Their Chianti Classico and Poggio alla Badiola are also highly praised. You can buy bottles in their small store, or eat a simple Tuscan meal at their unpretentious trattoria on the same road.

If you drive toward the tiny market town of Gaiole in Chianti, you'll pass Coltibuono. Follow the signs to **Badia a Coltibuono** (Loc. Badia a Coltibuono, 0577/ 744-832), a former abbey that's now a winery best known for its reliable Chianti Classico. The casual and elegant restaurant and wine bar have been tastefully redone and occupy an unbeatable setting overlooking surrounding green hillsides. A glass of wine here or a meal outdoors is to partake in the Tuscan good life. Guided tours of the wine cellar and abbey are offered from 2:30 PM to 4:30 PM, every half hour, from May to October. Call ahead to arrange wine or olive oil tastings (for groups of ten or more), or cooking classes (see page 219).

If you are touring Chianti as a day trip and plan to drive back to Florence at night, you might want to eat somewhere close to the city, such as San Casciano or **Mercatale**. Mercatale is a nondescript town, rebuilt in modern times, and not much worth visiting except to eat at **Tiratappi** (Via Sonnino 92, 055/821-8016; open Thursday through Tuesday 7:30 PM to 10:30 PM; credit cards accepted, €€), an intimate restaurant run by three young and enthusiastic partners. The food is Tuscan with slight twists. Start off with the outstanding *frittelline di pecorino con le pere* (delicious little fried balls of pear and pecorino) and a plate of mixed *bruschetta*. Continue with very fresh gnocchi of spinach and ricotta topped with cherry tomatoes, or *penette* with blue cheese and fried zucchini. Secondi are a little less exciting than the first half of the meal, but I would recommend the roast meats, sliced beef with balsamic vinegar, or pork topped with a bay leaf infusion. The signature dessert is a *zuccotino di gianduia,* a kind of semifreddo filled with chocolate-hazelnut goo. The wine list, as you might expect in this part of the world, includes plenty of superb choices at fine prices, and even gives short and interesting descriptions of each one (in Italian). We ended up with a full-bodied Chianti Classico from Macchiavelli, another Tre Bicchieri winner.

## 4. MONTALCINO, MONTEPULCIANO, PIENZA, AND MONDO X

Back when the term *Supertuscan* had yet to be coined and Chianti was served in bulging straw-covered flasks, the winemakers south of Siena had a head start on the rest of Tuscany due to the tradition of high quality— instead of just quantity—barrel-aged Brunello di Montalcino and Nobile di Montepulciano. And with the general tide that raised all boats in the 1980s, these wines, led by makers such as Avignonesi in Montepulciano and Col d'Orcia in Montalcino, became even better.

As in the Chianti region slightly to the north, where there's good wine you will also find good food. Many of the wineries of the area also serve hearty rustic meals in farmhouse settings to complement their full-bodied wines; and nearby Pienza, a pristine fifteenth-century hill town remade by a pope in his own image, is known for its excellent pecorino cheeses. This area is what Tuscan dreams are made of, blanketed with vines and olive trees growing on sloping sunlit hillsides. In this same region, in the hills just east of the town of Cetona, is a thirteenth-century Franciscan monastery that has been transformed into a sanctuary of extraordinary food as well as spritual rehabilitation.

## *Montalcino*

If you are coming south from Florence or Siena, head first to Montalcino, a pleasant if not altogether arresting hill town, built fortress-style for strategic purposes back in the days when catapulting boiling oil on your enemies was often a serious option. Now they have better uses for oil around here.

Just outside of town you'll find **Fattoria dei Barbi** (Loc. Podernuovi 170, 0577/848-277; www.fattoriadeibarbi.it), a full-service winery in every sense. You can eat lunch or dinner at their excellent restaurant, which features the outstanding Barbi *salumi; pici,* a local specialty pasta  and plenty of wild game. Of course this kind of heavy food goes extremely well with a bottle of their Brunello. When you're done, take a tour of the wine cellars where they age the Brunello in both French oak barriques and the bigger Slavic barrels. They also give selected tastings and sell bottles in the winery shop. In addition, they have a few apartments for rent by the week. The tasting room and tours go from 10 AM to 1 PM and 2:30 PM to 6 PM.

While in the area, you might want to stop in and visit other makers of fine Brunello, such as **Biondi-Santi** (Via Panfilo d'Oca, Montalcino, 0577/848-087). Tours of the cantina and tastings of their wines are by appointment only, but it's worth the trouble for the serious Brunello lover.

**Col d'Orcia** (Sant'Angelo in Colle, just outside Montalcino, 0577/808-011), famous for its fine Brunello, welcomes visitors for tastings only at the store on-site, which is open Monday through Saturday 8:30 AM to 10:30 AM and 2:30 PM to 6 PM. Unfortunately, no tours are given of the grounds and cellars.

*Visitors strolling through the arched gates of Pienza.*

## Pienza

About halfway between the two wine capitals of Montalcino and Montepulciano is Pienza, a town as systematically thought through in its creation as you are ever likely to see and which, because of its small scale and rural locale, completely retains its frozen-in-time aspect. Pienza was conceived and built in the fifteenth century under the auspices of Pope Pius II, who hailed from the small town that already stood here, then called Corsignano. A modest pontiff (he renamed the town after himself), but possessing good taste, he engaged architect Bernando Rossellino, a contemporary of Leon Battista Alberti, to oversee the building of stately Renaissance palaces and piazze. You can step into the Duomo, take a good look around the Palazzo Piccolomini next door, and stop to marvel at the geometric equilibrium achieved in this piazza, a model for many future Renaissance projects.

Aside from its architecture, Pienza is known for one thing: pecorino cheese. Pienza and the hills around it are the center of quality pecorino production in Tuscany, and all through the town and along the highways you'll see round after round of the pungent cheese for sale. Pecorino di Pienza is a cheese made of ewe's milk—usually pasteurized—shaped in smallish rounds and aged for various amounts of time to create a range of cheeses from fresh and light to hard and tart. The outer rind is sometimes covered in a dried tomato paste or ash, but this doesn't affect the flavor. Pecorino goes extremely well with pears as well as green apples; I also like to eat aged pecorino with a tangy *mostarda* or other sweet-spicy sauce, and it pairs nicely with the local full-bodied red wines. You will find delicious cheeses to buy both in Pienza, at the shops lining the main street, or on the farms in the surrounding hills.

Not far from Pienza, close to the slightly bigger towns of Trequanda and Sinalunga, is **Montisi**, a village so small it's not even marked on most maps. But in Italy one-horse towns often house two-star restaurants. **La Romita** (Via Umberto 1, 144, Montisi, 0577/854-186, fax: 0577/845-201; credit cards accepted, €€€) is not actually a Michelin star restaurant, but they are cooking sophisticated meals worthy of acclaim far beyond this tiny village. If you can, sit outside on the *terrazza* overlooking a typically stunning Tuscan valley. The interior is also pleasant, decorated with frescoes and an odd assortment of bric-a-brac. You can order either à la carte or from a choice of tasting menus. The *menu leggero* (light menu) consists of an antipasto, three small primi, and a dessert, whereas the *menu di campagna* (country menu) includes an antipasto, three primi, and two secondi, not to mention dessert if you have room for it. The antipasto is a large plate of unusual *crostini,* colorfully presented and topped with tomatoes, cheeses, *salumi,* liver pâté, onions, and lots of local olive oil. The kitchen focuses on old Tuscan dishes that have been largely forgotten, making use of porcini mushrooms and other delicacies. Secondi are mainly simple grilled and roasted meats scented with rosemary and thyme. The wine list is heavy on the old-school Tuscan labels, staying consistent with the theme. Service is extremely sober and solicitous; the owner is likely also to be your waiter. In addition to the superb kitchen, La Romita is a comfortable place to spend the night and enjoy their idyllic swimming pool.

### Montepulciano

In and around Montepulciano you can get your fill of Nobile di Montepulciano, second only to Brunello in this part of the world. It is made from a slight variation of the Sangiovese variety used in Brunello, but Nobile contains a small percentage of other varietals and is aged for a shorter time than Brunello, which usually renders it somewhat more affordable. The streets of hilly, medieval Montepulciano practically flow red with wine, and you'll find little *cantinette* all over the place offering wine to taste and buy.

While in the region, you might want to stop in at **Poliziano** (Loc. Montepulciano Stazione, Via Fontago 1, 0578/738-171, Az.agr.poliziano@iol.it), owned by Federico Carletti, which makes several refined Nobiles, as well as a Rosso and a Morellino di Scansano. They age most of their wines in small French oak barrels, giving them an elegant finish. You can tour the winery from 8:30 AM to 12:30 PM and 2:30 PM to 6:30 PM, except for Saturday and Sunday mornings. The winery also runs **Caffè Poliziano** (Via Voltaio del Corso 27, 0578/758-615; open daily 7 AM to midnight) in the center of town, where you can get a light bite to eat or a glass of their excellent wines.

## Mondo X

Imagine indulging in an outstanding eight-course tasting menu in an elegantly refurbished thirteenth-century Franciscan monastery high in the leafy hills near Montepulciano. Adding to the surreal experience, most of the food is grown and served by young recovering alcoholics and drug addicts who are part of Mondo X, a chain of spiritually focused rehab centers run by a charismatic Catholic priest named Padre Eligio. Yes, the whole thing is a little unreal, but also an unforgettable experience.

---

### La Frateria di Padre Eligio

**Convento St. Francesco, Cetona, 0578/238-261; fax: 0578/239-220**
**email: frateria@ftbcc.it**
**www.mondox.it**
**Open Wednesday through Monday 1 PM to 3PM and 8 PM to 10 PM**
**Credit cards accepted**
**€€€€**

Though officially La Frateria bears no Michelin stars, it is certainly on the level of the best restaurants in Italy in terms of food and service, and surpasses most of them in atmosphere and history. The elegant dining room, softened by fresh flowers and linens, is built into the old stones of the monastery, allegedly founded by St. Francis himself. The staff is made up of members of the Mondo X community, all immaculately groomed young men, who lead you to your table and proceed to serve the food and wine with care and attention. The star here, however, is chef Walter Tripoli, who has studied with master chefs in Piedmont and Paris, but seems to feel most at home with Tuscan traditions taken to a higher plane. The assorted dishes on his tasting menu show a sophistication rarely seen in Florence, but maintain the rustic flavor and flourish that distinguishes the unfussy cooking of this region.

Much of the fare—including the *spumante* served as an *aperitivo,* most of the vegetables, and even the meats—is made from ingredients grown and raised by the Mondo X communities. The meal begins with *spumante* and a platter of outstanding salami and prosciutto. The first few dishes are small and artfully presented, often with fish or poultry, and best accompanied with a white wine such as a Tufa di Greco from

Campania. Antipasti and primi might include a delicate whole smoked trout; a terrine of rabbit, prunes, and pine nuts that terrifically combines savory and sweet; and a more assertive orzo timbale with capers and green sauce.

Moving on to slightly heavier food, we were served wild boar ravioli in a smoked duck sauce in which the ravioli themselves were delicately striped like the Duomo of Siena. The secondo consisted of a very tender, barely seared fillet of beef in a light peppercorn sauce. Desserts are mercifully light here; if you still have room, you'll be able to enjoy the lemon sorbet with strawberry sauce or a similar confection, followed by a selection of excellent and original little cookies, each one different from the others.

A meal here is not cheap—around €80 per person—but the wine list is extremely reasonable, offering an excellent range of choices for under €25 a bottle on up to many of the fanciest vintages from the region. Plus, this is a complete experience, hardly comparable to dining at an ordinary fancy eatery in the city center. Either before or after your meal, ask to be taken on a tour of the monastery grounds as well as the cantina where they keep the wines. There are a few rooms (formerly monks' cells) that have been refurbished as an inn where guests can stay and enjoy the grounds and hospitality; they cost just under €200 per night.

## 5. Outlet Shopping and Good Food Around Montevarchi

A gaggle of tour buses gathers outside a long, low modern building amid the industrial clutter and lush green hillsides of the Valdarno area about thirty miles southeast of Florence. Taxis pour out a rush of avid visitors; rental cars and even people on foot gather around the guarded entrance. If it's a weekend, you'll probably have to take a number and wait for ten or fifteen minutes while chatting with other eager attendees. What is this mysterious structure? A modern art museum? A repository of Tuscan treasures from Giotto to Vasari? Not at all. This is the Prada outlet, and the giddiness of anticipation of those outside is a consumer frenzy in its purest manifestation. Travelers from Kyoto, Kansas, London, and Toronto can't wait to come inside and shop.

The small villages along the valley with their factories and industrial detritus have spawned a new kind of tourism in Italy. People now plan a trip to Prada, Gucci, and Dolce & Gabbana along with visits to the *David* and the Uffizi. Prices at these factory outlets are usually about 50 percent off retail (which is usually still quite expensive), though you can find even deeper discounts on certain items, especially at the very end of a season. I've seen women and men walk out with half a dozen bags, overflowing with shoes, purses, and all kinds of other booty.

The **Prada outlet**, also called **Space**, or **I Pellettieri d'Italia** (Route 69, 055/919-6528) is unmarked and thus difficult to find, just past the town of **Montevarchi** in a suburb called Levanella. Once you're in Levanella, keep your eye out for a long, low white building on your left; it's very likely you'll drive by it the first time, but don't worry—gas station attendants and *bariste* all over the area are used to pointing people in the right direction. The outlet is open Monday through Saturday 9:30 AM to 7:30 PM, Sunday 2 PM to 7:30 PM. In addition to the flagship Prada label, the outlet sells designs by Miu Miu, Helmut Lang, and Jil Sander. There is a café next door for coffee breaks.

If you want to hit the other outlets along this stretch, you will need to rent a car, as they are all in different towns right off the A1 Autostrada, but not accessible by train. If you are interested only in the Prada outlet, your least expensive and easiest choice of transport is to take a local train from Florence to Montevarchi (many trains heading in the direction of Arezzo stop there) and then a taxi from the station to the outlet. The short taxi ride will likely cost more than the train, but less than a luxury ride from Florence.

The **Dolce & Gabbana factory outlet** (Loc. S. Maria Maddalena, 49 Pian dell'Isola, Incisa, 055/833-1300; open Monday through Saturday 9 AM to 7 PM) is said to offer excellent deals, especially for men's clothing. You can also hit **The Mall** (Via Europa 8, 055/865-7775; open Monday through Saturday 10 AM to 7 PM; Sunday 3 PM to 7 PM) in Leccio Regello, which has outlets for Gucci, Giorgio Armani, Bottega Veneta, and Yves Saint Laurent.

Getting away from the fashion world, the designer glass manufacturer **IVV** has a factory store in the same vicinity (Lungarno Guido Reni 60,

055/944-444; open Monday through Saturday 9 AM to 1 PM and 4 PM to 8 PM; closed Monday morning) in San Giovanni Valdarno. Unfortunately, you won't find deep discounts on its selection of both elegant and more casual vases, Champagne glasses, and glass serving dishes, though it does have a larger selection than stores in Florence offering its wares, and it also has discounts on selected end-of-season items.

---

## Osteria di Rendola

**Via di Rendola 81, in the hills between Montevarchi and Mercatale Valdarno,**
**055/970-7490**
**Open daily 12:30 PM to 2 PM and 7:30 PM to 10 PM**
**Credit cards accepted**
**€€€**

Osteria di Rendola, set in the hills above Montevarchi, is fast becoming known as one of the top restaurants in Tuscany. Chef Francesco Berardinelli, also responsible for the kitchen at Beccofino (see page 45), opened this place and developed the menu. The kitchen is no longer in his hands, but the confident way in which Rendola combines the best aspects of Tuscan cuisine with judiciously used foreign ingredients and techniques is brilliant.

A meal might start with an *amuse-bouche* of delicate Parmesan flan topped with fresh tomato sauce, accompanied by a refreshing glass of *spumante.* The antipasto choices are all appealing, particularly the tuna tartare with baby vegetables and sesame oil and the beef carpaccio with chopped celery and chunks of Parmesan. The Asian-influenced tartare is beyond good, the raw pink fish absolutely fresh and buttery.

Primi are all more Italian in flavor, though still innovative. You can choose from dishes such as a spring risotto made with mussels, zucchini, and basil, or a *tortelli* stuffed with pigeon and topped with fava beans and pecorino, bathed in a succulent beef demi-glace. Secondi range from classic dishes such as a steak with salted potatoes and red wine sauce to slightly more unusual dishes like a saddle of rabbit wrapped in herbs and served with spinach and ricotta flan, or the slightly heavier lamb chops. In Florentine restaurants rabbit is often cooked beyond recognition and then drowned in heavy sauce, but here it was perfectly done.

For dessert the irresistible crème brûlée made with *farro*, the local peasant grain, is a perfect representation of the blending of old and new Tuscan cooking traditions, the kernels of *farro* giving the custard a little added texture. Also delicious is a mousse made of chocolate and hazelnut, always a winning combination.

In addition to being a restaurant, La Rendola is an *agriturismo* and a burgeoning winery. The wine list begins with a page of the Rendola offerings, followed by extensive listings of wines from Tuscany and Piedmont, a very small number from the rest of Italy, and a surprising number of French and German wines. If you are inclined to try the house brand, I would strongly recommend the Merlot, which is so far the very best of the bunch and quite reasonable at €25 per bottle for the 1999 vintage.

Osteria di Rendola is best reached by car. If you would rather use public transit, you can take a train to Montevarchi and catch a taxi to the restaurant (the ride takes about ten minutes and costs €10). The only problem is that the last train back to Florence leaves at 10:15 PM, so I would recommend booking your dinner for 7:30 PM, when the restaurant opens. You'll likely be the only diners for the first half hour, but that's not a problem. If you want to eliminate the fear of missing your train, arrange for your taxi driver to pick you back up after your meal at about 9:45 PM; this allows enough time to enjoy a wonderful, if not so leisurely, dinner.

## 6. WINE, FISH, AND FINE BEACHES IN THE MAREMMA

It wouldn't be incorrect to say that Sassicaia started it all. In the late 1960s the Marchese Mario Incisa della Rocchetta decided it would be nice to grow some imported French grapes and experiment with making a new kind of Tuscan wine at his Tenuta San Guido estate in Bolgheri. A world-class wine was born—Sassicaia—and a quiet renaissance in the area was underway.

This southwest portion of Tuscany, called the Maremma, centered around the unsensational town of Grosseto, has traditionally been a low-profile spot. You can barely find a paragraph on the area in most English guidebooks. Tuscans come here to hunt wild boar in winter, and the seaside—most of it developed in the nondescript contemporary Italian style—is frequented all summer by vacationing Italian families and visiting Germans. (In fact, most signs in the region are written in Italian and German.)

This sleepy region is starting to wake up, however. In the past fifteen years, the area has become a mecca for serious winemakers who want a piece of the Bolgheri limelight. It seems that the superior quality of the Maremma soil and the proximity to sea air have an especially positive effect on grapes—not to mention that several accomplished winemakers have brought the glamour of true quality, the highest awards in the business, and lots and lots of French grapes to the area, casting a certain amount of fairy dust over the major producers here: Tenuta San Guido, Ornellaia, Guado al Tasso. Along with these mainstays of any fine wine list, emerging producers such as Enrico Santini and Michele Satta are also turning out great product, and getting better every year.

In addition to its world-class wineries, the area has several points of interest, especially for the intrepid food lover. The completely unassuming port town of San Vincenzo offers a Michelin two-star eating experience by the sea, as well as a fun and funky casual seafood spot just down the road. And about an hour south of here in Alberese you can find a lovely protected nature area and Tuscany's most beautiful beach, Marina di Alberese, complete with white sands and turquoise waters, but without the chaos and endless rows of *ombrelloni* that you'll find at most Italian beaches.

### Visiting the Wineries

Wine tourism is a recently introduced concept for Tuscany, especially for this area, which hasn't had as much time as Chianti and Montalcino to get used to the idea. But with the biggest names in wine overrunning this region, it was only a matter of time before the marketing consultants from the Napa Valley and Champagne region in France were brought in.

If you simply show up in the Bolgheri region, excited about the prospect of visiting the home of your favorite wines, you are bound for disappointment. Instead of a slew of open tasting rooms, you'll find a series of barely marked villas sealed off to the drive-up visitor. However, you can still taste and buy the best local wines at **Enoteca Il Borgo** in Castagneto Carducci (Via Vittorio Emanuele, 0565/763-746; closed Mondays), and have a pizza or *aperitivo* in the charming hamlet of Bolgheri itself, one hill over, with great views of the surrounding hillsides.

It is possible to visit the best wineries of Bolgheri, but you have to jump through a couple of hoops to do it. Specifically you need to arrange all visits through the **Consorzio Strada del Vino** (Costa degli Etruschi, Loc. San Guido 45, Bolgheri 57020, 0565/749-768, fax: 0565/749-705, e-mail: sdv@infol.it, www.lastradadelvino.com). The multilingual staff will help you arrange either group or individual tours of Sassicaia, Ornellaia, Michele Satta, and other big names of the region. The tours are always guided, giving insight into the history of the wines and the techniques used to make them, and they always end with a tasting. Spring and summer are the best times to visit the area, though you can come any time of year except during the September harvest. It is best to call up to a month in advance to organize everything, though a week ahead will often suffice.

In terms of attracting and organizing visitors, the region is still not quite ready for prime time, but in five to ten years I predict it will become, if not as big a draw as Chianti, still a top destination.

## A Bolgheri Wine Rundown

**Tenuta dell'Ornellaia's** premier wine is without doubt the expensive and award-winning DOC Bolgheri Superiore, a mix of Cabernet Sauvignon and Merlot with a small amount of Cabernet Franc. The wine is aged for eighteen months in barriques and then in the bottle for another year. For us mortals, they make a less coddled and much more affordable red called Le Volte, as well as some very good whites. Formerly owned by an Antinori relative, it was bought in 2002 by a consortium that includes Frescobaldi and Robert Mondavi of California.

**Guado al Tasso,** the jewel in the vast Antinori family crown, produces a high-end Bolgheri DOC Superiore that uses all nonnative grapes—Cabernet, Syrah, and Merlot—and is stored in new French barriques for a year, then racked and aged in both barrel and bottle before being released. The winery also makes a white Vermentino and a rosé called Scalabrone.

**Podere Grattamacco** is a highly regarded maker of a Bolgheri Rosso Superiore called Grattamacco Rosso, as well as a Bolgheri DOC white, a grappa, and an olive oil.

**Tenuta San Guido,** domain of the Marchese Incisa della Rochetta, makes Sassicaia, the Supertuscan that started it all. Revolutionary for an Italian wine at the time (in the 1970s), the wine is a fairly straight-forward blend of Cabernet Sauvignon with 15 to 20 percent Cabernet Franc. It is aged in stainless steel, in barriques, and in the bottle before reaching the shelves. Sassicaia was the first mark to receive its own DOC designation, perhaps as acknowledgment for the trickle-down benefits it has bestowed on Italy's wine industry as a whole. In 2000 it published a coffee-table book devoted to the wine called, simply, *Sassicaia.*

**Michele Satta** is best known for its fine red called Piastraia, a potent combination of Cabernet, Sangiovese, and Merlot. It also produces an all-Sangiovese wine called Vigna del Cavaliere, which is aged in barriques for a year before reaching the stores. One of the most popular wines is Diambra, a light Bolgheri Rosso that goes well with food but won't overpower subtle flavors like chicken or fish. The winery's Bolgheri Bianco is also excellent.

**Enrico Santini** is a tiny producer who came out with his first vin-tage in 2000 but is already putting out an excellent product. Try the strong and deep red Poggio al Moro Bolgheri Rosso DOC, or one of his white wines, and look to see much more from this winery in the future.

## San Vincenzo

San Vicenzo is a popular seaside town made up of unrelentingly bland modern architecture. The one outstanding feature (other than a Michelin two-star restaurant) is a long pedestrian commercial zone that becomes site of a boisterous *passeggiata* (evening stroll) late into the night. The town is small, and if you don't keep a keen eye out, you could drive straight through it without finding the two excellent eateries here, both situated at the small port.

## Gambero Rosso

**Piazza della Vittoria 13, 0565/701-021, fax 0565/704-542**
**Open Wednesday through Sunday 12:30 PM to 2 PM and 8 PM to midnight**
**Credit cards accepted**
€€€€

San Vincenzo is an unlikely and somewhat inauspicious location for a two-star restaurant, which draws very little attention to itself as it overlooks a port, a turquoise sea, and a parking lot. But this tiny eatery has been plucked from obscurity and ranked with the best and brightest; it was voted best restaurant in the country by *Gambero Rosso* magazine (no relation despite the name), and given the nod by the extremely finicky people at Michelin. Gambero Rosso is the creation of Fulvio Pierangelini, recognized as one of the top chefs on the peninsula. He presides over the kitchen, while his wife, Emanuela, graces the dining room as both host and occasional waitperson. Pierangelini went up against Thomas Keller of the French Laundry restaurant and a list of other international toques to compete for the Master of Culinary Arts Award. And when *Wine Spectator* devoted a special issue to the food and wine of Tuscany, it raved, "No one in the region can cook as well as Fulvio Pierangelini, whose food exhibits vibrant clarity and intense flavor."

The dining room is surprisingly intimate, with just seven tables oriented west toward large windows giving out onto the sparkling sea. Numerous wait staff dressed in suit and tie attend to diners' every need (I was given a padded, silken stool on which to place my purse). Water is poured from a silver pitcher, and porcelain plates rest on top of silver chargers. The décor is elegant but quite simple: a tasteful flower arrangement adds a subtle flourish to the center of the room; white walls are decorated with unobtrusive modern paintings . . . in short, nothing to distract from the food. It can feel a bit formal, what with the servers standing about ramrod straight with hands behind their backs, but the overall effect is one of serenity.

Just as the dining room's focus is west toward the sea, so is that of the kitchen. Fresh fish, large and small, along with shellfish, make up the bulk of the menu. For an antipasto, you might choose between incredibly delicate scallops cooked in lemon butter and served in their own shells, or a salad of small red mullet. Primi include a perfect risotto with thick chunks of shellfish, bright pink crayfish, and salty mussels. One of the kitchen's signature dishes consists of a silky chickpea soup garnished with whole prawns. Another is the fresh-made fish ravioli topped with seafood-broth cream. But if you venture away from the sea for a dish you won't be disappointed. The chef has a way with pigeon, and his ravioli stuffed with pigeon and topped with a reduced cream sauce is divine. He also serves pigeon as a hearty secondo, along with a fillet of pork with delicate wine sauce. But the majority of secondi focus on fresh Mediterranean fish: gilt-head bream served in a sweet reduction of wine with pear, or sea bass wrapped in pancetta. All are cooked perfectly and matched with a delicate sauce, whether sweet or savory.

Desserts include a classic dark chocolate terrine; a semifreddo of *torrone* (almond nougat) with chocolate sauce; and an unusual assortment of *sorbetti* accompanied with little individual house-made cookies. The wine list deserves mention as well, not only for its excellently chosen selection of whites (important for all the fish) and reds, but also for the extremely reasonable prices. An outstanding bottle of local Ornellaia or other Tuscan best goes for around €20 to €25, depending on the vintage. Many diners here opt for the excellent five-course tasting menu, which includes many of Pierangelini's classic dishes.

## Zanzibar

**Piazza del Porto 2, 0565/702-927**
**Open daily 8:30 AM to midnight; Wednesday 8:30 AM to 5:30 PM**
**Credit cards accepted**
**€€**

In sharp contrast to the hushed formality at Gambero Rosso is Zanzibar, a very cool bar and restaurant just a few steps down the boardwalk. If Gambero Rosso is buttoned up, Zanzibar, with its mosaic-tile tables set outdoors next to billowing white drapery sheltering you from the sun, is the kind of place where you go with sand between your toes. At once extremely chic and minimalist in its interior design and casual in its attitude, Zanzibar is the kind of bar and fish restaurant you dream about finding at the beach: the mythical Margarita in a chilled glass, the perfect plate of fried fish. The restaurant is the creation of Giovanna Bellagotti, and though it juxtaposes dramatically against Gambero Rosso, it also owes much to the established Pierangelini, who first put this one-horse resort town on the culinary map.

After you've had your *aperitivo,* cold beer, or glass of local wine, the table is remade in preparation for dinner. The menu, handwritten on plain brown paper, is all fish (almost all of which are caught near San Vincenzo): fish soup, *fritto misto,* linguine with *frutti di mare,* and a changing selection of fish grilled over a live fire. The fish soup is heavier on the fish than on the soup, with whole prawns and other crustaceans sun-bathing on the rim of a bowl containing a scant but delicious red seafood-scented broth. The *fritto misto* (one of my favorite things to eat), served on brown paper, consists of small fish like sardines, anchovies, and red mullet. The one drawback is that you have to negotiate with a lot of bones when eating these kinds of fish whole.

Zanzibar has eliminated the concept of the full Italian meal (antipasto plus primo plus secondo), and it can be a relief to order just one dish for a meal, accompanied with a glass of Ornellaia Rosso or another local wine. San Vincenzo can consider itself very lucky to be the home base of two such different and exquisite eateries. After your meal, take a stroll through San Vincenzo's pedestrian district, where it seems as if the whole town, or possibly the whole region is out walking, eating gelato, even shopping, since the stores here stay open until midnight.

## Beaches of Southern Tuscany

If you're not too sated from the excellent food of San Vincenzo, you should visit one of this area's many fine beaches. Near Bolgheri, you'll find a plenitude of decent public beaches when you enter either at the **Marina di Donoratico** or the **Marina di Bibbona**. Take your pick between private clubs that provide *ombrelloni* and lounge chairs, and large swaths of public sand, cleaner and better cared for here than in other parts of Tuscany. If you have the time, the car, and the desire to visit the nicest beach in Tuscany, travel south past Grosseto for about an hour and a half until you reach the exit for the **Parco Naturale di Maremma**. Follow the signs first to the small town of **Alberese**, which houses the parking office for the **Marina di Alberese**. At the office you can purchase the right to park in the parking lot of the beach. There is a separate ticket office around the corner for visiting the park itself—what, did you think they'd make it easy for you? Rangers offer guided tours of the most interesting hikes in the park fairly early in the morning in summer, and for the rest of the day you can buy a ticket that lets you wander around specific open areas of the park. Public access is limited because of fire danger in summer, but during the rest of the year you can visit the entire park without restrictions.

To get to the beach, once you've bought your parking ticket, retrace your tracks and then turn west to the Marina, where you'll encounter a barrier bar into which you insert your ticket and are allowed to pass. You then drive along an evocative lane of umbrella pines to the parking lot for the Marina di Alberese, from which you can walk along several miles of uncorrupted white sandy beach. The turquoise water here is the perfect temperature for swimming amid the gentle waves.

### Il Giardino dei Tarocchi

If your path takes you farther south from Alberese, an artistic marvel awaits just outside the medieval hilltown of **Capalbio**. The iconoclastic French-American artist Niki de Saint-Phalle is best known for her colorful, childlike, kinetic sculptures in the fountain outside the Centre Pompidou in Paris, but in fact her magnum opus, which took decades and dozens of assistants to create, lies in the hinterlands of southern Tuscany. The massive figures that make up her Giardino dei Tarocchi (Tarot Garden) are visible even from the Via Aurelia as you approach the site. The artist built a wonderland of giant playful figures, some as big as buildings, covered with a sea of mosaic tiles, mirrors, and decorated ceramic. Saint-Phalle's signature "nana" figures—giant, surreal maternal personae— preside over the central fountain. Nearby you'll find an idiosyncratic chapel that looks like an igloo; a two-story piazza; and a female figure

*A fanciful sculpture at the Giardino dei Tarocchi.*

that, once entered (yes, it's all quite Freudian), becomes a psychedelic living quarters, complete with mirror-covered bedroom and bathroom, where the artist actually lived for part of the time she worked on the project. The figures large and small all correspond to symbols from tarot cards, but also seem to represent various aspects of humanity. The garden is truly a unique and inspiring experience, especially for kids ecstatic at the opportunity to touch and crawl all over art with a capital A. (Loc. Garavicchio, 0564/895-122, www.nikidesaintphalle.com, email: tarotg@tin.it; open daily May 13 through October 20 from 2:30 PM to 7:30 PM and November through May on the first Sunday of each month from 9 AM to 1 PM—call first to confirm; €12, €6 for students and children between seven and sixteen, children under seven enter free.)

When you are done here you might also explore Capalbio, where you can walk on the walls, have an ice cream, or take in a meal at one of the multitude of trattorias.

## *Scansano*

If you'd like to continue your wine tasting in southern Tuscany, head east from Alberese to Scansano, home of the Morellino grape (a variant of Sangiovese) and birthplace of some very good red wines. The area is in the rarely visited hills to the southeast of **Grosseto**.

**Erik Banti,** a dashing figure and modern Renaissance man, has been making wine in the area since the early 1980s. In 1994 he relocated his base to Scansano (Loc. Fosso dei Molini, Scansano 58022, 0564/508-006, fax: 0564/508-019, www.erikbanti.com, email: info@erikbanti.com; open Monday through Friday 8:30 AM to 12:30 PM and 2 PM to 6 PM, Saturday 10 AM to 1 PM and 4 PM to 7 PM). In addition to Morellino, he has just harvested a new acreage of Sangiovese and is also growing Merlot, Cabernet Sauvignon, Syrah, and Primitivo on recently acquired land. Unlike many wineries of the region, Banti welcomes visits and offers free wine tastings *(accidenti!)*. Tastings are open to the public Monday through Friday 8:30 AM to 12:30 PM and 2 PM to 6 PM (April through October). The estate's wine shop, which he describes as "California style," also sells *salumi* and cheeses, and is open on weekends. Already recognized as a pioneer for the Morellino grape, Banti is now clearly at the forefront of accessible wine tourism in southern Tuscany.

# GLOSSARY

## A

Acciuga = Anchovy
Aceto = Vinegar
Aceto balsamico = Balsamic vinegar
Acido = Sour, acidic
Acqua = Water
Acqua frizzante = Sparkling water
Acqua naturale = Still water
Affogato = Gelato dunked in espresso
Affumicato/a = Smoked
Aglio = Garlic
Agnello = Lamb
Albicocca = Apricot
Albume = Egg white
Alice = Anchovy (alt. spelling)
Alimentari = Small food shop
Alla spina = On tap (e.g., beer, Coke)
Al rubinetto = From the tap (water)
Alloro = Bay leaf
Al vapore = Steamed
Amaro = Bitter
Ananas = Pineapple
Anatra = Duck (also *anitra*)
Antipasto = Appetizer
Aperitivo = Before-dinner drink
Arachide = Peanut
Aragosta = Lobster
Arancia = Orange
Aringa = Herring
Arista = Roast pork
Arrosto = Roasted
Asparagi = Asparagus
Astice = Small lobsterlike crustacean

## B

Babà = Little cake soaked in rum
Baccalà = Salt cod
Basilico = Basil
Barbabietola = Beet
Bavarese = Cold puddinglike dessert
Bevande = Beverages
Bicchiere = A glass
Bietola = Chard
Bignè = Éclair
Birra = Beer
Biscotti = Cookies
Bistecca = Steak
Bocconcini = Little bites
Bollito = Boiled
Bombolone = Doughnut
Bottarga = Dried mullet roe
Bottiglia = Bottle
Braciola = Chop (e.g., pork chop)
Branzino = Sea bass (also *spigola*)
Bresaola = Thin-sliced cured beef
Brioche = Croissant
Brodo = Broth
Bruciato = Burned
Bruschetta = Grilled bread slice rubbed
     with garlic and olive oil
Budino = Pudding
Buccia = Peel, rind (e.g., of an orange)
Burro = Butter

## C

Caccia = Wild game
Cacciucco = Fish stew, specialty
     of Livorno

Cachi = Persimmons
Caffè = Coffee
Caffeina = Caffeine
Caffettiera = Coffeemaker
Caldo = Hot
Cameriere = Waiter
Candito = Candied
Cantucci[ni] = Biscotti
Capperi = Capers
Caprino = Goat cheese
Caraffa = Carafe
Carciofi = Artichokes
Carne = Meat
Carota = Carrot
Carpaccio = Anything served raw and
    thin sliced, usually a meat or fish
Carta = Menu
Carta dei Vini = Wine list
Cassa = Cash register
Castagna = Chestnut
Cavallo = Horse, horsemeat
Cavatappi = Bottle opener
Cavolfiore = Cauliflower
Cavolo = Cabbage
Cavolo nero = Tuscan black cabbage
Ceci = Chickpeas
Cena = Dinner
Cenare = To dine
Cervelli = Brains
Cetriolo = Cucumber
Ciabatta = Slipper-shaped bread
Ciliegia = Cherry
Cima di rapa = Turnip leaf (bitter green)
Cinghiale = Wild boar
Cioccolata calda = Hot chocolate
Cioccolato = Chocolate
Ciotola = Bowl (also *scodella*)
Cipolla = Onion
Cocco = Coconut
Cocomero = Watermelon
Coda di rospo = Monkfish
Colazione = Breakfast

Coltello = Knife
Condividere = To share (also *fare
    in due*)
Coniglio = Rabbit
Conto = The bill
Contorno = Side dish
Coperto = Cover charge
Cotta/o = Cooked
Cozze = Mussels
Crema = Cream or custard
Crema chantilly = Whipped cream
Crespelle = Crepes
Crosta = Crust
Crostata = A tart, usually filled
    with jam
Crostini = Little toasts, usually covered
    with liver pâté
Crostoni = Open-face sandwiches
Crudo = Raw
Cucchiaio = Spoon[ful]
Cucchiaino = Little spoonful
Cucina = Kitchen (also used for cuisine)
Cucinare = To cook

**D**
Datteri = Dates
Decaffeinato = Decaffeinated coffee
Degustazione = Tasting menu
Disossato = Deboned
Dolce = Sweet
Dolci = Sweets, desserts

**E**
Enofilo = Oenophile
Enoteca = Wine shop, wine bar
Erbe = Herbs
Etto = 100 grams (about $1/4$ pound)
Extravergine = Extra virgin (olive oil)

**F**
Fagioli = Beans (usually "white beans"
    in Tuscany)
Fagiolini = Green beans

Faraona = Guinea hen
Fare la scarpetta = To soak up sauce
    with bread
Farro = Ancient wheat variety,
    sometimes translated as emmer
Fave = Fava beans
Fegato = Liver
Fegatini = Chicken or rabbit liver
Fettina = Thin slice
Fettunta = Tuscan word for *bruschetta*
Fichi = Figs
Fichi di India = Prickly pears
Filetto = Fillet (usually beef)
Finocchio = Fennel bulb
Finocchiona = Tuscan *salame* made
    with pork and spiced with fennel
Fior di latte (sometimes *fiordilatte*) =
    Fresh cow's milk mozzarella
Fiori di zucca = Zucchini flowers
Fondente = Melted chocolate
Forchetta = Fork
Formaggio = Cheese
Forno = Oven (also bread bakery)
Fragola = Strawberry
Freddo = Cold
Fresco = Fresh, also cool or cold
Frigorifero (also *frigo*) = Refrigerator
Frittelle = Sweet fritters
Fritto = Fried
Frutta = Fruit
Funghi = Mushrooms
Fuso = Melted

### G
Gamberetto = Baby shrimp
Gambero = Shrimp
Gamberone = Big shrimp
Gelato = Ice Cream
Ghiaccio = Ice
Gnocchi = Dumplings made from
    potato or semolina
Golosa/o = A glutton

Gorgonzola = Italian blue cheese,
    from Lombardy
Grana = Aged cow's milk cheese from
    the north, similar to Parmesan
Granchio = Crab
Granita = Liquidy sorbet
Grappa = Hard alcohol made from wine
    pressings
Grasso = Fat
Grigliata = Grilled
Guanciale = Cheek meat
Guscio = Peel or shell (e.g., of a nut,
    egg, fava bean)

### I
Insalata = Salad
Insalatone = Big salad
Integrale = Whole wheat
Inzimino = A dish of squid (usually)
    cooked in spicy tomato sauce
In umido = Braised in sauce
Involtino = Anything rolled in a
    cylindrical shape

### L
Lampone = Raspberry
Lampredotto = Boiled intestine
Lardo di Colonnata = Cured lard from
    Colonnata
Latte = Milk
Lattina = Can
Lattuga = Lettuce
Lenticchie = Lentils
Lepre = Hare
Lesso = Boiled, steamed
Lievito di birra = Yeast
Limoncello = Lemon liqueur served
    cold after dinner
Limone = Lemon
Litro = Liter
Lombatina = Veal chop

## M

Macedonia = Fruit salad
Macinato = Ground
Maiale = Pork
Mais = Corn
Mancia = A tip
Mandorla = Almond
Manzo = Beef
Marmellata = Fruit jam
Marzapane = Marzipan
Mascarpone = Sweet fresh cow's milk
    cheese, from Lombardy
Mela = Apple
Melanzane = Eggplant
Melone = Melon
Menta = Mint
Mezzo kilo = Half a kilo (about 1 pound)
Mezzo litro = Half liter
Mezzo-stagionato = Semi-aged (cheese)
Miele = Honey
Minestra = Soup, usually containing
    rice or pasta
Mirtillo = Blueberry
Misto = Mixed
Mora = Blackberry
Mortadella = Bologna
Mostarda = Mustard (also *senape*)
Mostarda di frutta = Tangy fruit chutney
Mozzarella di bufala = Prized
    mozzarella made from buffalo milk

## N, O

Nespola = Loquat, medlar
Noce = Nut (usually walnut)
Nocciola = Hazelnut
Nostrale = Locally raised
Oca = Goose
Olio = Oil
Olio di oliva/uliva = Olive oil
Olio di semi = Sunflower seed oil
Orata = Gilt-head bream
Osso = Bone

## P

Padella = Pan
Pancetta = Salt-cured bacon
Pane = Bread
Panino = Sandwich (or sandwich roll)
Panna = Cream
Panzanella = Florentine summer bread
    salad
Pappa al pomodoro = Florentine
    tomato-bread soup
Parmigiano = Parmesan cheese
Passato = Thick vegetable purée soup
Pasta = Pasta as used in English; dough;
    a pastry such as *brioche*
Pasto = A meal
Patata = Potato
Pecorino toscano = Tuscan cheese
    made from ewe's milk
Pentola = Pot
Pepe = Pepper
Peperoncino = Dried hot red pepper
Peperone = Pepper (bell, red, etc.)
Peposo/a = Tuscan beef stew
Pera = Pear
Pesce = Fish
Pesce spada = Swordfish
Petto = Breast
Piatto = Plate
Piccante = Spicy
Piccione = Pigeon
Pici = Thick handmade spaghetti
Pinoli = Pine nuts
Pinzimonio = Raw vegetables with salt
    and oil for dipping (Tuscan)
Piselli = Peas
Pizzico = A pinch (e.g., of salt)
Pollo = Chicken
Polpetta = Meatball
Polpo = Octopus
Pomodoro = Tomato
Pompelmo = Grapefruit
Porchetta = Pork stuffed with herbs and
    cooked slowly on a spit

Porcini = Aromatic mushrooms available fresh in the fall and dried year-round

Porro = Leek

Pranzo = Lunch

Pranzare = To have lunch

Prezzemolo = Parsley

Prosciutto = General term for ham

Prosciutto cotto = Cooked ham

Prosciutto crudo = Raw cured ham

Prugna = Prune

Puntarelle = Bitter, pointy salad green

Purè = Mashed potatoes

## Q, R

Quaglia = Quail

Ragù = Meat sauce for pasta

Ribollita = Tuscan bean soup

Ricetta = Recipe

Ricevuta = Receipt (also *scontrino*)

Ricotta = Light, fresh cheese made from either cow's or sheep's milk

Ripieno = Stuffed

Riso = Rice

Risotto = Slow-boiled rice dish

Rombo = Turbot

Rosmarino = Rosemary

Rucola = Arugula (also *ruchetta*)

## S

Salame = Salami

Sale = Salt

Salmone = Salmon

Salsa = Sauce

Salsiccia = Sausage

Saltato = Sautéed quickly in oil

Salumi = General term for cured meats

Salvia = Sage

Sarde = Sardines

Scalogno = Shallot

Scampi = Crayfish

Scarola = Escarole

Scamorza = Cow's milk cheese that comes shaped like a pear with golden rind

Schiacciata = Tuscan version of focaccia

Scodella = Bowl (also *ciotola*)

Scontrino = Receipt (also *ricevuta*)

Semifreddo = Sweet frozen mousse

Sedano = Celery

Senape = Mustard seed

Seppia = Squid

Sfogliatelle = A flaky, ricotta-stuffed pastry

Soffritto = Mix of carrot, celery, and onion used as a base for most stocks and sauces

Speck = Smoked prosciutto, typical of Alto-Adige

Soppressata = Headcheese

Spezzatino = Tuscan stew

Spiedino = Skewer

Spigola = Sea bass (also *branzino*)

Spinaci = Spinach

Spumante = Italian sparkling white wine

Spuntino = Snack

Stagionato = Aged (as in cheese)

Stracotto = Tuscan pot roast

Strutto = Lard (uncured)

Sugo = Meat sauce

Surgelato = Frozen

Susina = Plum

## T

Tacchino = Turkey

Tagliata = Sliced, or plate of sliced steak

Taleggio = Pungent, tangy cow's milk cheese, from Lombardy

Tartufo bianco = White truffle

Tartufo nero = Black truffle

Tè = Tea

Tè detèinato = Decaffeinated tea

Tiepido = Warm

Timo = Thyme

Tomino = Small round of goat or other
    soft cheese, often baked

Tonno = Tuna

Torta = Cake, pie, tart

Torta della nonna = Florentine custard
    tart

Tovaglia = Tablecloth

Tovagliolo = Napkin

Triglia = Red mullet

Trippa = Tripe

Trota = Trout

### U

Uovo = Egg

Uovo sodo = Hard-boiled egg

Uva = Grape

Uva passa = Raisins (also *uvetta* and
    *sultana*)

### V

Vaniglia = Vanilla

Verdure = Vegetables

Verza = Dark leafy round cabbage

Vino = Wine

Vino della casa = House wine

Vino novello = New wine, no aging

Vino sfuso = Wine from a vat

Vin santo = Sweet dessert wine, from
    Tuscany

Vitello = Veal

Vitellone = Veal slaughtered between
    twelve and eighteen months

Vongole = Clams

### Z

Zabaglione = Custard made with egg,
    cream, and Marsala wine

Zafferano = Saffron

Zampone = Pig's foot

Zenzero = Ginger

Zibibbo = Sicilian dessert wine (also
    name of the grape)

Zucotto = Tuscan dessert of sponge
    cake, ricotta, and whipped cream

Zucca = Squash, pumpkin

Zucchero = Sugar

Zucchine = Zucchini

Zuppa = Soup

# INDEX

## A

addresses, 11
Al Antico Ristoro di Cambi, 59
Alberese, 254
Alessi, 142
All'Antico Vinaio, 32, 106, 108
Alpina, Gelateria L', 205
Amadei, 201
Amon, 108
Angie's Pub, 111
Antica Gastronomia, 80, 158
Antica Macelleria Cecchini, 172, 236
Antica Macelleria Falorni, 172, 235
Antica Mescita di San Niccolò,
        Osteria, 77
Antica Porta, 96–97
Antinori family, 30, 46, 163
*antipasti*, 4–5
*aperitivi*
    about, 135
    Capocaccia, 137
    Dolce Vita, 136
    Gilli, 136–37
    La Torre, Caffè, 137
    Riffrulo, Il, 136
Apicius, 213–14
Arezzo, 228
Artimino, 231, 232
Asia Masala, 158
Associazione Italiana Sommeliers
        (AIS), 222
Azzarri, 159, 160

## B

*baccalà alla livornese*, 47
Badia a Coltibuono, 219, 237–38
Badiani, 206

baked goods. *See also* bread
    Becagli, 187
    Boutique dei Dolci, La, 194
    Buscioni, 186–87
    Castaldini, 188–89
    Cosi, Patrizio, 190
    Dolci & Dolcezze, 190–91
    Donnini, 192
    Galli, Forno Stefano, 199
    Gilli, 192
    Gualtieri, 193
    Italiano, Caffè, 195
    Mattei, Antonio, 188
    Migone, 195
    Mini, 195–96
    Mr. Jimmy's, 194
    Nannini, Alessandro, 196–97
    Paszkowski, 197
    Petrarca, 198
    Rivoire, 198
    Robiglio, 199–200
    Ruggini, 200
    Scudieri, 200
    types of, 185, 188
Baldovino, Enoteca, 114, 132
Baldovino, Trattoria, 60
Balducci, 114–15
Banti, Erik, 256
Barbi, Fattoria dei, 239
Baroni, 152, 160
Barrique, Enoteca le, 61
bars, 135–37, 183–84. *See also* wine bars
Bartolini, 175
beaches, 253–54
Becagli, 187
Beccofino, 45–46, 132–33
Benci, Osteria de', 40, 62

Biagio Pignatta, 231
Bibbona, Marina de', 253
Bibe, 84–85
Biondi-Santi, 239
*biscottini di Prato*, 188
*bistecca alla fiorentina*, 15–16
Bizzarri, 159
Boccadama, 63–64, 133
Bolgheri, 29, 31–32, 247–50
Bolognese, La, 166
Bonatti, 143
books, 179–81
Borgo, Enoteca Il, 249
Borgo Antico, 64–65, 156
Bottega delle Chiacchiere, La, 167
Boutique dei Dolci, La, 194
Braccini, 169
bread, 19. *See also* baked goods
   *pane toscano*, 19
   *schiacciata*, 23
Brindellone, I', 78
brunch, 55
Brunello di Montalcino, 35
Bugialli, Giuliano, 214–15
burgers, 111
Buscioni, 186–87
buses, 12
Bussotti, 143–44
butchers, 152, 157, 172–73, 235, 236

**C**
Cabiria, 156
*caffè. See* coffee
Caffè dei Costanti, 228
Caffè Italiano, 195
Caffè Italiano, Osteria, 65
Caffè Italiano, Pizzeria, 97–98
Cantina Orlandi del Gallo Nero, 237
Cantine di Greve in Chianti, Le, 235
Cantinetta Antinori, 46–47
Cantinetta dei Verrazzano, 19,
   115–16, 183
Capalbio, 254–55
Capezzana, Tenuta di, 220–21
Capocaccia, 55, 116, 137

Carabé, 206
Carmignano, 29, 230–31
Carraia, La, 207
Carrozza, 208
Casa del Vino, 133
Casalinga, 63, 78–79
Cascine Market, 176
Castaldini, 188–89
Castellina, 237
Catinari, 201
Cavini, 209
*cavolo nero*, 16–17
Cavolo Nero (restaurant), 49–50
Cecchini, Antica Macelleria, 172, 236
Cecchini, Dario, 135, 172, 236
Cent'Anni, 86
Cento Poveri, 50
Central Market, 152–54
Cerreto Guidi, 233
cheese
   course, 8
   pecorino, 19–20, 241
   purchasing, 152, 157
Chianina beef, 16
Chianti (region), 234–38
Chianti (wine)
   Classico, 28
   history of, 25, 26
   other, 29
Chiaroscuro, 189
children, eating with, 63
chocolate
   about, 201
   Amadei, 201
   Castaldini, 188–89
   Catinari, 201
   De Bondt, Paul, 201
   Dolci & Dolcezze, 190–91
   Gilli, 192
   Gualtieri, 193
   Hemingway, 193
   Migone, 195
   Olandese Volante, L', 197
   Procacci, 163–64
   Rivoire, 198

Robiglio, 199–200
Scudieri, 200
Slitti, 201
Vestri, 202
Cibreo, Caffè, 189–90
Cibreo, Ristorante, 42–43
Cibreo, Trattoria (Cibreino), 66
Cinta Senese pigs, 22–23
Cioni, Carlo, 232
coffee
  Castaldini, 188–89
  Chiaroscuro, 189
  Cibreo, Caffè, 189–90
  Cosi, Patrizio, 190
  Dolci & Dolcezze, 190–91
  Donnini, 192
  Gilli, 192
  Hemingway, 193
  Italiano, Caffè, 195
  Mini, 195–96
  Nannini, Alessandro, 196–97
  Petrarca, 198
  at restaurants, 9
  Robiglio, 199–200
  Ruggini, 200
  Scudieri, 200
  Torrefazione Fiorenza, 202
  vocabulary for, 187
Coin Casa, 176
Col d'Orcia, 239
Colivicchi, 169
Colonnata, 17
Consorzio Strada del Vino, 249
Conti, 160
contorni, 7
Convivium, 161
cookbooks, 180–81
cooking classes
  about, 213
  Apicius, 213–14
  Badia a Coltibuono, 219
  Cooking in Florence, 214–15
  Cordon Bleu, 215–16
  Culinary Arts, 220

Divina Cucina—Judy Witts Francini, 216–17
  Faith Willinger, 218
  Tenuta di Capezzana, 220–21
  Jeff Thickman, 217
  Toscana Saporita, 221
  Zibibbo—Benedetta Vitali, 218–19
Cooking in Florence, 214–15
coperto, 10
Coquinarius, 117
Cordon Bleu, 215–16
Cosi, Patrizio, 184, 190, 191
Culinary Arts, 220

D
Da Delfina, 232–33
Da Fernando, 162
Da Noi, 120–21
Da Ruggiero, 82
Da Stefano, 48
Da Ventura, 226–27
Danny Rock, 111
D'Azeglio, Bar, 117–18
De Bondt, Paul, 201
Del Soldato, Macelleria, 152, 157
digestivi, 9
Dioniso, 124–25
Divina Cucina, 216–17
Divinus, 51
DOC and DOCG regulations, 27
Dolce & Gabbana outlet, 245
Dolce Vita, 136
dolci, 8–9
Dolci & Dolcezze, 190–91, 196
Donnini, 192
Donoratico, Marina di, 253

E
EDI House, 98–99
Edison, Libreria, 180
Eito, 125–26
enoteca, definition of, 2, 131. See also
  restaurants; wine bars; wine shops
Enotria, 134
euro, introduction of, 10–11

excursions
  Chianti region, 234–38
  Da Delfina and the Medici Villas, 230–33
  Maremma, 247–56
  Montalcino, Montepulciano, Pienza, and Mondo X, 238–43
  Montevarchi, 244–47
  Piero Trail, 226–28
  transportation for, 225–26

## F

Falorni, Antica Macelleria, 172, 235
Federazione Italiana Sommeliers (FISAR), 223
Feltrinelli International, 180
Festa dell'Unità, 124
*fiaschetteria,* 2
*finocchiona,* 22
Firenze Nova, 99–100
fish, 47–49, 152, 172, 174–75
Fonterutoli, 237
Fontodi, Tenuta, 236–37
food fairs, 229
*formaggi. See* cheese
*forni,* 184. *See also* bread
Forteto, Il, 152
Francini, Judy Witts, 216–217
Fratelli Briganti, 85
Fratellini, I, 24, 110
Frateria di Padre Eligio, La, 243–44
Frescobaldi family, 33–35, 52
Frescobaldi Wine Bar, 52–53
Fuor D'Acqua, 48
Fuori Porta, 138–39
Fusion Bar at Gallery Hotel Art, 55

## G

Galli, Forno, 19
Galli, Forno Stefano, 199
Gambero Rosso, 251–52
Gambi, 144
gelaterias
  about, 205
  Alpina, Gelateria L', 205

Badiani, 206
Carabé, 206
Carraia, La, 207
Carrozza, 208
Cavini, 209
Neri, 209
Perchè No?, 210
Veneta, 210
Vestri, 210–11
Vivoli, 211
Ghiotta, La, 121
Giacosa, 135
gifts, 175–79
Gilli, 136–37, 192
Gottino, I', 110
grappa, 9, 39
Greve, 234
Grosseto, 256
Gualtieri, 193
Guscio, Il, 67–68
GustaVino, 53–54, 139

## H

Habitacion Liquida, La, 126
hamburgers, 111
Hemingway, 55, 193
holidays, 3–4

## I

ice cream. *See* gelaterias
Ieri, Macelleria, 152
IGT wines, 26, 27–28, 37
India, 126–27
*insalate,* 8
*insalatone,* 8
international food
  about, 123
  Amon, 108
  Asia Masala, 158
  Dioniso, 124–25
  Eito, 125–26
  Habitacion Liquida, La, 126
  India, 126–27
  Momoyama, 127–28
  Nin Hao, 128

Rose's, 129
ViviMarket, 165–66
Italiano, Caffè, 195
IVV, 245

**J, K**
Johns, Pamela Sheldon, 212, 220
kitchenware, 175–79

**L**
La Torre, Caffè, 137
Lanini, Macelleria, 173
*lardo di Colonnata*, 17
Latini, Il, 63, 69
light meals. *See also* sandwiches and
    snacks
  about, 107
  Baldovino, Enoteca, 114
  Balducci, 114–15
  Cantinetta dei Verrazzano, 115–16
  Capocaccia, 116
  Coquinarius, 117
  Da Noi, 120–21
  D'Azeglio, Bar, 117–18
  Ghiotta, La, 121
  Mangiatoia, La, 121
  Oliandolo, 118
  Rocco, Tavola Calda da, 118–19
  Rose's, 119
  Santo Bevitore, Il, 119–20
Luca Menoni, Macelleria, 157

**M**
Mall, The, 245
Mangiatoia, La, 121
Maremma, 29, 31–32, 247–56
Maremma, Parco Naturale di, 254
Mariano, 111–12
Mario, Trattoria, 81
markets. *See also* specialty shops
  about, 149–50
  Cascine Market, 176
  hours, 150
  Mercato Centrale, 152–54
  Mercato Sant'Ambrogio, 157

Mattei, Antonio, 188
Mazzetti, Lina, 21
meat
  butchers, 152, 157, 172–73, 235, 236
  Chianina beef, 16
  *salumi*, 22–23, 167–68
Medici Villas, 230–31, 233
menus, 4–5, 7–9
Mercatale, 238
Mercato Centrale, 152–54
Mercato Sant'Ambrogio, 157
*mescita*, 2
Mesticheria Mazzanti, 177
Migone, 195
Millesimi, 31, 145
Mini, 195–96
Mr. Jimmy's, 194
Momoyama, 127–28
Mondo X, 243–44
Montalcino, 35, 239
Montepulciano, 36, 242–43
Monterchi, 228
Montevarchi, 244–47
Montisi, 241
Morellino di Scansano, 32, 256
Morganti, 156, 162
Museo Civico, 227
Museo Leonardiano, 233

**N**
Nannini, Alessandro, 196–97
Negroni, 135
Nerbone, 112, 152
Nerbone a Greve, 235
Neri, 209
Nin Hao, 128

**O**
Ognissanti, Enoteca, 145–46
Olandese Volante, L', 197
Oliandolo, 118
olive oil, 17–18
Omero, 87
Ortolano Ciasky, L', 171

*osteria*, definition of, 1. *See also*
    restaurants
Osvaldo, 88
outdoor eating areas, 67
outlets, 244–46

## P
Paggeria Medicea, 231
Pagnotti, Forno, 19
pancetta, 22
Pandemonio, 54, 56
Pane & Co., 167
Pane e Vino, 56–57
*pane toscano*, 19
Paolo e Marta, Pizzicheria, 168
Paperback Exchange, 181
Parione, 57–58
pasta, 166
Pasta Fresca di Giancarlo Bianchi, 166
*pasticceria*, definition of, 184. *See also*
    baked goods
pastries. *See* baked goods
Paszkowski, 197
pecorino cheese, 19–20, 241
Pegna, 163
Perchè No?, 210
Perseus, 70
Petrarca, 198
Piansa, 183
Piazzetta, La, 63, 100–101
Picchi, Fabio, 41, 42–43, 91
Pienza, 240, 241–42
Piero Trail, 226–28
Pinchiorri, Enoteca, 44–45
Pitti Gola e Cantina, 139–40, 181
Pizzaiuolo, Il, 101
pizzerias
  about, 95–96
  Antica Porta, 96–97
  Caffè Italiano, Pizzeria, 97–98
  EDI House, 98–99
  Firenze Nova, 99–100
  Piazzetta, La, 100–101
  Pizzaiuolo, Il, 101
  Santa Lucia, 102

Spera, Pizzeria, 103–4
Tarocchi, I, 104–5
Poggio a Caiano, 230
Poliziano, 242–43
poultry, 172–73
Prada outlet, 245
*primi*, 5
Procacci, 163–64
produce, 152, 154–55, 156, 157,
    169–71
prosciutto, 22, 23
Pugi, 113

## Q, R
Quattro Leoni, 71–72
Querceto, Castello di, 236
Rendola, Osteria di, 246–47
reservations, 2
restaurants (general)
  child-friendly, 63
  days off and holidays, 3–4
  dining times, 3
  for locals, 68
  menus, 4–5, 7–9
  with outdoor areas, 67
  paying at, 10–11
  pricing key, 13
  reservations, 2
  terms for, 1–2
  tipping, 11
  useful phrases, 6
  vegetarian, 73–74
restaurants (specific). *See also*
    international food
  Al Antico Ristoro di Cambi, 59
  Antica Mescita di San Niccolò,
    Osteria, 77
  Baldovino, Trattoria, 60
  Barrique, Enoteca le, 61
  Beccofino, 45–46
  Benci, Osteria de', 62
  Bibe, 84–85
  Boccadama, 63–64
  Borgo Antico, 64–65
  Brindellone, I', 78

Caffè Italiano, Osteria, 65
Cantinetta Antinori, 46–47
Capocaccia, 55
Casalinga, 78–79
Cavolo Nero, 49–50
Cent'Anni, 86
Cento Poveri, 50
Cibreo, Ristorante, 42–43
Cibreo, Trattoria (Cibreino), 66
Da Delfina, 232–33
Da Stefano, 48
Da Ventura, 226–27
Divinus, 51
Fratelli Briganti, 85
Frateria di Padre Eligio, La, 243–44
Frescobaldi Wine Bar, 52–53
Fuor D'Acqua, 48
Fusion Bar at Gallery Hotel Art, 55
Gambero Rosso, 251–52
Guscio, Il, 67–68
GustaVino, 53–54
Hemingway, 55
Latini, Il, 69
Mario, Trattoria, 81
Omero, 87
Osvaldo, 88
Pandemonio, 54, 56
Pane e Vino, 56–57
Parione, 57–58
Perseus, 70
Pinchiorri, Enoteca, 44–45
Quattro Leoni, 71–72
Rendola, Osteria di, 246–47
Romita, La, 241–42
Ruggiero, Da, 82
Ruth's Kosher Vegetarian
    Restaurant, 73
Sabatino, 82–83
Scoglietto, Lo, 48–49
Sedano Allegro, 73
Targa, 89–90
Tiratappi, 238
Tranvai, Il, 83
Tre Merli, 72, 74
Tre Soldi, 90–91

13 Gobbi, I, 74–75
Vecchia Bettola, 75–76
Vegetariano, Il, 73
Zanzibar, 252–53
Zibibbo, 91, 93
*ribollita*, 20
Ricchi, Caffè, 156
Richard Ginori, 177
Riffrulo, Il, 136
*ristorante*, definition of, 1. *See also*
    restaurants
Rivoire, 198
Robiglio, 199–200
Rocco, Tavola Calda da, 118–19
Romanelli, Leonardo, 79–80, 131
Romita, La, 241–42
Rose's, 119, 129
Rosso di Montalcino, 35
Rosso di Montepulciano, 36
Ruggiero, Da, 82
Ruggini, 200
Ruth's Kosher Vegetarian Restaurant, 73

**S**
Sabatino, 82–83
*sagre*, 229
*salame toscano*, 22
*salumi*, 22–23, 167–68
San Vincenzo, 250–53
sandwiches and snacks. *See also* light
    meals
    about, 107
    All'Antico Vinaio, 108
    Amon, 108
    Angie's Pub, 111
    Danny Rock, 111
    Fratellini, I, 110
    Gottino, I', 110
    Mariano, 111–12
    Nerbone, 112
    Pugi, 113
    Sartoni, Forno, 109–10
    Stenio, 113
    tripe sellers, 109
Sansepolcro, 227

Santa Lucia, 102
Sant'Ambrogio Formaggi, 157
Sant'Ambrogio market, 157
Santo Bevitore, Il, 119–20
Santo Spirito, Piazza, 156
Sartoni, Forno, 19, 109–10
Sbigoli, 178
Scansano, 32, 256
*schiacciata*, 23
Scoglietto, Lo, 48–49
Scudieri, 200
seasons, eating with, 154–55
*secondi*, 7
Sedano Allegro, 73
shipping, 160
shopping. *See also* markets; specialty
    shops
  etiquette, 151
  outlet, 244–46
  vocabulary, 151
siesta, 150
Silvestri, Pescheria, 174
Slitti, 201
Slow Food movement, 79–80, 158
snacks. *See* sandwiches and snacks
Soderi, Macelleria, 152
*soppressata*, 22
spaghetti, 85
specialty shops. *See also* markets
  about, 149–50
  Antica Gastronomia, 158
  Asia Masala, 158
  Azzarri, 159
  Bartolini, 175
  Bizzarri, 159
  Bolognese, La, 166
  Bottega delle Chiacchiere, La, 167
  Braccini, 169
  Coin Casa, 176
  Colivicchi, 169
  Convivium, 161
  Da Fernando, 162
  Edison, Libreria, 180
  Feltrinelli International, 180
  hours, 150

Lanini, Macelleria, 173
  Mesticheria Mazzanti, 177
  Morganti, 162
  Ortolano Ciasky, L', 171
  Pane & Co., 167
  Paolo e Marta, Pizzicheria, 168
  Paperback Exchange, 181
  Pasta Fresca di Giancarlo Bianchi, 166
  Pegna, 163
  Pitti Gola e Cantina, 181
  Procacci, 163–64
  Richard Ginori, 177
  Sbigoli, 178
  Silvestri, Pescheria, 174
  Sugar Blues, 74
  Tassini, 165
  Telerie Toscane, Le, 178
  Tirrena, Pescheria, 174–75
  Veneziano, 179
  Vettori, 171
  Vice Versa, 179
  Zagli, Macelleria, 173
Spera, Pizzeria, 103–4
Stenio, 113
Sugar Blues, 74
Supertuscans, 26, 36–37

T
take-out food, 120–21
Targa, 89–90
Tarocchi, Giardino dei, 254–55
Tarocchi, I, 104–5
Tassini, 165
*tavole calde*, 2
taxis, 12–13
Telerie Toscane, Le, 178
Tenuta di Capezzana, 220–21
Tenuta Fontodi, 236–37
Thickman, Jeff, 217
tipping, 11
Tiratappi, 238
Tirrena, Pescheria, 174–75
Torrefazione Fiorenza, 202
Toscana Saporita, 221
transportation, 12–13, 225–26

Tranvai, Il, 83
*trattoria*, definition of, 1. *See also*
    restaurants
Tre Merli, 72, 74
Tre Soldi, 90–91
13 Gobbi, I, 74–75
tripe sellers, 109

**V**

Vecchia Bettola, 75–76
vegetarian restaurants, 73–74
Vegetariano, Il, 73
Veneta, 210
Veneziano, 179
Verrazzano, Castello di, 235
Vestri, 202, 204, 210–11
Vettori, 171
Vice Versa, 179
*vin santo*, 39
Vinci, 233
*vini novelli*, 37–38
Vino al Vino, 235
Vino Nobile, 36
Vino Olio, 146, 160
Vitali, Benedetta, 41, 42, 91, 92, 218–19
ViviMarket, 165–66
Vivoli, 207, 211
Volpi e L'Uva, Le, 140–41

**W**

Willinger, Faith, 218, 220
wine
    Antinori family, 30
    Bolgheri and the Maremma, 29,
      31–32, 247–50
    Brunello and Rosso di Montalcino, 35
    Carmignano, 29
    Chianti, 25, 26, 28–29, 234–38
    classes, 222–23
    dessert, 9

    DOC and DOCG regulations, 27
    Frescobaldi family, 33–35
    future of, 35
    history of, 25–26, 34
    IGT, 26, 27–28, 37
    Morellino di Scansano, 32, 256
    Supertuscans, 26, 36–37
    tours, 234–38, 239, 242, 248–49, 256
    *vin santo*, 39
    *vini novelli*, 37–38
    Vino Nobile and Rosso di
      Montepulciano, 36
    white, 38
wine bars
    about, 131–32
    Baldovino, Enoteca, 132
    Beccofino, 132–33
    Boccadama, 133
    Casa del Vino, 133
    Enotria, 134
    Fuori Porta, 138–39
    GustaVino, 139
    Pitti Gola e Cantina, 139–40
    Volpi e L'Uva, Le, 140–41
    Zanobini, 141
wine shops
    about, 142
    Alessi, 142
    Bonatti, 143
    Bussotti, 143–44
    Gambi, 144
    Millesimi, 145
    Ognissanti, Enoteca, 145–46
    Vino Olio, 146

**Z**

Zagli, Macelleria, 173
Zanobini, 141
Zanzibar, 252–53
Zibibbo, 91, 93, 218–19

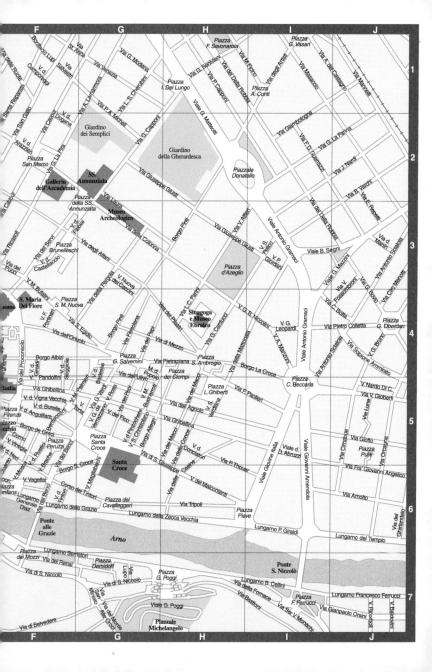

EMILY WISE MILLER is a food and travel writer based in Florence. She has written and edited travel guides to Italy, Great Britain, and the Pacific Northwest; was a restaurant critic for Sidewalk.com; and has contributed to the *San Francisco Chronicle, Salon,* and other publications.